THE ENTHUSIAST'S GUIDE TO EXPOSURE

49 Photographic Principles You Need to Know

JOHN GREENGO

THE ENTHUSIAST'S GUIDE TO EXPOSURE:
49 PHOTOGRAPHIC PRINCIPLES YOU NEED TO KNOW

John Greengo

johngreengo.com

Project editor: Maggie Yates
Project manager: Lisa Brazieal
Marketing manager: Mercedes Murray
Copyeditor: Maggie Yates
Layout and type: WolfsonDesign
Cover design: WolfsonDesign
Indexer: Maggie Yates

ISBN: 978-1-68198-258-8
1st Edition (1st printing, August 2017)
© 2017 John Greengo
All images © John Greengo unless otherwise noted

Rocky Nook Inc.
1010 B Street, Suite 350
San Rafael, CA 94901
USA

www.rockynook.com

Distributed in the U.S. by Ingram Publisher Services
Distributed in the UK and Europe by Publishers Group UK

Library of Congress Control Number: 2016960856

Printed in China.

To Mom and Dad:

Anything worth doing
is worth doing right.

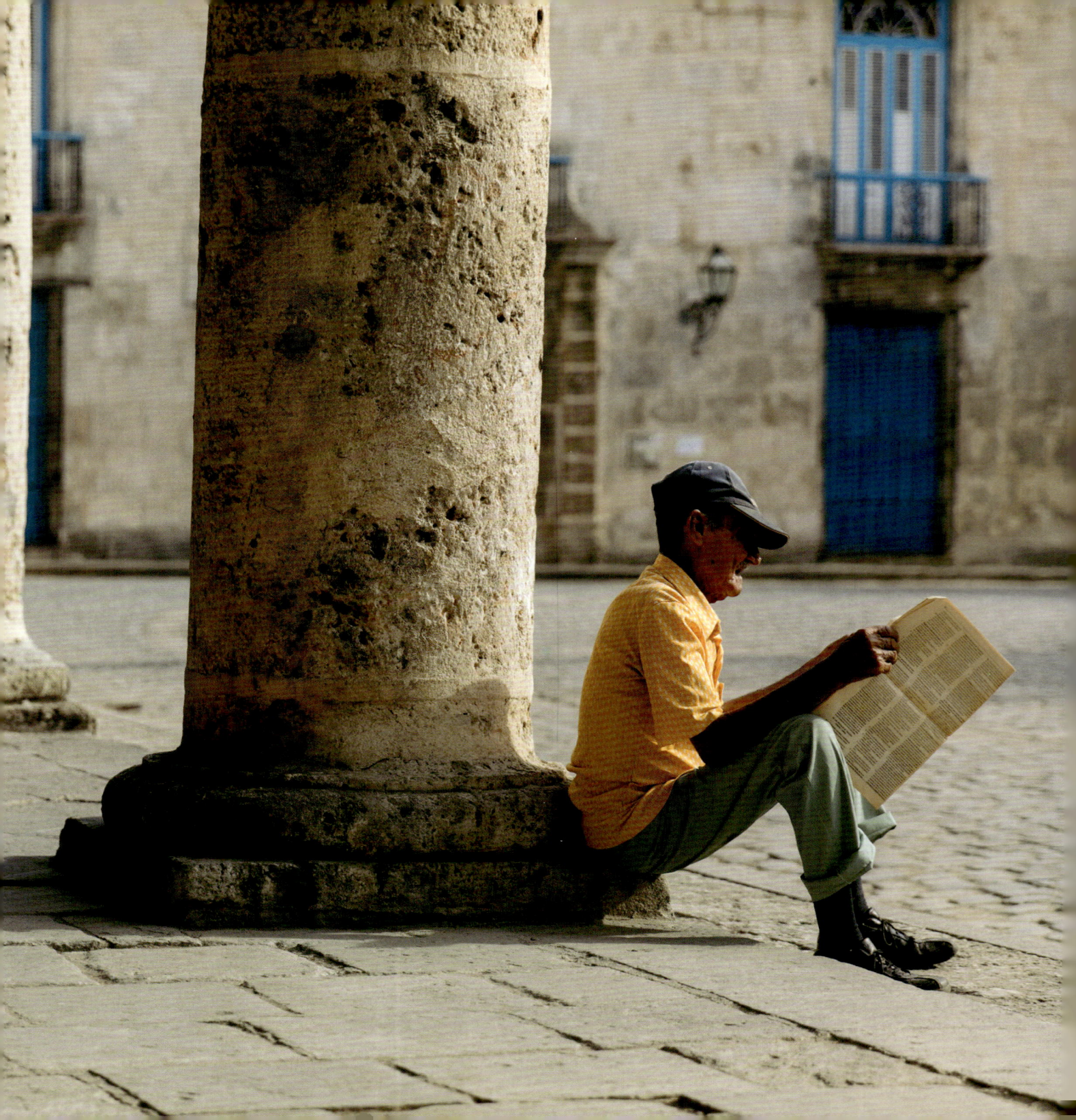

CONTENTS

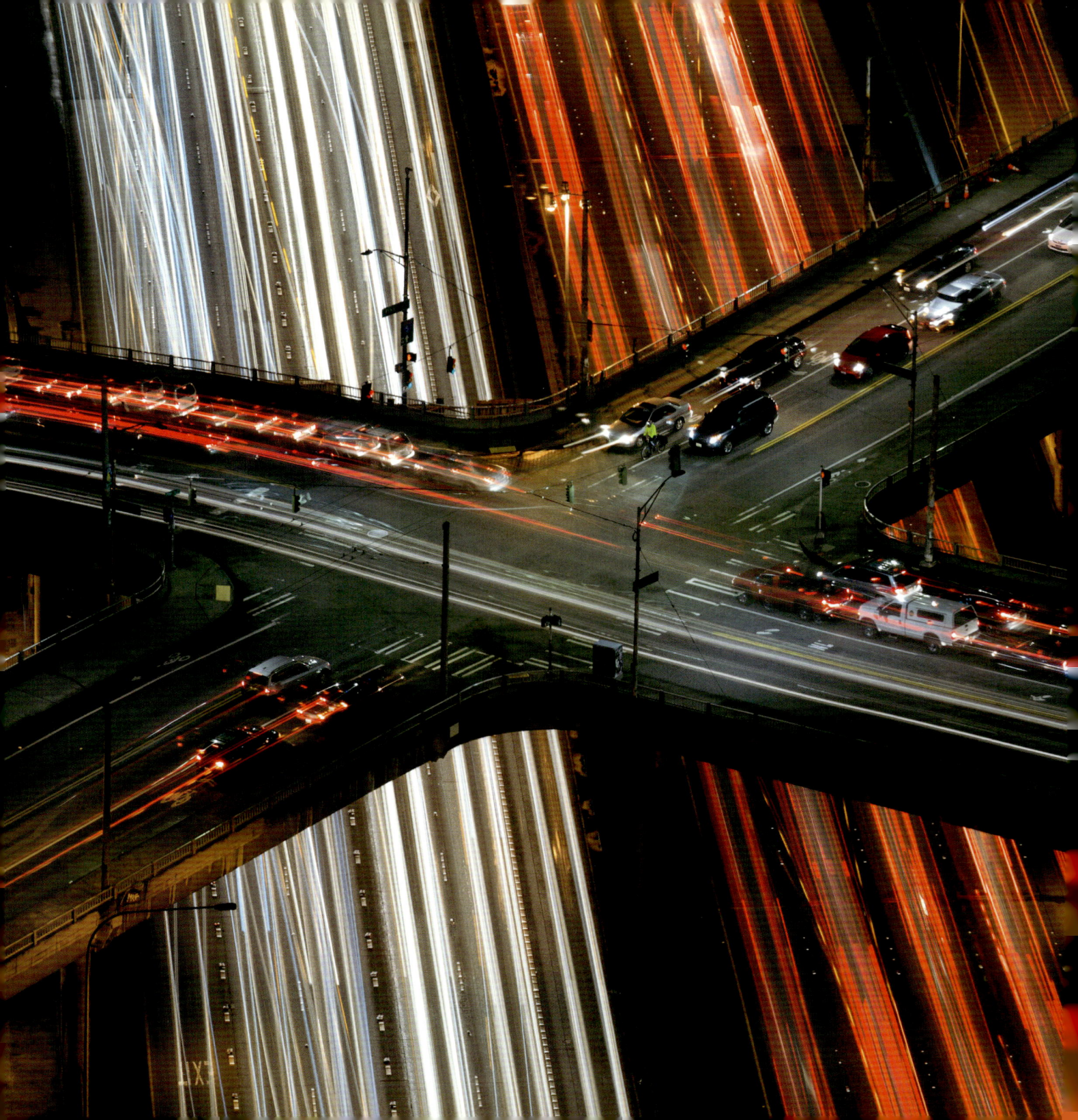

CONTENTS

1

THE BASICS OF LIGHT

CHAPTER 1

Photography represents a wonderful mixture of art and technology, but ultimately every photo will be judged primarily on its artistic merit. Long before any image is final, there are many technical issues that must be addressed. The first of those issues is the light. One must understand how the camera works and how best to adjust the settings to achieve the optimum results. There are many criteria that must be understood—some under your control, some not—and all are a part of a chain of decisions that must be considered before the shutter is clicked.

1. WHAT IS EXPOSURE?

EXPOSURE IS LIGHT striking the sensor in our digital cameras; or, if you prefer the old-school photographic process, exposure is light hitting the film. How this is achieved profoundly affects the outcome of the final photograph. Getting it right can be bit of a puzzle, but when you know how the pieces work, the process becomes quite easy.

Just the Right Amount

Certainly the quantity of light is very important—we don't want to let in too much or too little light; we want just the right amount. There are a variety of tools you can use to measure the intensity of the light that will hit your digital sensor or the film in your camera. Use this measurement value to decide how to set up your shot according to what we want to achieve for that particular photograph.

Most cameras offer several automatic exposure modes that meter the light and choose "optimal" settings, but this technique comes with a catch: even though your modern camera is filled with a vast array of advanced electronics, it can't tell what you are photographing or intuit the style of photograph you desire.

For simple photos, these auto exposure programs are just fine. If you want to concentrate on other things, put your camera into full auto mode and let the camera sweat the details for you. All modern cameras will to a good job at automatically exposing the right amount of light to give a decent resulting photograph. If you aren't happy with the way your photos are turning out, or you are looking to showcase your own vision, you'll need to start taking manual control.

It's More Than Quantity

Beyond getting the correct amount of light, the way in which the light is recorded has a profound effect on your final image. The photographic exposure tools we use are known as the exposure triangle. The three points of this triangle are shutter speed, aperture, and ISO. The combination of these three parameters offers a plethora of available options for interpreting a given scene.

Great photographs often involve interesting subjects in interesting actions. How you frame, compose, and expose your photo will have a great impact on how your subject is viewed.

With the tools of the exposure triangle, you can control the camera's settings to emphasize the elements that are most important and diminish those that are less so.

This interpretation of the scene is what makes a photograph unique to the photographer. Rarely do two photographers choose to capture a subject in exactly the same way. Everyone sees and thinks differently about their subjects. Controlling this creative process is one of the best attributes of photography; not only do you get to record what you see and experience, you can add your creative ideas to the mix to create unique photos that reflect the way you see the world.

Harnessing the exposure system is key to taking control of your photographs. Each of the individual elements is rather simple to understand. It's only when using all the elements together that you see the multitude of options available. This incredible variety is a good thing. It will give us the greatest freedom when it comes to creating a unique photograph. First we must master each individual part of the exposure triangle, which isn't difficult at all. Let's get started.

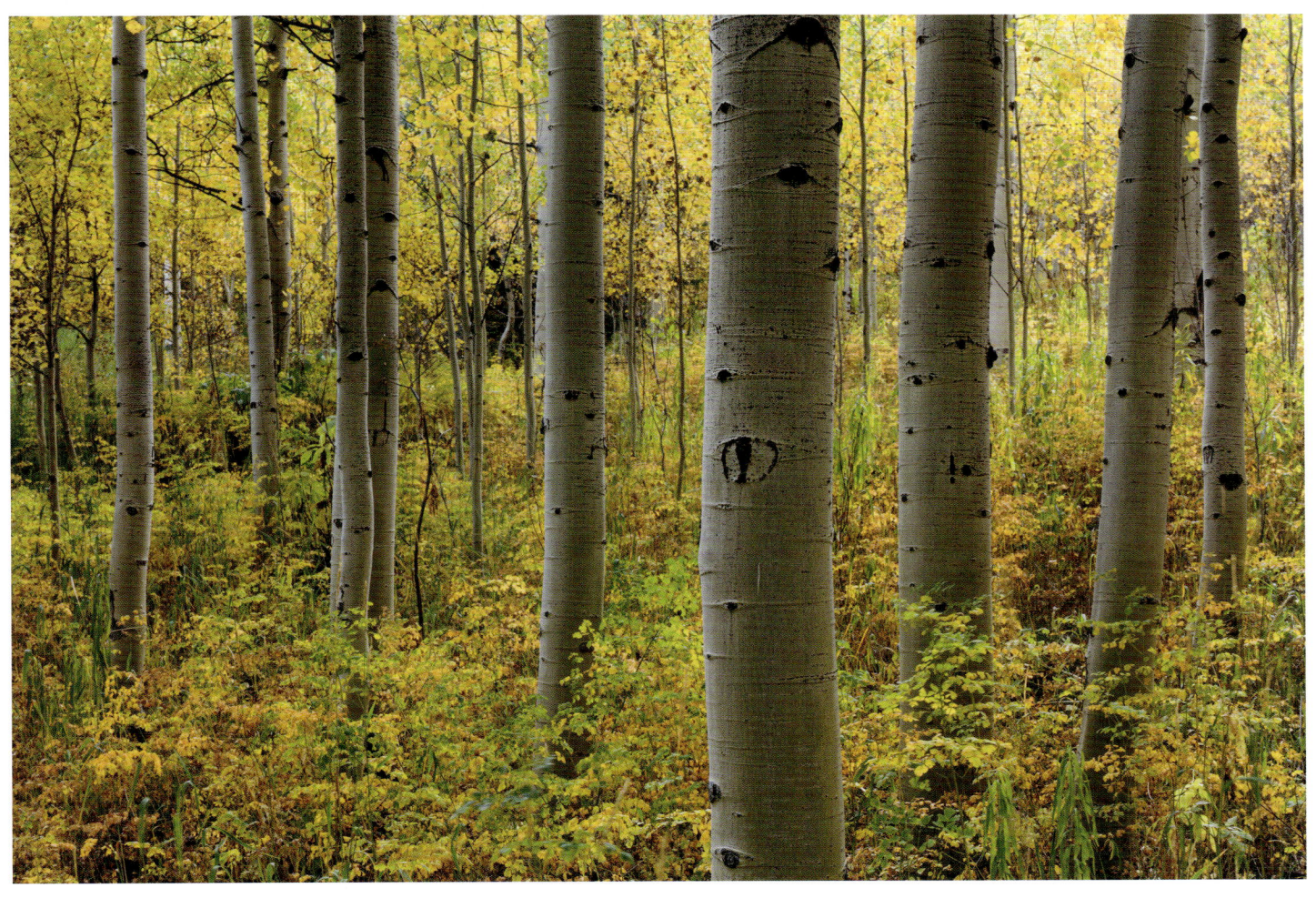

1.1 Taking control of your camera's exposure system will ensure that your photos are captured and displayed in the manner that you think looks best.
1/2 sec.; f/16; ISO 100; Canon 5DSR; EF24-70mm f/4L IS USM @ 55mm

2. PHOTOGRAPHY IS ABOUT LIGHT

PHOTOGRAPHY IS ABOUT light. In fact, the very definition of the word *photography* is "to write with light." Understanding the properties of light and how to control them are at the very core of mastering photography. The tools we use to control the light—the light meter, shutter speed, aperture, and ISO—are the tools we must master to take control of our photographs.

Hard vs. Soft

A basic but important difference in lighting scenarios is hard light versus soft light. Take a bright sunny day in a city with tall buildings. On the streets, you'll see shafts of intense light interspersed with deep shadows from the buildings. This is hard light. The gradation between light and shadow is a hard or abrupt edge. Hard light is the product of a single bright light. It can be compounded by dark surroundings or an environment that lacks reflective surfaces to bounce the light around.

Photographs taken with hard light often feature high contrast, and can have a very sharp look to them. This type of lighting is sometimes used to make edgy portraits or photographs that evoke a sense of mystery.

Soft light features a gradual transition from light to shadow. It's created by a diffuse light source, whether that diffusion is natural or artificial. Great soft light can be found on a foggy morning or an overcast day, when sunlight is diffused by cloud cover.

Subjects lit with soft light tend to be easier to look at because the transitions between light and dark are gentle. This is why most lights in your home have a light shade—to diffuse the light and soften the area it effects. Soft light will be enhanced in environments that have lots of natural reflectors—for instance, a white room or a snow-covered landscape.

Control the Light

As a photographer, you are in control of the light that hits the sensor or the film. You'll be choosing when and where you'll be taking photos, and those decisions will result in different lighting scenarios. If you choose to work in a studio, you'll be in more control of the light in the environment—how many lights, how many reflectors, and the power of the light. If you are a control freak, this is the place to be.

Most of us work in the real world with natural light, where there is a limited set of controls to choose from. Consider the environment: is it morning or afternoon? Is it a sunny day or cloudy one? Each of these variables will have a profound impact on your photos.

The choice of when to photograph is often made for us by the availability of the subject. All too frequently, we will be stuck with a less-than-ideal lighting situation and little ability to change it. We do, however, have control of our camera and its exposure system. With just a few controls and a few key adjustments, we can make the best of a less-than-ideal lighting situation.

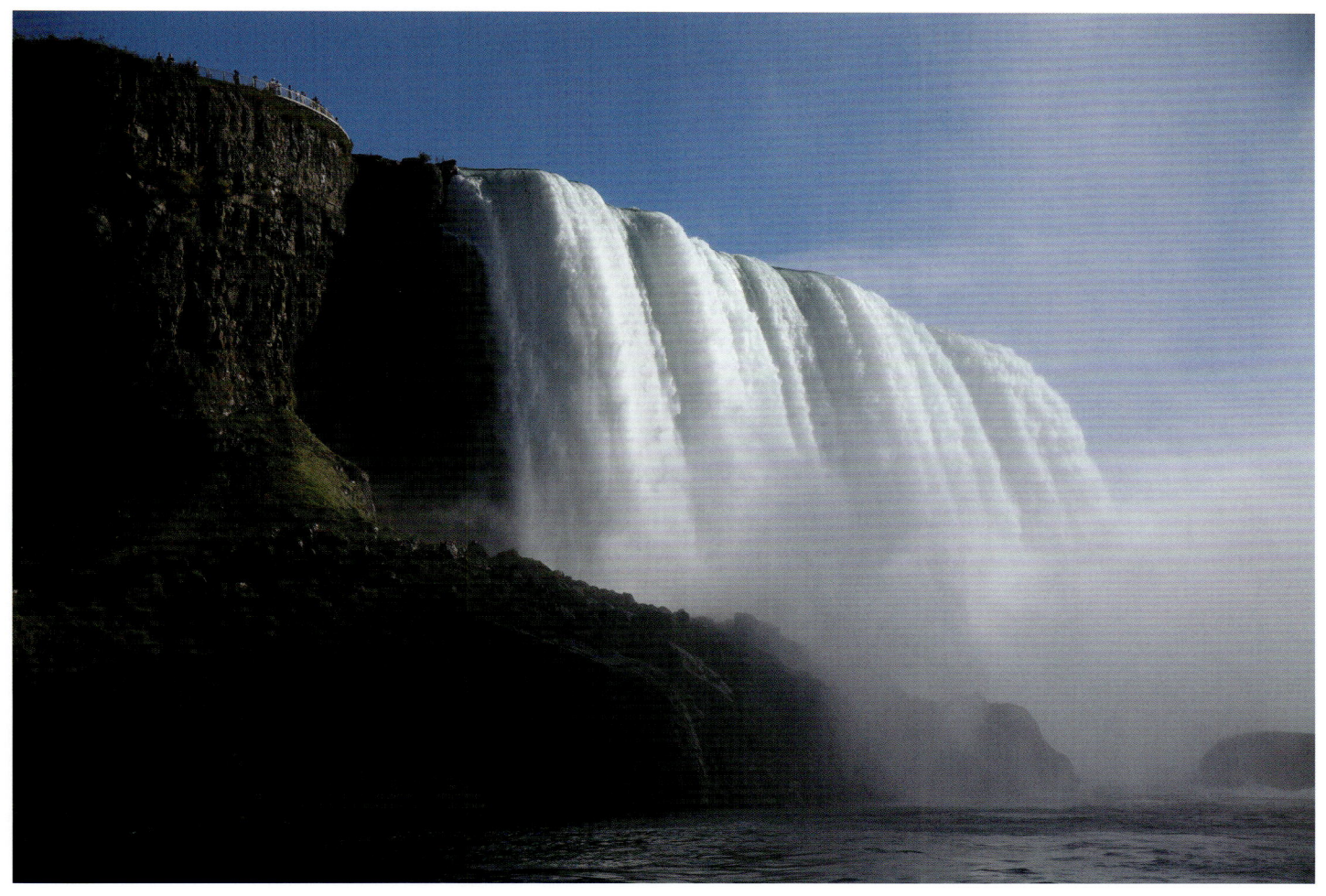

2.1 Some scenes will range from bright sunlight to deep shadows, which can be a good thing if it adds to the visual drama of the image.
1/1000 sec.; f/5.6; ISO 100; Canon 5D Mark IV; EF24-70mm f/4L IS USM @ 57mm

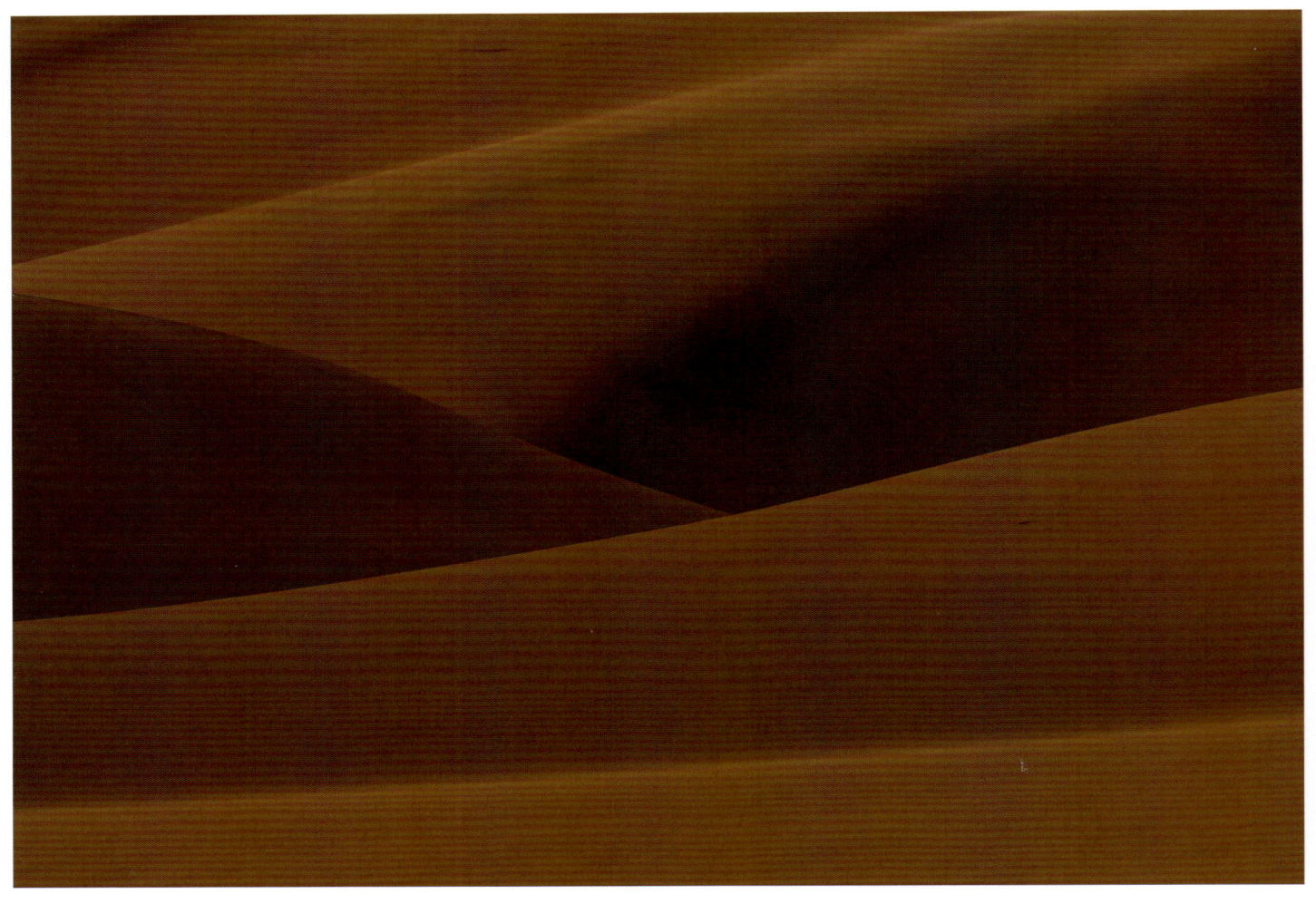

2.2 Sand dunes under soft light allow us to see the subtlety of the lines and shapes in the sand.
1/2 sec.; f/16; ISO 100; Canon 5DSR; EF100-400mm f/4.5-5.6L IS II USM @ 170mm

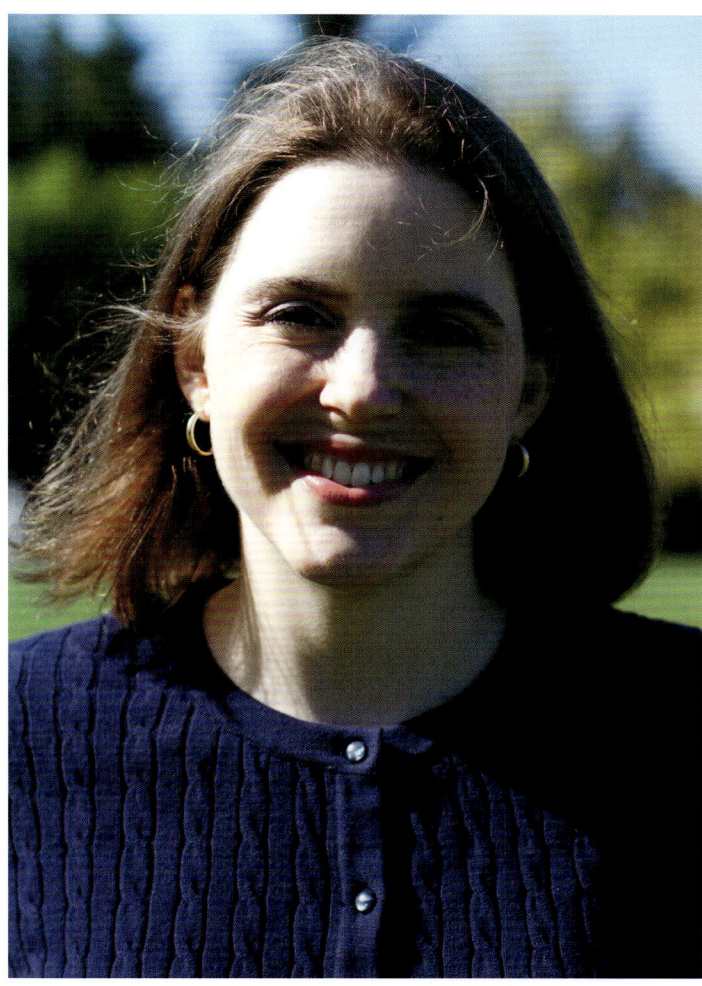

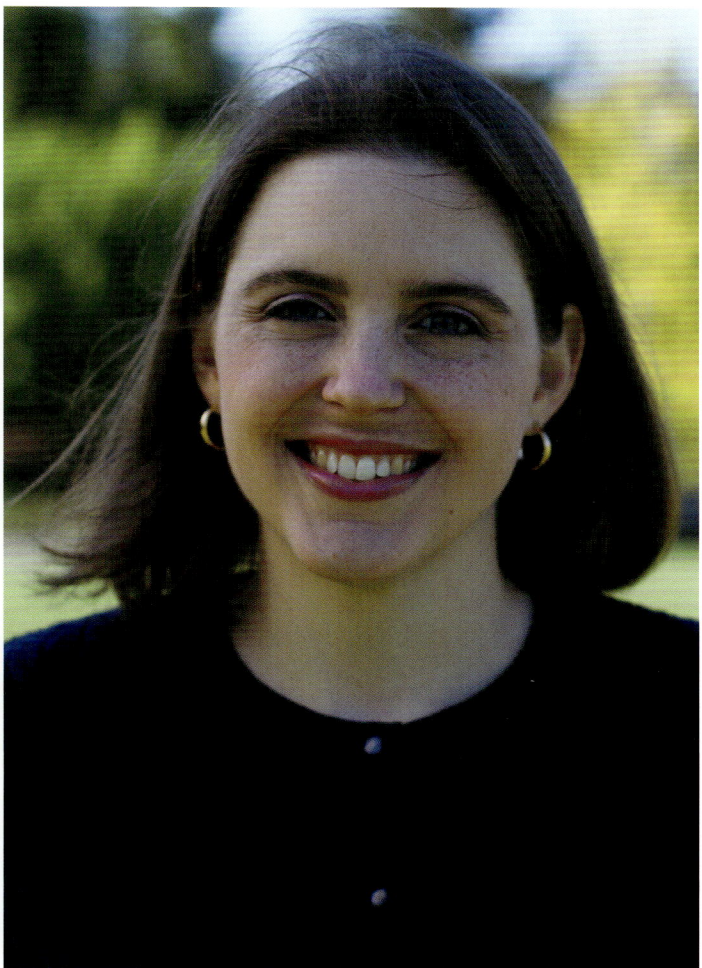

2.3 Hard light is created on sunny days when the sun mixes with shadows. Areas in the shadows will be hard to see because cameras cannot capture detail in bright sun and deep shadows at the same time.
1/1000 sec.; f/2.8; ISO 100; Canon 7D; EF50mm f/1.4 USM

2.4 The softer light created by a diffuser eliminates the direct sunlight and allows the subject to be more easily seen.
1/1000 sec.; f/2.8; ISO 100; Canon 7D; EF50mm f/1.4 USM

3. THE CHARACTERISTICS OF LIGHT

THERE ARE MANY ways to characterize light: quantity, direction, size, color, and range. All of these are important to the final photograph, but some are more significant when it comes to the technical world of exposure. In order to achieve optimum exposure, we need to have a solid understanding of what aspects of light affect the exposure system and how we can work with them.

Quantity

Do you want to know how much light there is? Use a traditional handheld light meter (yes, they still make them) to get an exact reading. One of the options on most of these light meters is to measure light in terms of Exposure Value (EV).

In this system, 0 (zero) equals an easy-to-remember setting that is extremely low light. A reading of 0EV is equal to ISO 100, a shutter speed of 1 second, and an aperture of f/1.0. This is about the amount of light you'd encounter on a dark street with just a single common light in the distance. EV2 is twice as bright (think: two lights). A typical work or home interior might be around 8EV, a cloudy day around 12EV, and a bright sunny day 15EV.

The EV number system was designed with photographers in mind. Each numeric increase in EV allows us to decrease shutter speed by one stop or close our aperture by one stop. However, because the standard EV scale was designed around ISO 100, using a different ISO setting means recalculation is necessary.

Most photographers don't use handheld meters or work with the EV system anymore, but the concept helps illustrate the idea of light quantity. Brighter scenes will require faster shutter speeds and/or smaller aperture openings. It is, however, somewhat limited: it only tells us the total amount of light landing on a particular spot on the sensor or film, and not the specific brightness values from different areas within our scene.

Range

The range of light in a particular scene is not something the average person thinks too much about. Human vision adapts to various lighting conditions very quickly. When we look at a bright object our pupils constrict to block the excessive light, and when it gets dark, our pupils open wide to let in more light.

The camera, on the other hand, is capturing a single exposure for the entire scene and must settle on one set of settings. Furthermore, the camera's sensor is limited in the range of brightness that it can record, at least in comparison with the remarkable versatility of the human eye.

Imagine a scene in a sunny park: bright sun reflecting off lily pads on the surface of a pond, and a thick grove of trees at the edge of the park. As a photographer, we need to decide how to bias our exposure for the highlights or the shadows.

If the highlights are most important to us, we can adjust the exposure so that the lily pads in the pond keep their natural green color rather than becoming overexposed. We'll do this by making our photo a little bit darker overall to protect our highlights from getting too bright. A consequence of this exposure will be that everything in the shadows will be rendered very dark to pure black.

We could, on the other hand, shoot for the shadows and let in enough light to clearly see a couple sitting on a bench in the shadow of the trees. This will be achieved by making our image a bit brighter so that we can see into the shadow region a little be better. The effect of this choice will be that the lily pads will be rendered as a collection of blobs of pure white, lacking any color or detail. Neither option is specifically right or wrong—just a choice we must make depending on our desired outcome.

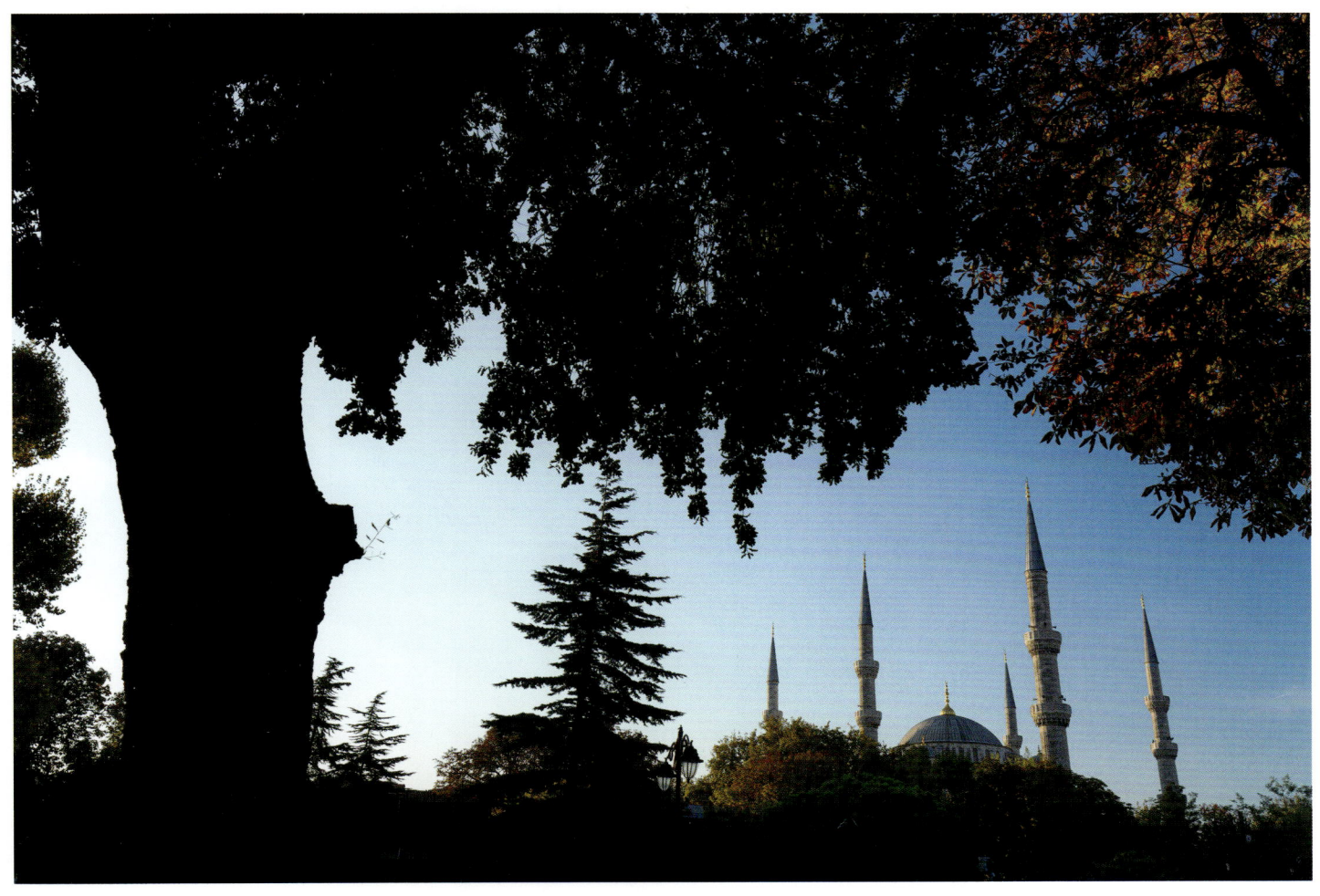

3.1 It can be difficult to properly expose scenes with areas of both shade and sunlight. In some cases, you'll have to choose whether subjects in the sun or subjects in the shade are more important for the exposure.
1/80 sec; f/5.6; ISO 100; Canon 5D Mark IIIl EF24-70mm f/2.8L USM @ 26mm

Color

All light has color, and that color can strongly affect your image and the impact of your photograph. For instance, sunlight is pure white. As it passes through the atmosphere, the light may be perceived as yellow, orange or red.

The lights in our homes and offices have a wide range of colors depending on the type of bulb being used. Tungsten or incandescent bulbs emit a warm reddish-orange color. Fluorescent bulbs traditionally were limited to a slightly off-white greenish color, like an office with lots of cubicles. Modern fluorescent lights are now available in a variety of color temperatures. Take a look at their packaging to see what color they are.

White Balance

To control the color of our image, we will work with a camera feature called White Balance. This can be set to one of several preset options that will correct for a variety of common lighting scenarios (daylight, cloudy, shade, tungsten, flash). There are also manual options that will allow the camera to correct for almost any conceivable lighting situation. In order to use the manual option on your camera, you may need to check your instruction manual.

One very challenging situation to work with is a mixed lighting scenario.

This could happen at a stage play or concert where the color of the lighting changes from moment to moment. At the beginning of the song, everyone may be bathed in blue light, but by the end, the stage is illuminated in red light. This is truly a photographic nightmare scenario, but there are ways to deal with it.

An equally challenging problem occurs when there are two strong light sources with different colors. This could happen at a banquet hall where the room lights are warm in color and the natural light coming through the windows on one side of the room is neutral in color. If you need to shoot photos at a variety of locations within that environment, every image will have a slightly different mix of the two light sources.

One solution to these problems would be to adjust the White Balance setting for each scenario. This is a bit time consuming, but it can work. Another solution is to shoot with a RAW image file format. The RAW format allows for adjustment after the fact, without damage to the original file. In a wide variety of photo-editing software programs there will be a temperature slider that will allow you to adjust the color in a blue to yellow spectrum. This allows you to shoot your subject without regard to the color, since you know you will be able to fix it later.

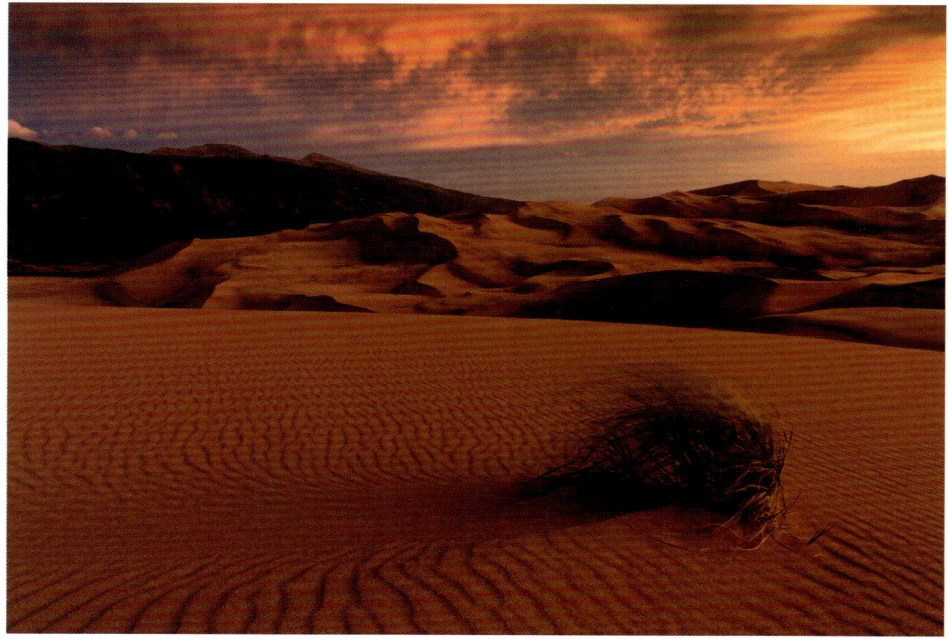

3.2 Light from the setting sun passes through more of the Earth's atmosphere than it does when it's shining from an overhead angle. This affects the color of the light.
1/2 sec.; f/11; ISO 100; Canon 5DSR; EF24-70mm f/4L IS USM @ 32mm

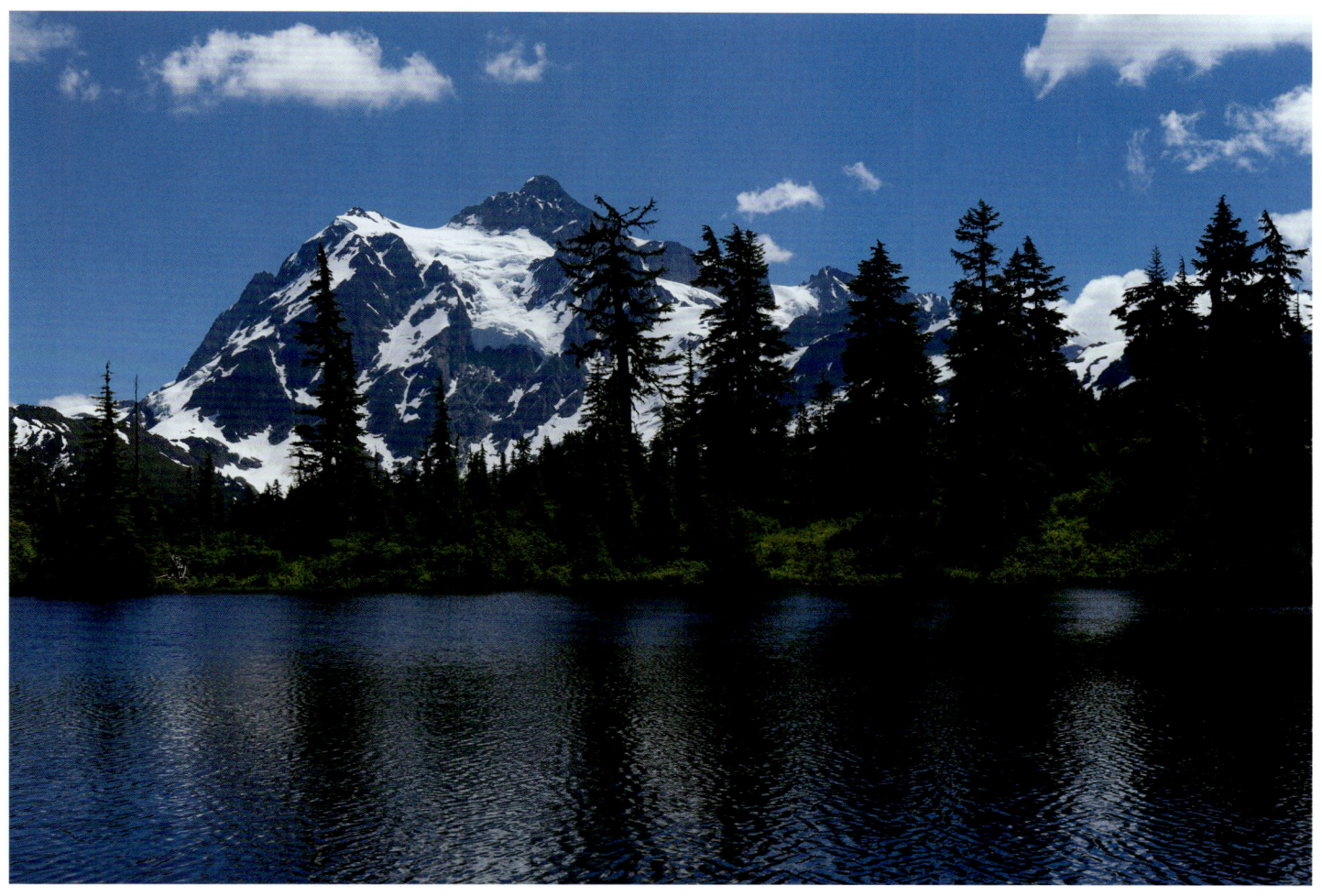

3.3 Bright, sunny days are known for their hard light in the middle of the day. Areas in the sun are easy to see, but shadows can be hard to see because of the vast difference between sunlight and shade.
1/125 sec.; f/8; ISO 100; Canon 5D Mark III; EF16-35mm f/4L IS USM @ 35mm

4. THE LIGHT METER AND METERING MODES

ALL MODERN CAMERAS have a light meter—a device that measures the amount of light that will strike the sensor. The light meter takes that information and then makes a recommendation to the photographer as to how much light should be allowed in. The camera delivers this information to you via the exposure indicator (sometimes referred to as the light meter): generally a linear scale ranging from -3 to +3. This scale may be horizontal or vertical; it may only range from -2 to +2; or, it may only show you a numeric value, like -1 or +2. Look in the viewfinder to locate the indicator. You may also see one on the top or back LCD, as well.

Put your camera in the Manual exposure mode (M on the mode dial) and adjust the shutter speed and aperture until you see the exposure indicators changing. You may need to adjust your ISO to something other than AUTO for this to work.

The concept is pretty easy. The meter will read a setting of 0 (zero) when you have achieved the recommended setting for the exposure. In the automatic exposure modes, the photos you take will likely look like just about right: not too bright, not too dark. This if fine for most situations, but there can be complications depending on your subject.

18% Gray

The camera gauges 0 (zero) on the exposure indicator as the best exposure for a scene based on the assumption that the average brightness of your scene, and all scenes, is equal to 18% gray, which is a middle gray between black and white. This may or may not be true, but it's how the camera makes its recommendations.

Bright Scenes

You'll need to second-guess your exposure meter with scenes that are predominantly bright or dark. Imagine a snow-covered mountain in bright sun—your camera doesn't know that the subject is mostly white; it just thinks the subject is super bright. The meter believes that all subjects are gray, so the camera will recommend an exposure that results in the mountain looking like it's covered in dirty, gray snow.

To resolve this issue, you need to let the camera know that your subject is much brighter than 18% gray. Instead of setting your exposure to 0 (zero), set the exposure indicator to somewhere in the +1 or +2 range by adjusting the shutter speed or aperture. For brighter scenes, set the meter to the + (positive/overexposure) side of the scale, because the scene you are capturing is brighter than an average scene.

Dark Scenes

With dark environments, we'll use the opposite technique. Imagine a forest with a thick canopy above and dark trees, foliage, and dirt on the ground. If you shoot an exposure with the indicator at the 0 (zero) mark, the scene will be much brighter in the photo than in real life. It might look pretty good on the back of the camera, but it doesn't represent the true brightness of the scene. To correct for this, you'll need to set the exposure indicator somewhere in the -1 or -2 range.

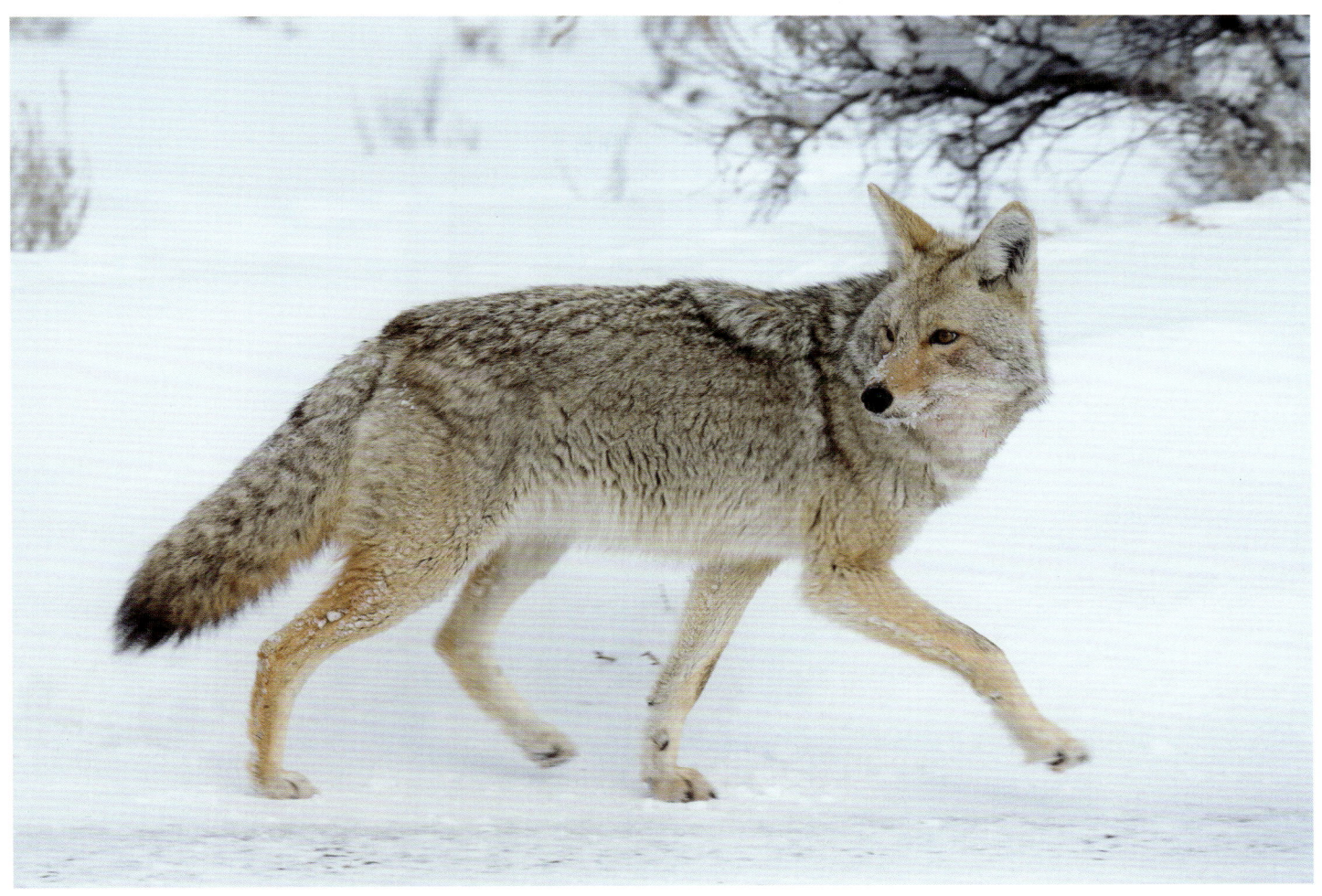

4.1 Light-colored subjects, which reflect more light than average, can fool your camera's light meter. You'll need to overexpose these types of shot to compensate for the amount of light in the scene.
1/320 sec.; f/8; ISO 100; Canon 5D Mark III; EF70-200mm f/4L IS USM @ 135mm

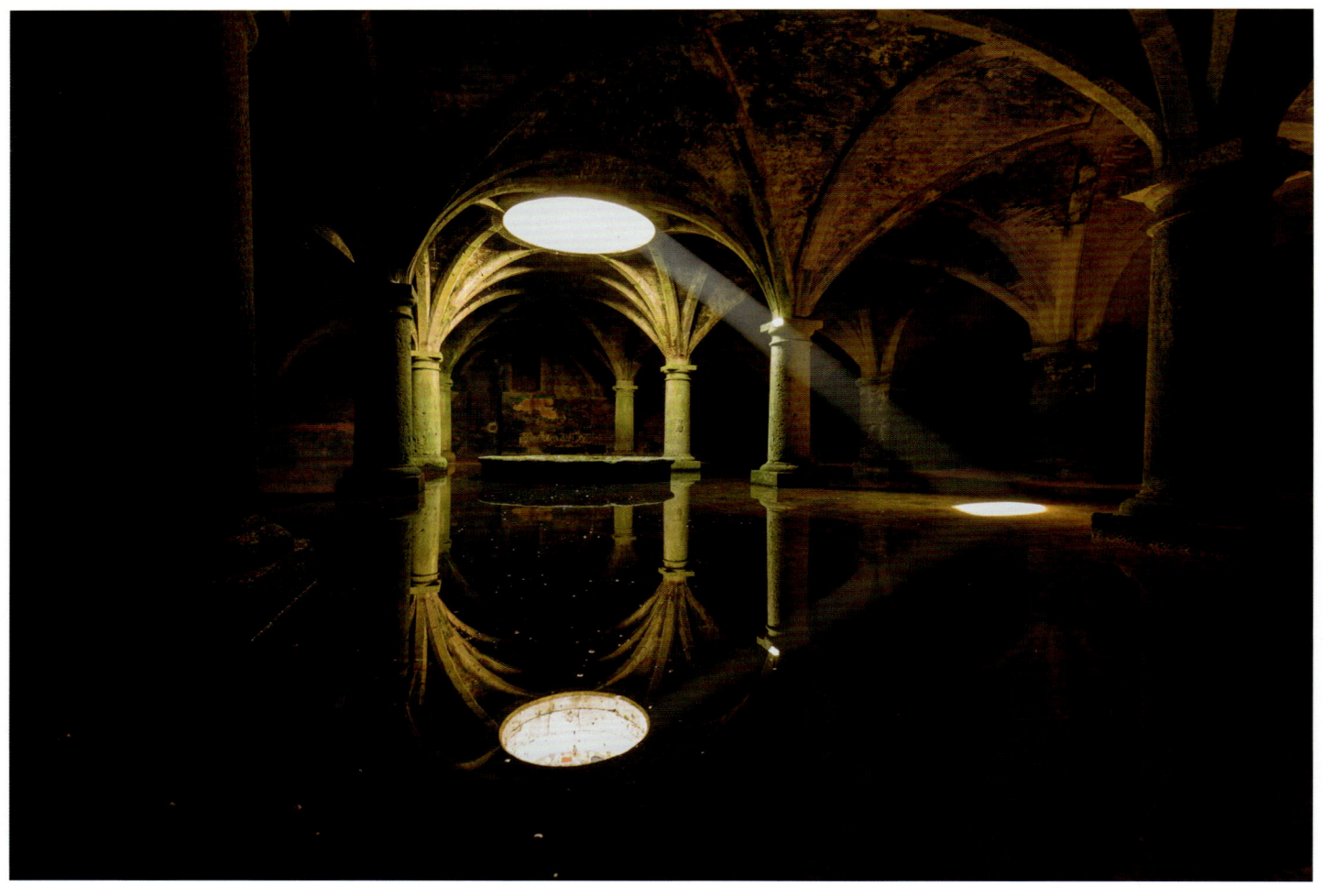

4.2 Shots of very dark environments can fool your camera's light meter. You'll need to underexpose these types of shots to compensate for the amount of light in the scene.
1/8 sec; f/5.6; ISO 800; Canon 5D Mark III; EF16-35mm f/4L IS USM @ 16mm

Wiggle Room

Modern digital cameras and their advanced sensors have a bit of leeway in the exposure, meaning it doesn't have to be perfect in camera. If the exposure is a little too bright or too dark, we can always fix it in postproduction with adjustments in your photo editing software. Most images can withstand a "push" or "pull" of a couple of stops. Some cameras can handle adjustments as much as 5 stops. Despite this flexibility, the standard recommendation is to try and get it right in the camera if possible.

The Metering Mode

The cameras exposure recommendation is for middle gray (18%), but from where in the frame is this reading being taken? Cameras have several ways of reading the amount of light entering the lens. These are called the metering modes.

Old cameras used a metering mode called center-weighted metering. In this system, the camera measured everything inside and outside of a big circle in the middle of the frame, and weighted the result with a 60% emphasis on the inside of the circle. For subjects that mostly filled the frame and were of an average brightness, this system worked perfectly well.

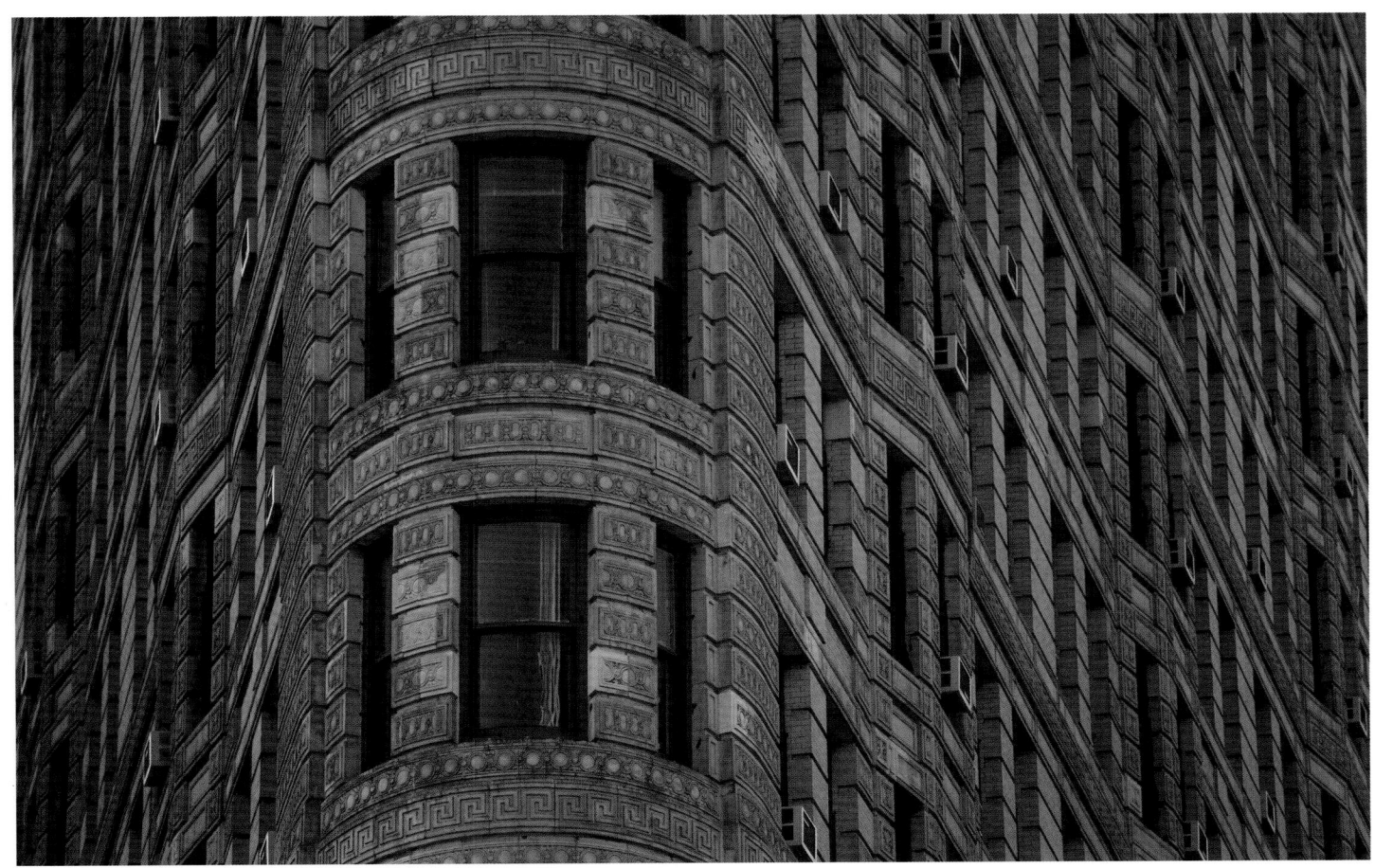

4.3 The Flat Iron building in New York City is of average brightness. Metering the light reflected off this building will give a correct reading because the building is near the 18% gray that all cameras read.
1/250 sec.; f/4; ISO 100; Canon 5D Mark IV; EF70-200mm f/4L IS USM @ 200mm

The Spot Meter

The next evolution in metering, used to obtain a more precise reading—perhaps the measure of light on a person's cheek or a bird perched on distant tree—was the spot meter. Spot metering measures the light inside a very small circle within the viewfinder's frame. This circle, often just around the focusing area in the middle of the frame, comprised only 1-5% of the total area in the frame.

This metering system proved accurate when only a small portion of the total scene was middle gray (18%). The problem with this system is that it is a very precise tool; pointing it at the wrong subject (anything not 18% gray) yields images that are under- or overexposed. Be forewarned: don't absentmindedly leave your camera in spot metering!

The Multi-Segment Meter

The next step in the evolution of the meter was a system that used multiple points to read the light. The information was then run through an algorithm to achieve an optimal exposure recommendation. At first, these systems were using 5 points of data; then 9; then 15; and beyond. Today, some cameras have over 100,000 detection points.

The number of points don't matter as much as how that data is crunched. These multi-segment metering systems don't just average all the data, they work hard to try and figure out what the scene is. Modern systems can detect a human in the frame, or "see" a bright yellow object in the upper portion of the frame and assume a landscape scene.

These systems are generally very good at figuring out the best exposure. They are what I recommend to all photographers for most situations. The name for this metering system varies by manufacturer: Matrix, Evaluative, and Multi-Segment are among the more popular names.

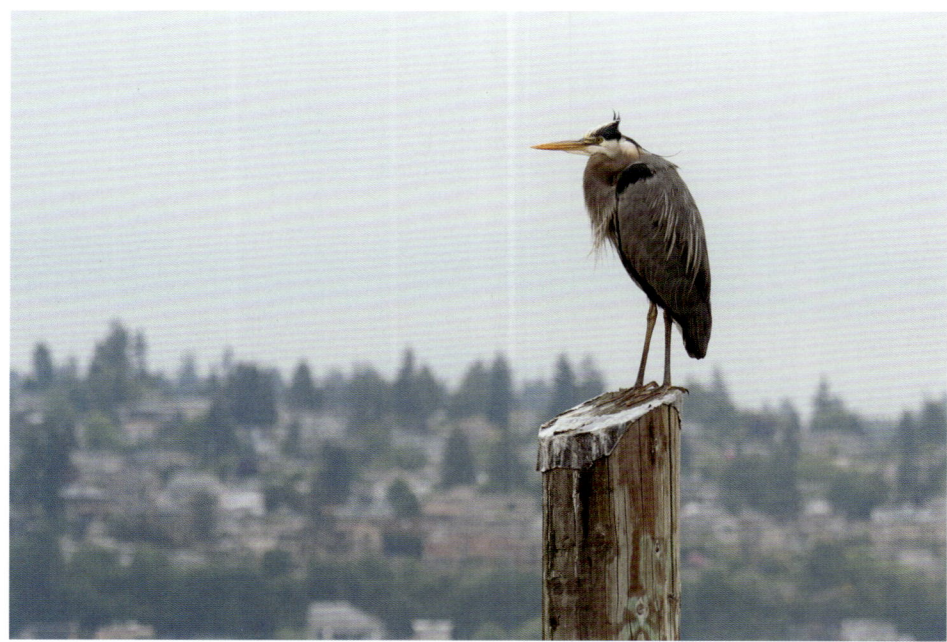

4.4 Subjects with bright (or dark) surroundings can be properly metered using a spot meter.
1/2500 sec.; f/4.5; ISO 400; Canon 40D; EF70-200mm f/4L IS USM @ 135mm

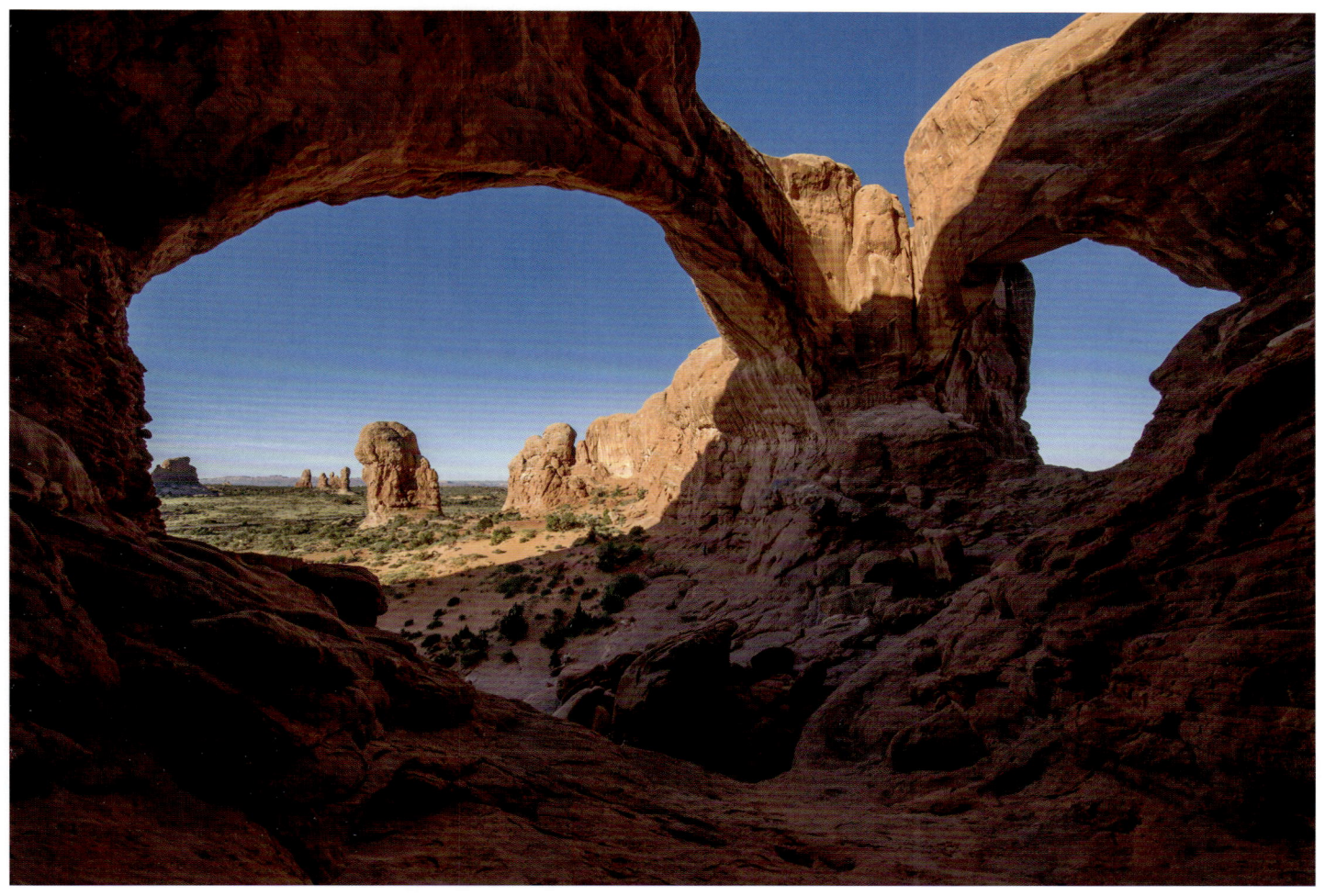

4.5 The multi-segment meter can analyze an entire scene and produce a reasonable average of the light and dark regions in the shot to maintain as much exposure information as possible.
1/100 sec.; f/11; ISO 100; Canon 5D Mark III; EF11-24mm f/4L USM @ 11mm

5. THE HISTOGRAM

THE HISTOGRAM IS a graphic display of the amount of light striking the sensor. It's a more modern and detailed method of determining the incoming light than the traditional light meter. The shape of the histogram shows us information about the range of brightness and how the tonal areas are related.

The traditional light meter measures light in a specific area, then indicates the average with a single number on a scale that typically ranges from -3 to +3. This simplistic system fails to convey the complex subtitles of light in many scenes. The histogram does a much better job of offering an easy-to-read analysis of both the amount and the range of light.

The histogram comes in two styles: brightness and RGB. (Check your camera's menu to see if you have the option to switch between the two.) The brightness histogram shows the range of pixel brightness of a particular scene; the RGB histogram separates that same information into red, green, and blue color channels.

What Am I Looking At?

The histogram is a rectangular graph in which the X-axis (along the bottom of the graph) represents the range of brightness in pixels, with pure black on the far left and pure white on the far right. The Y-axis (along the vertical side of the graph) represents the relative number of pixels at a particular level of brightness. The taller the row, the more pixels there are with a certain tonal value. Pure black pixels (those that have received zero light) are at the far left. (This could mean that the object is either black or has not received enough exposure for its true brightness to be apparent.) The right end of the spectrum represents pixels that are pure white, either because there is a pure white object in the frame or because that object has been overexposed.

Pixels in the middle of the histogram are somewhere between white and black. If we want to work with our images after we have taken them, it's these pixels in the middle that are the most pliable. We can make them a bit darker or a bit lighter quite easily.

Pixels on the far left or the far right are limited in how much they can be manipulated. We therefore want to capture an exposure that puts as much information as possible in the middle of the histogram.

If we increase our exposure, we are making our image brighter. In such cases, the histogram shape will trend to the right. If we decrease our exposure, the histogram shape will be denser on the left side of the graph, indicating the image is darker than average.

Most cameras offer the option to see a histogram of any image that is played back, but you may need to make a setting change on your camera to bring up this information. Many (mirrorless) cameras can show a live histogram in the electronic viewfinder while you are composing your image. Check your camera to see if this is possible.

Capturing exposures in which everything is represented by points in the middle of the histogram isn't always possible, since the range of brightness in the real world is greater than what sensors can record. In these situations we'll need to make a compromise on the exposure by adjusting it a little to the left (dark) or to the right (bright), depending on what is most important to us in the photo.

The Right Side

The most critical area to look at in most histograms is the right edge (the highlights). In most cases, we don't want pixels that are pure white unless we are photographing a light source or a shiny reflection. Many photographers "protect the highlights" by making sure the histogram doesn't have any points touching the far right barrier.

Blinkies

Some cameras offer a feature called Highlight Alert (or similar), sometimes referred to as "blinkies." With this mode engaged, all pixels that are overexposed will blink in the image on the LCD. With the blinkies turned on, it's very easy to see what data is being lost to overexposure. It will be up to you to change the exposure if this overexposure isn't acceptable. You'll need to look at the real scene with your own eyes and determine if that information is important and how bright it should actually be. In general, if you see a large area of blinkies, it means you need to darken your exposure.

The Left Side

The second most important area on the histogram is the far left, where the black pixels are represented. We usually don't want to see areas of pure black in the scene. However, dark areas in a photograph are far more common than bright areas. These dark areas are frequently shadows, and you'll need to determine how important it is to see detail in that shadowed area. If you do want to see information in the shadows, you'll need to adjust your exposure so that the histogram is not weighted too far to the left.

Examples

A graph with a big hump on the left shows the brightness of a photo with lots of dark pixels. A graph with a big hump on the right means a photo with lots of light pixels. A photo of a panda or zebra would result in a spike on the left (dark pixels) and a spike on the right (light pixels). A photo of an elephant would likely have a big hump of information in the middle, indicating middle gray. Every image is unique, as is every accompanying histogram. The more you study the histograms of your images, the more you'll be able to comprehend their information.

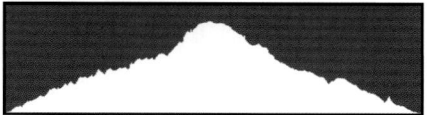

5.1 A typical histogram will have a mound of information in the middle, often tapering off as it reaches the edges.

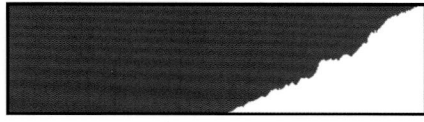

5.2 A histogram that represents an image of overexposure, or excessive brightness, will be "piled" up on the right side of the graph.

5.3 A histogram that indicates too much darkness, or underexposure, will be shifted far to the left side of the graph.

Histogram General Guidelines

- Try to keep most of the information in the middle of the graph.
- Remember that pixels on the far right are pure white.
- Remember that pixels on the far left will be pure black.
- It's better to give your subject more light than less light (so long as you don't overexpose important areas).

6. THE EXPOSURE TRIANGLE

THE EXPOSURE TRIANGLE refers to the three key parameters that control the exposure process in the camera: shutter speed, aperture, and ISO. By adjusting any of these settings, we can change our exposure to make the image brighter or darker. However, adjusting any one of these controls not only makes the image brighter or darker, it changes some other aspect of the image, as well.

The shutter speed affects subjects that move; the aperture affects the depth of focus; and ISO adjustments show more or less noise.

Don't worry about the specifics of these right now; we'll look more closely at each of these in upcoming sections.

Optimum Exposure

To achieve optimum exposure, first determine your subject and consider how you'd like the image to look. You may be taking a portrait of a person, and you'd like to throw the background out of focus so it's not a distraction. Perhaps you're capturing a photograph of a bird in flight and you'd like to freeze the motion of the wings.

Once you've picked the most important elements and decided how you're going to photograph them, set your exposure with these goals in mind. Understanding the exposure triangle simply involves understanding each of the three elements. The better you understand each of them the better you will be able to make decisions out in the field. In the following sections we will cover each of these three parts of the exposure triangle. This is a good time to have your camera nearby to practice making these adjustments.

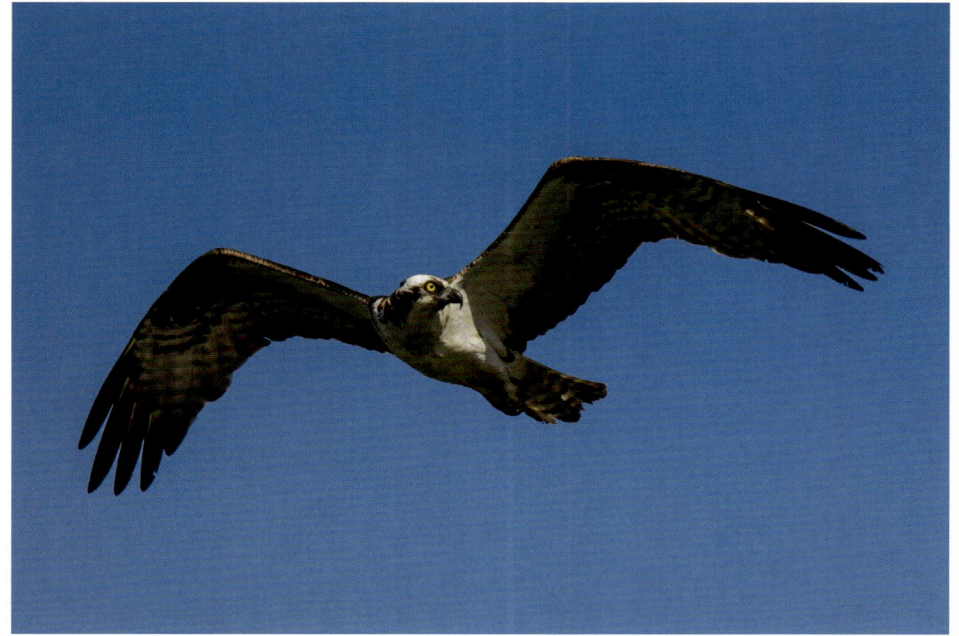

6.1 Working the exposure triangle begins with deciding how you want your photo to look. If you want to freeze the action of a fast-moving subject, you'll start by setting a faster shutter speed.
1/320 sec.; f/4; ISO 200; Canon 40D; EF300mm f/2.8L IS USM + 1.4x Extender II @ 420mm

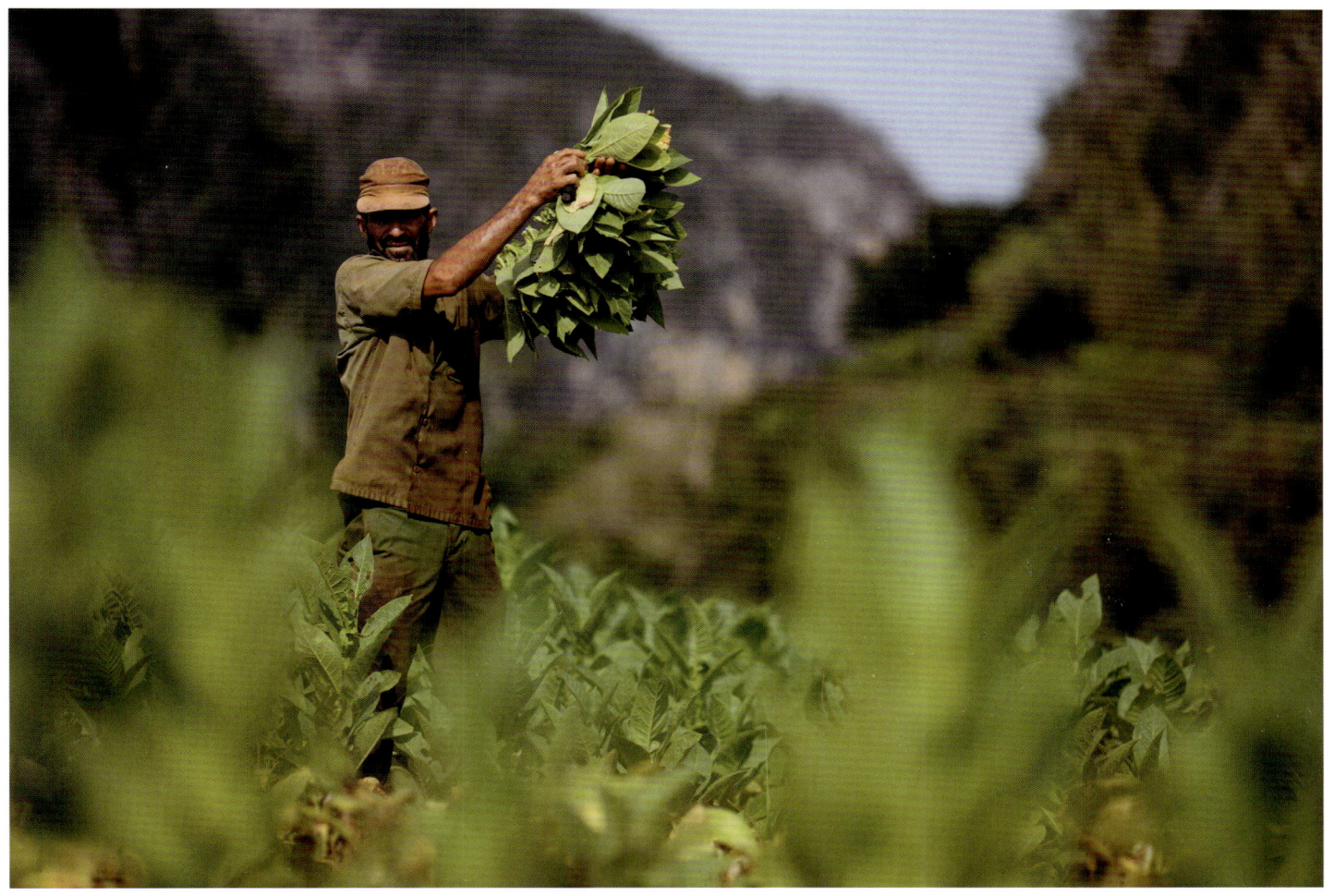

6.2 If you want your subject to stand out from the background, you'll need to set a large aperture opening. Once the aperture is set, you'll need to set the shutter speed and ISO according to the light levels in the scene.
1/1600 sec.; f/2.8; ISO 100; Canon 5DSR; EF200mm f/2.8L II USM

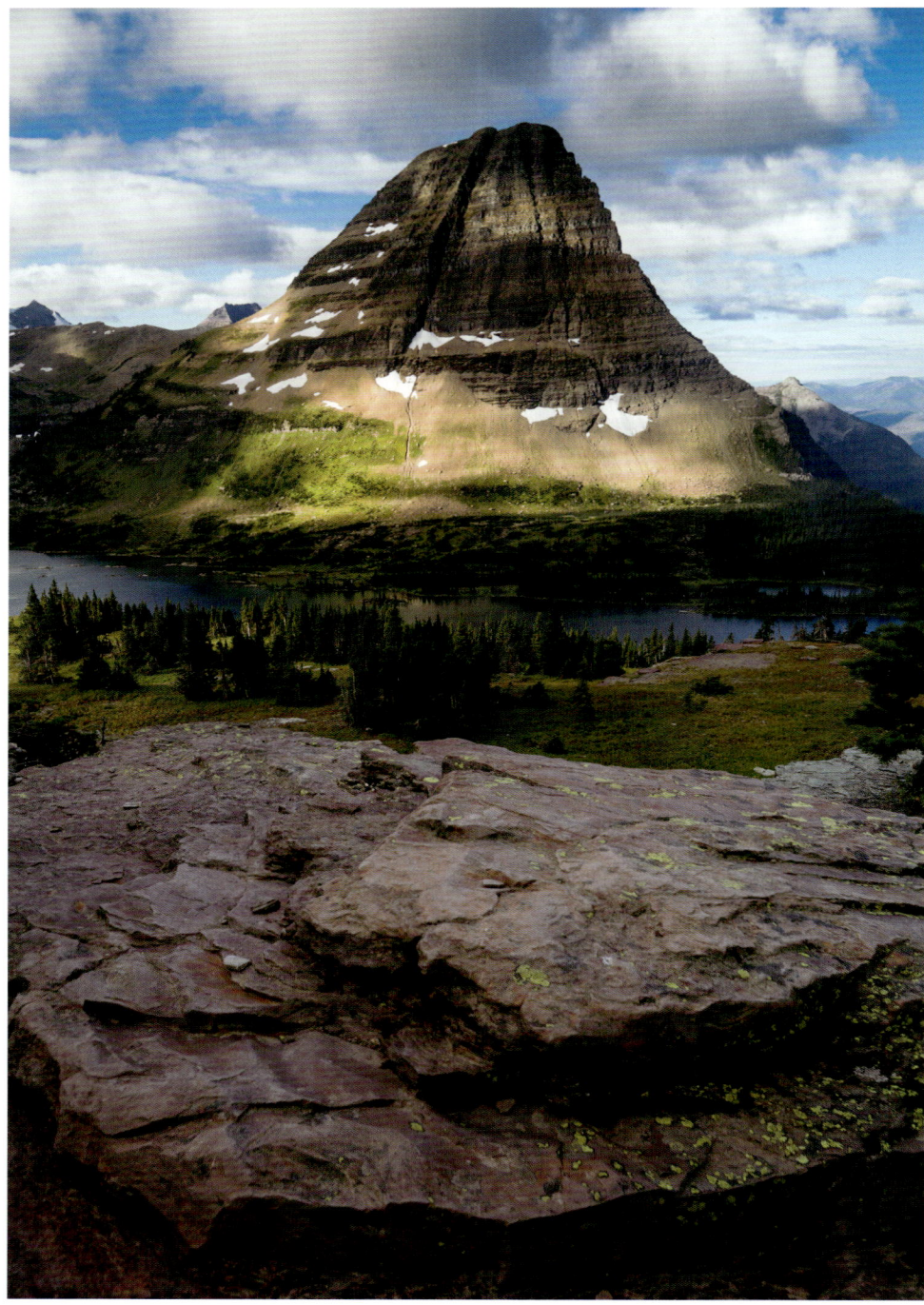

6.3 To capture subjects that have an expansive depth of field, you'll need to use a very small aperture. Landscape photographers frequently close their apertures down to f/11 to f/22 in order to hold focus from foreground to infinity.
1/15 sec.; f/14; ISO 100; Canon 5DSR; TS-E24mm f/3.5L II

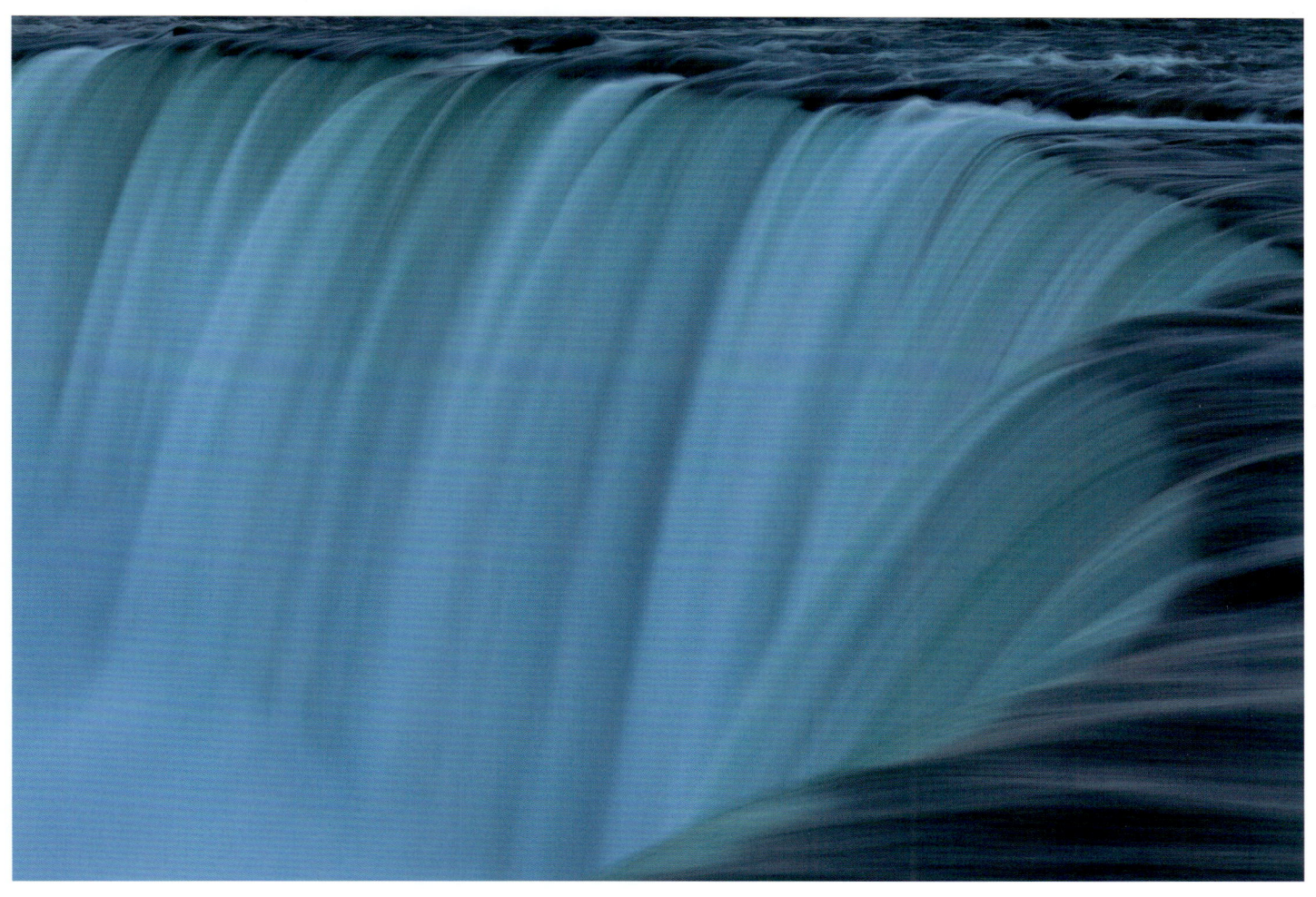

6.4 To blur the appearance of a waterfall, you'll need to use a slow shutter speed.
1 sec.; f/22; ISO 50; Canon 5D Mark IV; EF70-200mm f/4L IS USM @ 97mm

2

SHUTTER SPEEDS

CHAPTER 2

Perhaps the most enduring aspect of photography is the ability to stop time and capture life in a brief moment. That unique visual moment separates photography from all the other arts. No other medium can capture life so clearly and communicate it so easily. At the heart of this ability is the camera's shutter. It's critical to understand how the speed of the shutter, whether very fast or very slow, affects the final image so that you can tell your story more precisely. In photography, the difference between a hundredth of a second and a thousandth of a second is the difference between getting a great shot and not getting a useable shot at all.

7. HOW THE SHUTTER WORKS

THE SHUTTER SPEED describes the amount of time each pixel on the sensor is exposed to light. The actual speed of the shutter movement doesn't change at all; the amount of time the shutter is left open changes. "Exposure time" is a better description of this aspect of photography.

Most photographers understand that the shutter speed describes the shutter unit opening and closing for a specified period of time. The actual workings of the shutter are a bit more complicated. The shutter is like a door that opens and closes, exposing the sensor to light. But it's not like your everyday hinge door; it's more like sliding doors.

The camera's shutter comprises a group of quick-moving blades (generally 3–5) that are made from very lightweight materials. The blades overlap slightly, like shingles on a roof, to block light from passing through. When the shutter release is pressed, all the blades recede quickly out of the way in order to let the light through. The sensor is then exposed to light coming through the lens for the specified

amount of time. To end the exposure, a second set of blades from the opposite side will follow the motion of the first set.

This two-curtain system ensures that each pixel is exposed to light for the exact same amount of time. If there were only one set of blades, they'd have to make a return trip, thus exposing the pixels on one side of the sensor for more time than those at the other.

There is a slight problem with this system. Even with the best of technology, both the blades and the motors that power them have a limit of how fast they can go. If the second curtain waits for the first curtain to open completely before starting its closing motion, the fastest shutter speed possible on most cameras would be about 1/250 of a second.

In order to get faster shutter speeds, the camera employs a little trick: the second curtain begins to close shortly after the first curtain has begun to open to let light on the sensor. The two shutters working in tandem are, in effect, scanning light onto the sensor in a narrow strip.

Mirrorless Camera Shutters

This process of exposing the sensor to light describes how a traditional SLR camera works. Mirrorless cameras, on the other hand, must first have the shutter open in order to gather information on the sensor to be displayed in the electronic viewfinder or on the back LCD monitor of the camera.

When the shutter release is pressed on a mirrorless camera, the shutter unit moves into position to block the sensor. The sensor is then prepared to receive light. The first shutter opens and the second shutter closes, just like in an SLR. In order to return an image to the viewfinder, the second shutter needs to open so that light may strike the sensor and the information can be sent to the viewfinder.

This extra step at the beginning and end is necessary since SLRs use a mirror to view through the lens and a mirrorless camera uses the image coming directly off the sensor.

8. ELECTRONIC SHUTTERS

MECHANICAL SHUTTERS HAVE been a part of photography since the very beginning, when the "shutter unit" was a lens cap or a hat in front of the lens. With modern digital cameras, a new option has arisen: the electronic shutter. This new system will transform the way cameras are made and operated.

An electronic shutter isn't really a shutter at all—it's simply a sensor that can turn on and off very quickly. Doing away with the traditional shutter will save money, weight, and space. This complex apparatus sometimes causes blurring when the shutter unit opens so quickly that it causes a vibration throughout the camera at the moment the light is recorded by the sensor.

In theory, an electronic shutter is very simple. Turn all the pixels on to record the light striking them, then turn them off a fraction of a second later. With current technology, this process is not so simple.

The most common sensor in today's cameras is a CMOS (Complementary Metal Oxide Sensor), chosen for its high resolution, low noise, and efficient use of power. The CMOS doesn't record light with a simple on/off system. The CMOS uses a sequential system in which it turns on one pixel, then the next one in that row, and so forth until it gets to the end of the row and moves on to the next. This scanning process results in moving objects being slightly distorted. Moving cars look like they are leaning forward or backward depending on their movement. Cameras that are moved sideways will record buildings and trees that are leaning strongly to the left or right.

There are many cameras on the market right now that offer the option of either electronic first shutters or full electronic shutters. Because of the problem with moving subjects, these shutters are usually best employed when photographing stationary subjects. The main reasons to use an electronic shutter are for the silent, vibration-free operation or for reducing exposure time with stationary subjects.

Silent

New possibilities arise when using truly silent shutters or those that may have the very slight sound of the aperture closing down. Think about photographing in situations where any noise could be considered a distraction, like a stage play, a courtroom, or when photographing wild animals.

Vibration Free

Vibration from shutter movement or shutter bounce is not a rampant or significant problem, but it can affect photographs of subjects with very precise setups, like those common in macro or astrophotography, or shots with very high megapixel cameras.

With an electronic shutter, there are no moving parts—thus there is nothing to cause a vibration when the shutter unit opens up. This problem seems to peak in significance when the camera is on a tripod and set to a shutter speed around 1/8 of a second. The shutter unit quickly opens up and causes the entire camera to vibrate for a short period of time, resulting in a photo with a slight blur. A silent shutter completely solves this problem.

Exposure Control

While the modern sensors can't turn all the pixels on and off simultaneously, some can do it with a scanning process resulting in shutter speeds of 1/16,000 and 1/32,000, which are faster than the modern mechanical shutters can muster. At these very high shutter speeds, each pixel is turned on for a very short amount of time, but the scanning process across the sensor takes about 1/20 of a second. It's for this reason that the electronic shutter speeds are not useful for moving subjects but are quite practical for stationary ones.

If you were to shoot in bright sunlight with a low ISO and a wide aperture of f/1.2, your resulting exposure may require a shutter speed of 1/16000s–1/32000s. Most standard cameras will have a top shutter speed of 1/4000s–1/8000s.

The solution, with a traditional mechanical shutter, is to stop the lens down to f/2 or f/2.8, or to use a neutral density filter; both solutions may have a negative impact on the final photo. With an electronic shutter you can select 1/16000s or 1/32000s and get the shot without stopping the lens down or adding a filter.

I have no doubt that we'll see more advanced electronic shutters in the future. Eventually this technology will get faster, or a new type of sensor will be introduced to solve the current problems. The only problem with having only electronic shutters in all cameras is the loss of that traditional "click" sound with each exposure. You'll need to decide whether you'd prefer a silent shutter or one with a digital "click" sound effect added.

THE SHUTTER SPEED will impact a photograph in two ways: how much light falls on the sensor and how sharp or blurry an object that moves will be rendered.

The amount of light is pretty easy to understand. Let's start by moving from one full second to two full seconds. Twice the time equals twice the light. A shutter speed of 1/2 second means half the light as a one-second exposure.

On traditional cameras, the shutter speeds are approximately doubled or halved in sequence. For instance, the available shutter speeds are listed as: 1s, 2s, 4s, 8s, 15s, 30s as the exposure times get longer, and 1/2s, 1/4s, 1/8s, 1/15s, 1/30s, etc., as the exposure gets shorter. In theory, we can go as far as we want in either direction. In reality, most cameras will top out at 1/4000s or 1/8000s. This is due to mechanical limitations on the shutter unit. On the long end, most cameras will bottom out at 30 to 60 seconds

Camera displays, in the viewfinder or on the back or top of a camera, will often display one second as 1" (with the quotation mark indicating that the number is equal to or greater than a full second). All other numbers are fractions.

Thus, 60 means 1/60 of a second and 4 means 1/4 of a second.

Bulb

With most modern cameras, you can use a setting called "Bulb" that will allow you leave the shutter open as long as you like. To use this feature, press the shutter release a first time to open the shutter. When you want to end the exposure you'll press the shutter a second time to close the shutter. This might be handy for exposures that take place at night or in a very dark environment. Most photographers will limit this feature to exposures between 1 and 10 minutes since anything longer will exhibit excessive noise that detracts significantly from the photo. A tripod and remote cable release are important tools in this situation because they allow you to keep the camera steady, and you can start and stop the exposure without touching the camera.

One Stop

Going from 1" to 2" is often said as exposing for one more stop of light. "One stop of light" simply means we have doubled the amount of

light being received by the sensor. We can work this in reverse as well: 1/2s is one stop less light than 1". To change by one stop of light is to either double or cut in half the amount of light.

In order to be as exact as possible, shutter speeds are available in third stops. Going from 1 to 2 seconds looks like this: 1", 1.3", 1.7", 2". Set the camera to manual and turn the shutter speed dial to see for yourself. For example, working our way down from 1/1000s we have 1/800, 1/640, and 1/500. Some cameras may show slightly different numbers; for instance, some cameras display 2, while others display 0"5 to indicate 1/2 of a second.

The reason we have third stops and not fourth or tenth stops is that it's about the smallest difference a person can see when comparing two photos side by side. Tenth stops would allow us to be very precise, but would also require us to rotate our shutter speed dial a whole lot more! So if you wanted to make a photo that is just the slightest bit brighter or darker, you should adjust the exposure by 1/3 of a stop.

10. FAST SHUTTER SPEEDS TO STOP THE ACTION

MOST CAMERAS WILL have shutter speeds that range from 1/4000 to 30 seconds, with some models extending beyond these settings. In terms of exposure, shutter speeds are a great way of controlling the amount of light entering the camera, since every camera has so many from which to choose.

Beyond using shutter speeds for exposure control, we can also use them to affect the look of moving objects in the frame. Moving objects can be rendered either frozen or blurry depending on the chosen shutter speed and the movement of the subject.

What Is a Fast Shutter Speed?

A fast shutter speed is one that is quick enough to freeze the motion of a moving object. Generally speaking, shutter speeds of 1/30s and longer can be considered slow; speeds of 1/250s and shorter can be considered fast.

For fast human action, like running or dancing, 1/500 should freeze the action. With casual human motion, like walking or talking, 1/60 will likely do a good job at stopping the motion. These examples are very general rules of thumb, and there are many exceptions.

Your average runner going through the local park will likely be frozen with a shutter speed of 1/500s, but a professional athlete may need 1/1000s or 1/2000s. For a slug moving through the garden, a shutter speed of 1/30s may do a perfectly good job. The concept of a fast shutter speed is all relative to the motion of the subject, but 1/250s and faster is a good rule of thumb.

Right and Wrong Shutter Speeds

When it comes to right and wrong shutter speeds, it all depends on the desired outcome of the photographer. Don't ask another photographer what shutter speed to use unless you are trying to get your photo to look just like theirs!

Sometimes we want our subject to be frozen so that we can clearly see every detail, from the shoelaces to the hair blowing in the wind. Other times we want to create a more artistic abstract of a moving subject with the blurred lines showing their movement during the exposure.

The Best Fast Shutter Speed

For subjects that move, there does seem to be a best fast shutter speed and a best slow shutter speed. The best fast shutter speed is the slowest one that clearly stops the motion of a subject.

If you want to freeze the action of a subject, you'll use a faster shutter speed, possibly 1/250s or faster. If the subject shows movement or looks blurry at 1/250s, go to the next faster shutter speed of 1/500s. Continue that experiment until you get to a shutter speed that will clearly freeze the motion of your subject. An overly fast shutter speed will certainly stop the motion of the subject, but it also lets in less light, meaning you'll have to compensate by changing the aperture or ISO setting.

Let's take the example of a runner that could be frozen at 1/500s. In this case, let's say that 1/500s is doing a perfectly good job freezing the action. For the rest of the exposure, suppose we have an aperture of f/4 and an ISO of 100.

Suppose we now change our shutter speed to 1/8000s to stop every last bit of possible motion. What's the effect? Going from 1/500s to 1/8000s is 4 stops of light less. In other words, our image just got 4 stops darker and we'll need to compensate for this by changing either the aperture or the ISO, or a combination of the two.

We could open up the aperture by 4 stops (f/4 to f/2.8 to f/2.0 to f/1.4 to f/1.0), but there are very few f/1.0 lenses available, so this is an unlikely option.

We could make our image brighter by raising the ISO (ISO 100 to 200 to 400 to 800 to 1600), which would compensate for the 4-stop change. The problem here is that sensors will have more noise at ISO 1600 than they will at ISO 100 and our image will not be as clean and smooth in detail as a result.

Back to our running subject, which was frozen at 1/500s: by going to 1/8000s to freeze more action, we've lost 4 stops of light. If you recall, we said 1/500s was doing a perfectly good job of freezing the action, so going faster would have no discernible benefit. Losing 4 stops of light does cause a negative impact on our other settings. Changing the aperture to compensate may not be a viable option, and changing the ISO results in a noisier image. A 1/500s shutter speed is the best fast shutter speed in this case, because it sufficiently stops the motion of the runner and allows the aperture and ISO to be set with optimum settings.

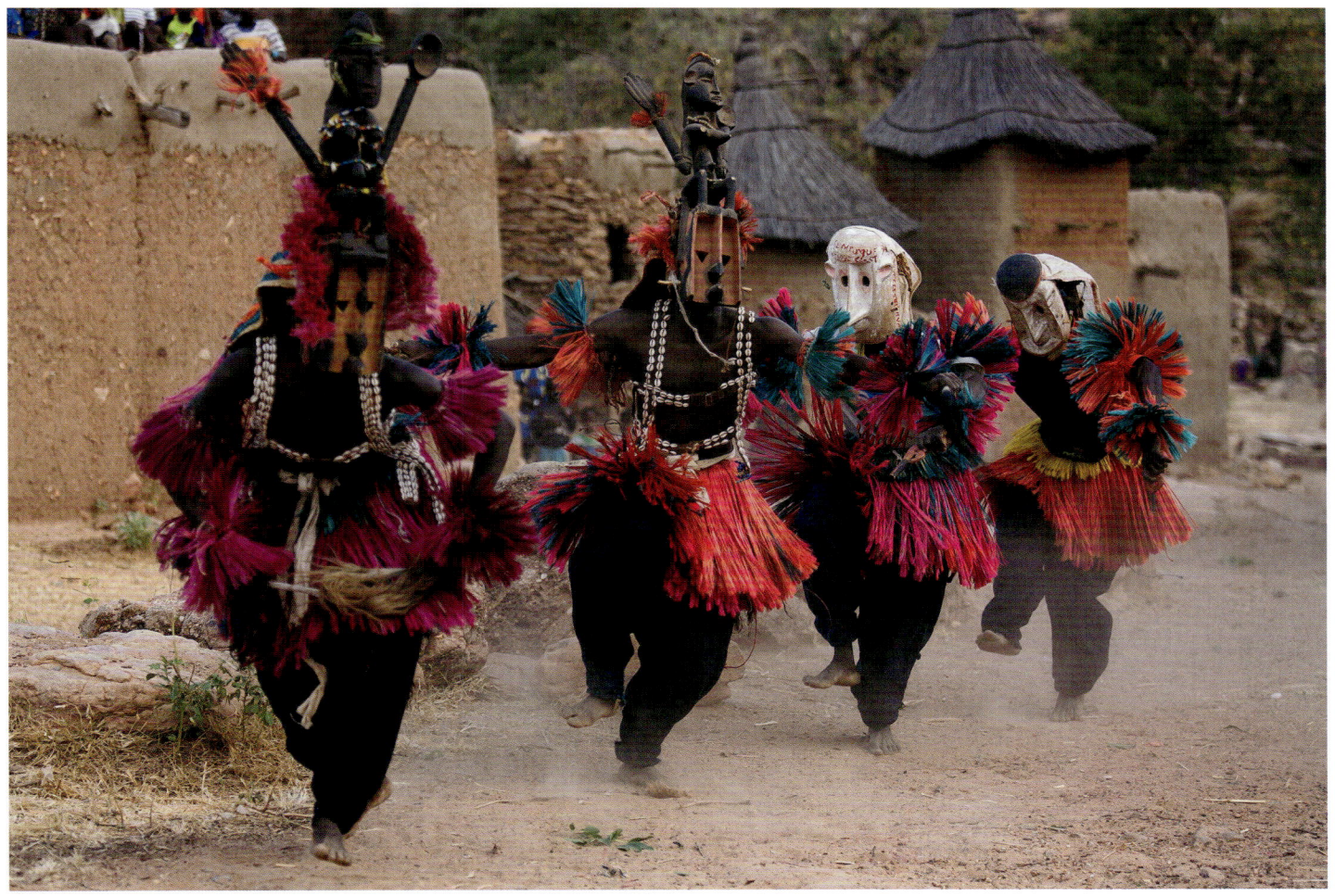

10.1 A shutter speed of 1/500s or faster is recommended for stopping fast human action.
1/500 sec.; f/2.8; ISO 200; Canon 5D; EF70-200mm f/2.8L USM @ 85mm

Share Your Best Shots in Which You Freeze the Motion of Your Subject!

Once you've captured a great shot in which you've frozen the motion of your subject, share it with the *Enthusiast's Guide* Community! Follow @EnthusiastsGuides and post your image to Instagram using the hashtag #freezemotion. You can also search that hashtag to see and be inspired by other photographers' shots.

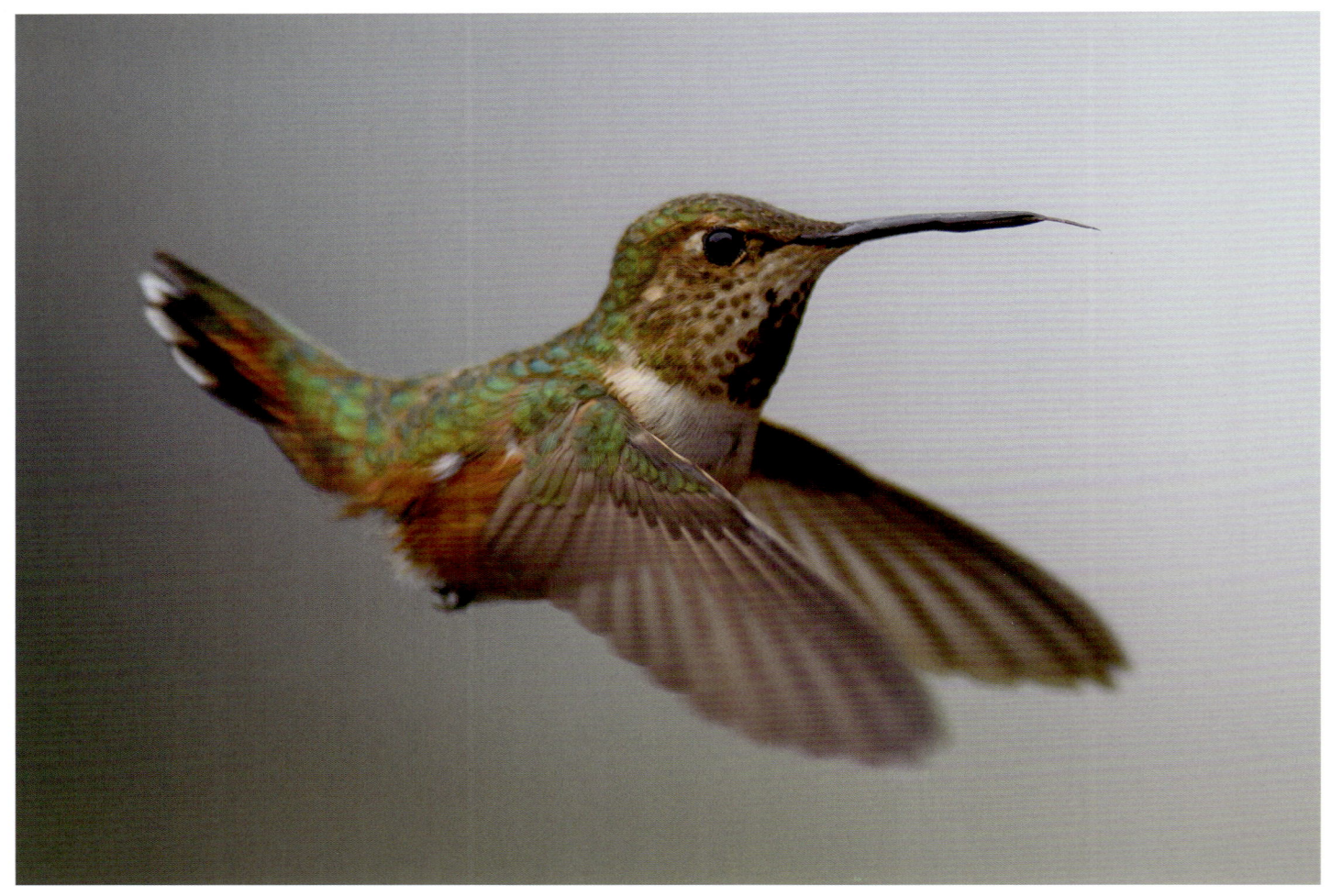

10.2 With a shutter speed of 1/2000s, the shutter has frozen the motion of
this hummingbird but not its wings.
1/2000 sec.; f/2.8; ISO 800; Canon 7D; EF300mm f/2.8L IS USM

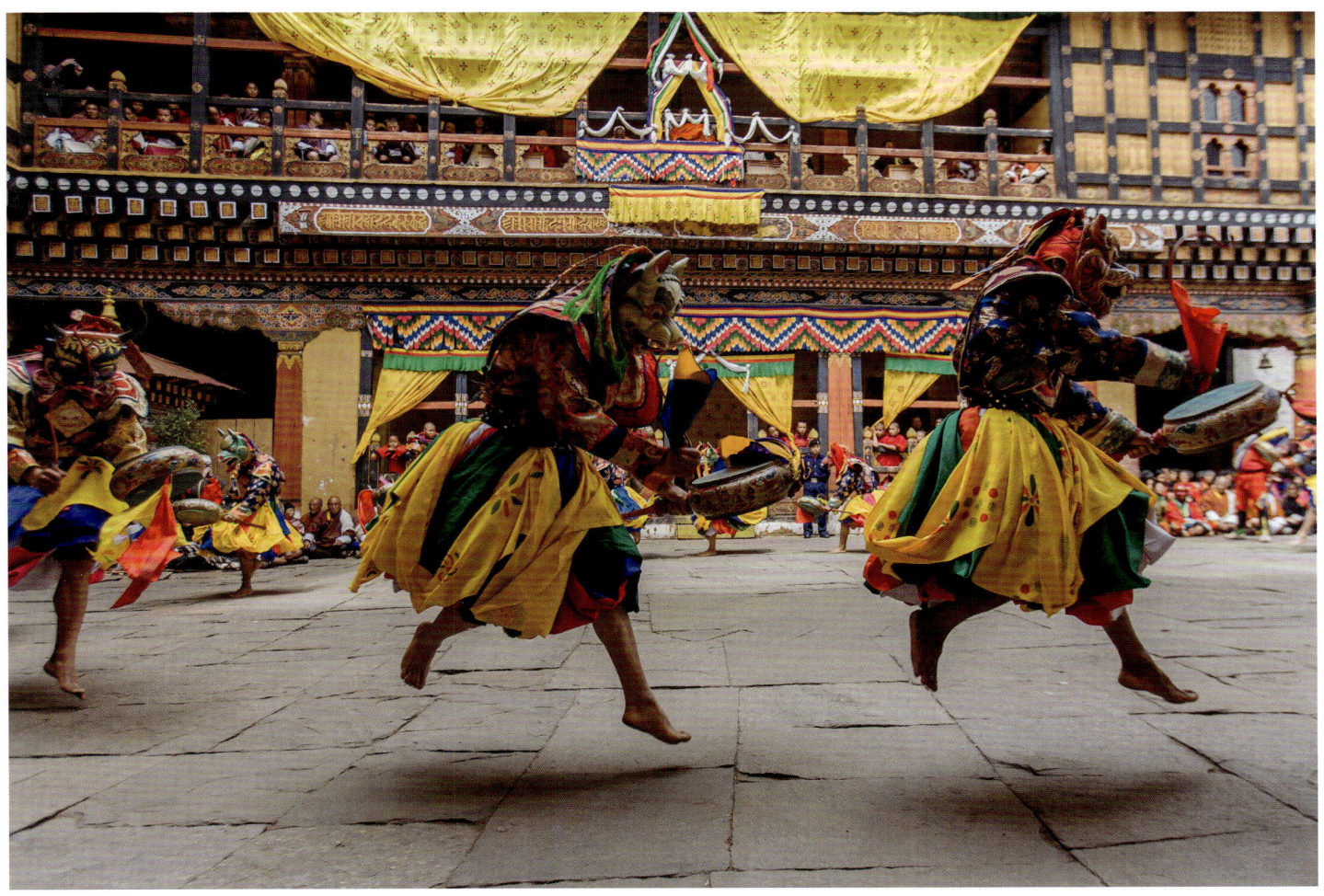

10.3 A shutter speed of 1/500s or faster is recommended for stopping fast human action.
1/500 sec.; f/4; ISO 200; Canon 5D; EF16-35mm f/2.8L USM @ 20mm

11. SLOW SHUTTER SPEEDS TO BLUR MOVEMENT

TO RENDER A moving object blurry, you can use a slow shutter speed. Why would anyone want a blurry subject? There can be lots of reasons for this: to show motion, to add mystery, or to hide details. Photography is a visual art, and slow shutter speeds are one way we can choose to render a scene in a visually unique manner.

What Is a Slow Shutter Speed?

Slow shutter speeds, like fast ones, are all relative to the motion of the subject. For those who like to keep things simple, shutter speeds of 1/30s and longer can generally be considered a slow shutter speed.

With our example of the runner in the park (the one where a 1/500 froze the action), a shutter speed of 1/30s will likely result in a trail of blurred streaks where the runner moved while the shutter was open. For a very fast moving subject like a hummingbird, 1/500s may be considered slow. Once again, it's all relative.

Subject Movement vs. Camera Movement

An important distinction between the types of blur you will get in a photo has to do with *what* is moving: the subject or the camera. With a camera secured to a tripod, it's the subject's movement that will create the blur streaks. Think of a night scene with car taillights streaking across the frame during a very long exposure.

If you move the camera while set to a slow shutter speed, everything will be blurry. The slower the shutter speed and the more movement of the camera, the blurrier the image will be.

Panning

If you move the camera to follow a moving subject, keeping it in the same location in the frame, you are panning with your subject. This is a common technique among sports and action photographers who are capturing several images in a row with the subject in about the same position in the frame. Panning with a slow shutter speed creates a distinctive look.

If a car is driving down the street and you follow it in the viewfinder, keeping it in the same location in the frame while also using a slow shutter speed, the car will be mostly sharp, but the background will be blurry. The sharpness of the car will depend on how precisely you are able to match your panning motion with that of the car. The blurriness of the background will depend on what shutter speed you have chosen and how fast you move the camera.

These slow shutter speeds combined with panning can result in some interesting photos and can be a lot of fun to experiment with. Expect lots of mistakes. With a bit of practice, you are sure to end up with a few winners.

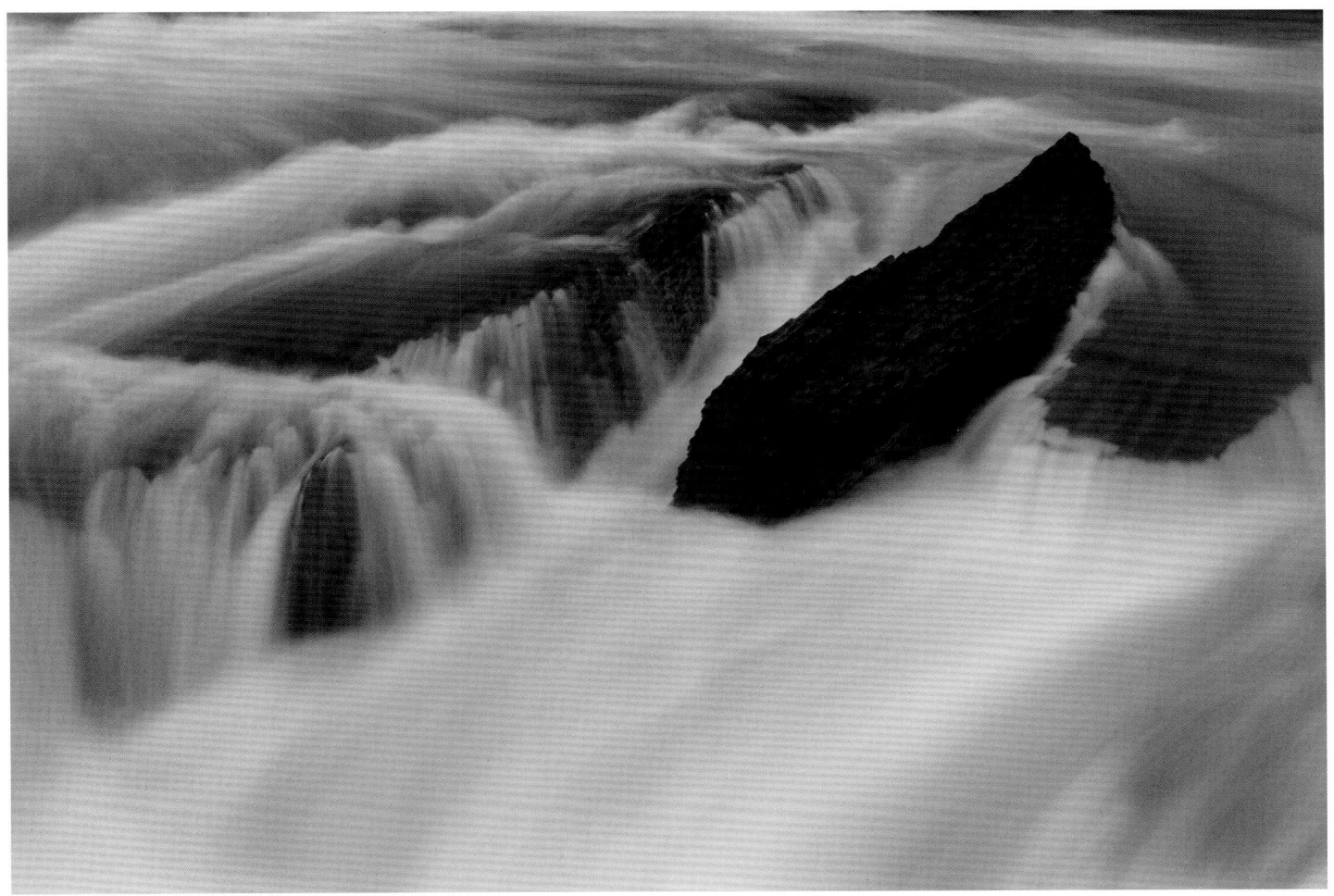

11.1 Capturing the flow of a river with a slow shutter speed (1s) was traditionally done out of necessity, but now is more of an artistic choice.
1 sec.; f/32; ISO 50; Canon 5D Mark II; EF70-200mm f/4L IS USM @ 78mm

Share Your Best Shots in Which You Blur the Motion of Your Subject!

Once you've captured a great shot in which you've blurred the motion of your subject, share it with the *Enthusiast's Guide* Community! Follow @EnthusiastsGuides and post your image to Instagram using the hashtag #blurmotion. You can also search that hashtag to see and be inspired by other photographers' shots.

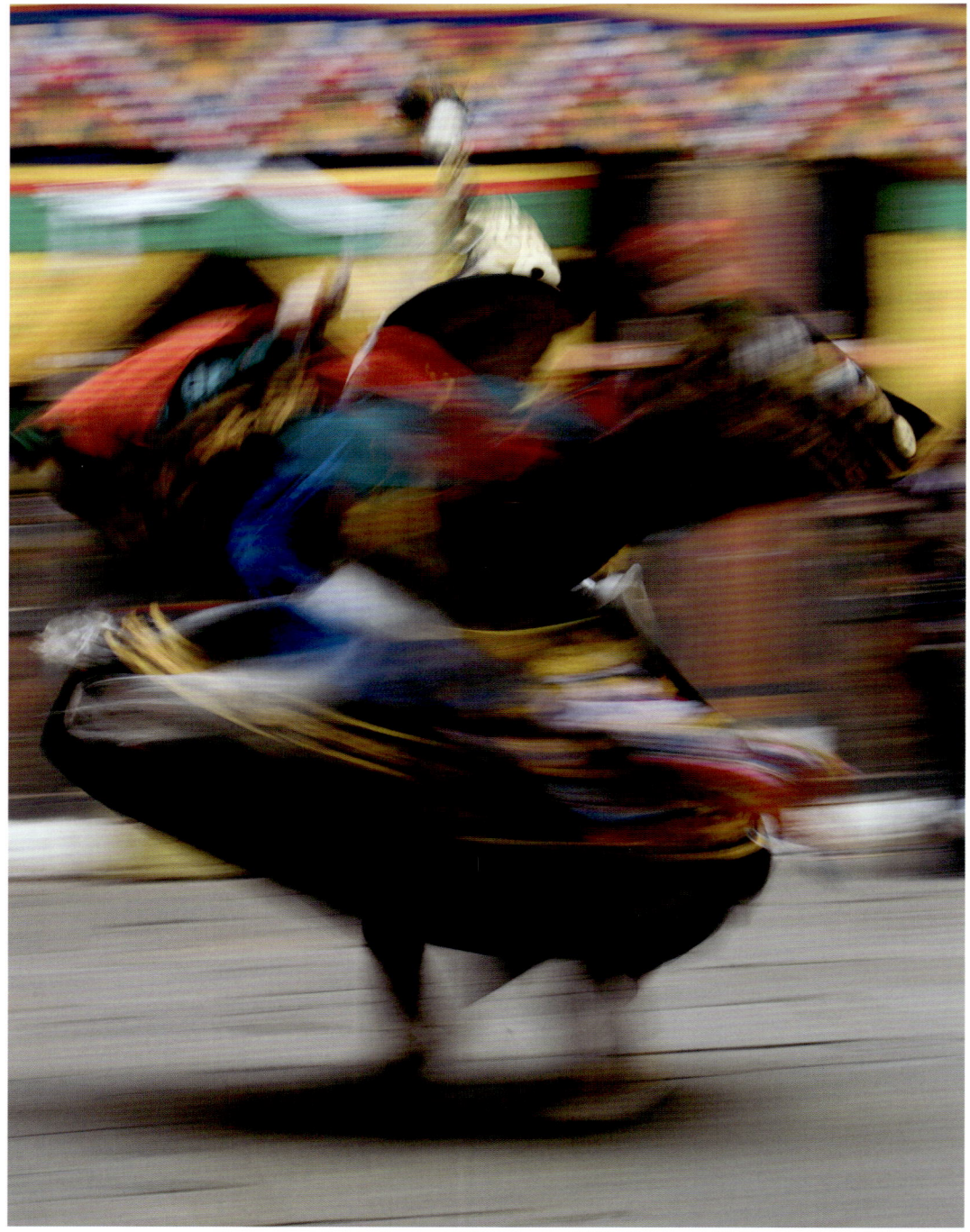

11.2 Try experimenting with different shutter speeds and moving subjects. This image, captured at 1/15s, was created by panning the camera with a dancing subject that was moving and spinning.
1/15 sec., f/16, ISO 200, Canon 5D, EF70-200mm f/2.8L IS USM @ 78mm

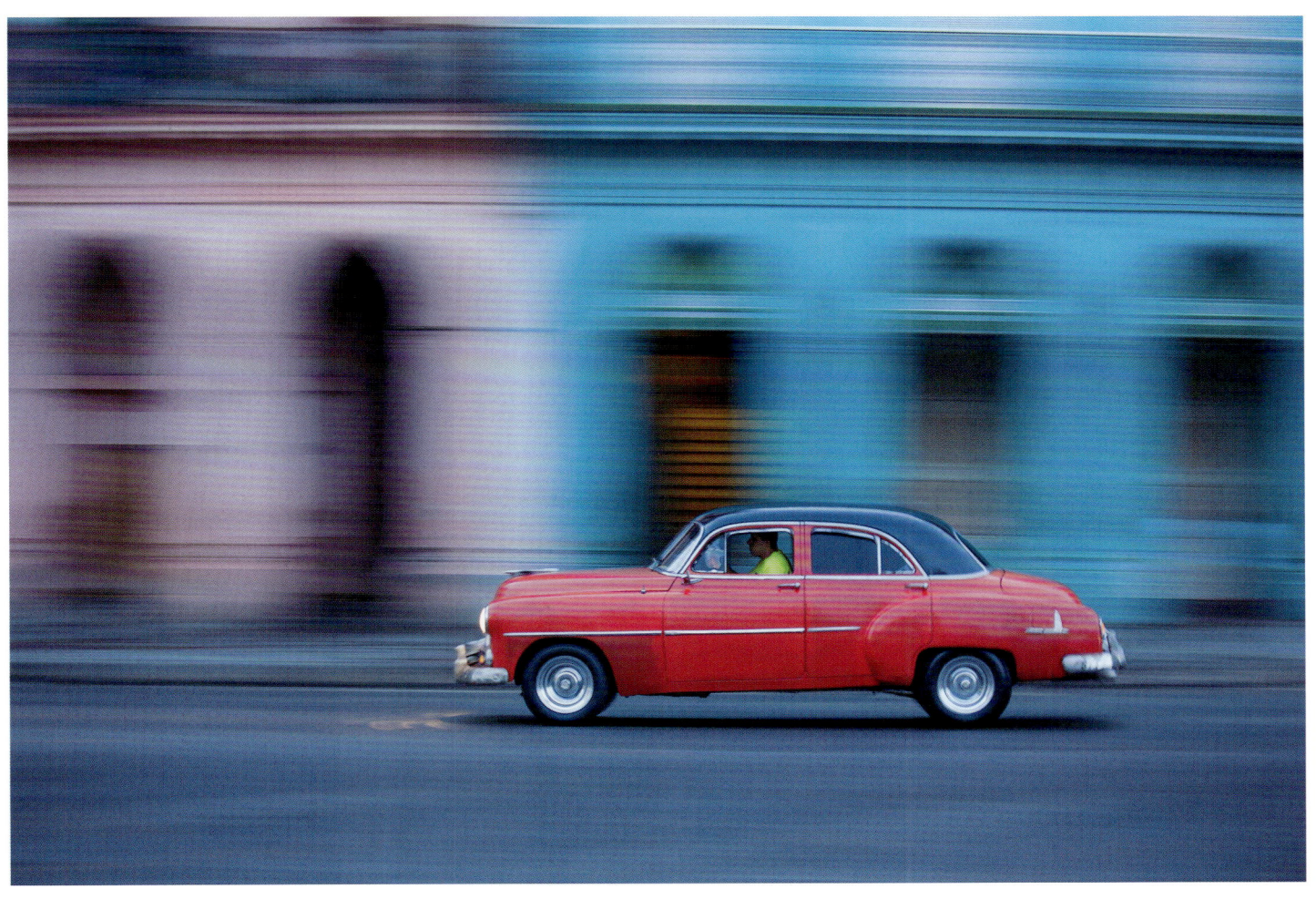

11.3 The key to panning is to use a slow shutter speed (1/8s here) and to keep the camera lined up and on pace with your subject as it moves.
1/8 sec.; f/4; ISO 400; Canon 5D Mark III; EF70-200mm f/4L IS USM @ 70mm

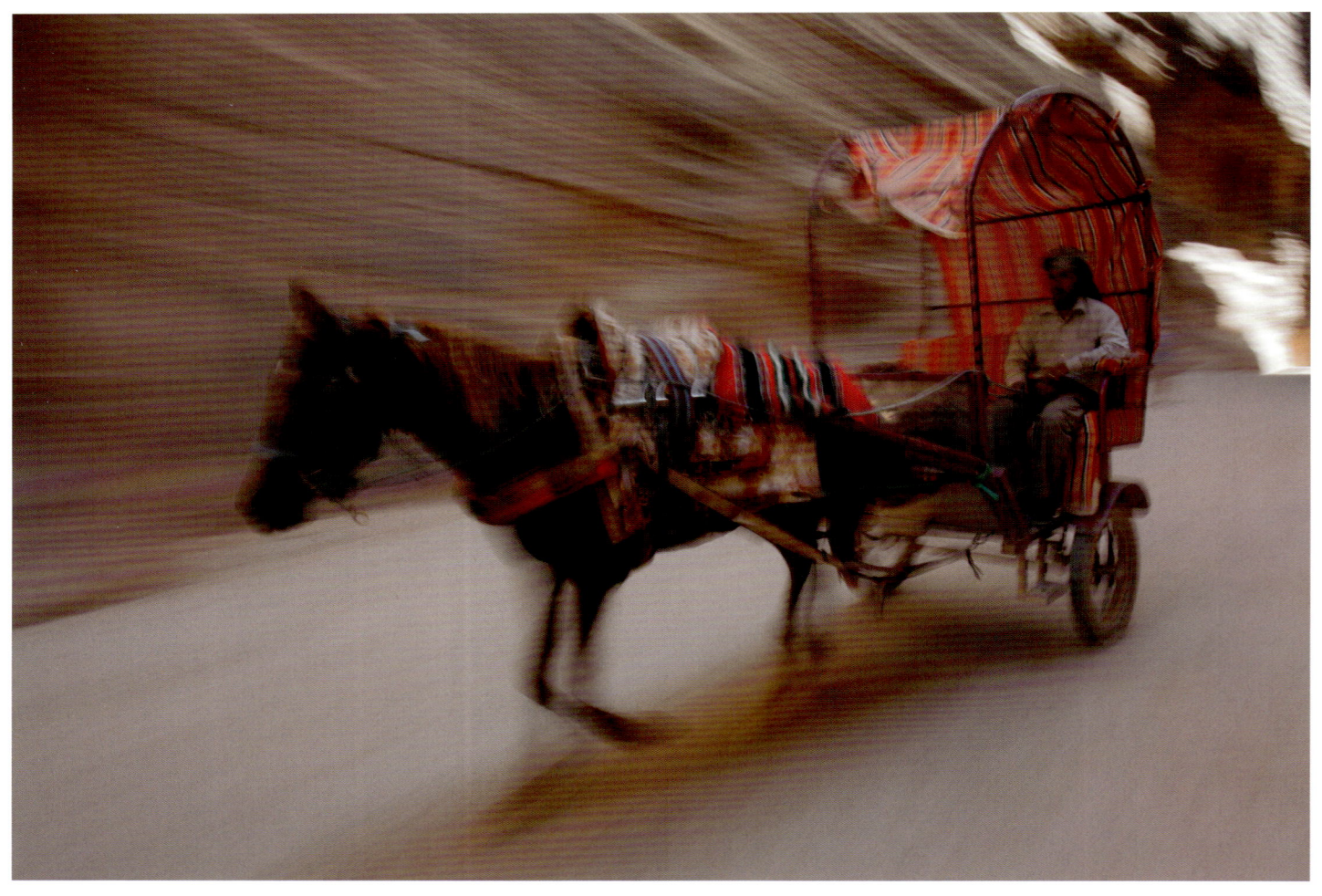

11.4 Panning with very slow shutter speeds (1/8s here) can lead to
very interesting results.
1/8 sec.; f/11; ISO 100; Canon 5D Mark II; EF17-40mm f/4LUSM @ 25mm

Subject Size Matters

The size of the blur will depend on the motion of the subject and the length of the exposure, but the relative size of the subject in the frame is also important. If a field of flowers is being blown about by a wind, flowers that are closest to the camera will appear to be more blurry than ones in the background. All the flowers may be moving the same amount, but the ones closest to the camera will appear the largest and thus show the most motion.

Subject Direction Matters

One more factor that comes into play in the world of blur is the direction of motion by the subject. Think about a fast-moving car going left to right across the frame. Its position is changing as it moves. Now consider that same car from a head-on point of view. As it approaches you, its position in the viewfinder of the camera doesn't change, but its size does, getting larger as it gets closer.

If the car is far away, the rate of size change relative to the frame is smaller than if the car is close. Subjects moving toward or away from the camera do not show as much relative movement as subjects that move across the frame. As a result, you'll need faster shutter speeds to stop action that happens across the frame, but you can use slower shutter speeds with action that approaches the camera.

The Best Slow Shutter Speed

Optimum results from slow shutter speeds is a matter of personal taste. Getting the perfect blur on a panning shot of car driving down the street or a wispy blur of a waterfall in the forest is often achieved though test shots at different shutter speeds.

Handholding the Camera

Blurry images caused by handholding the camera with too slow of a shutter speed are one of photography's most common mistakes. The shutter speed you need to be at for a sharp image can depend on many variables.

Shutter speeds below 1/60s are often referred to as slow, and will frequently result in blurry handheld images. Longer focal length lenses offer greater magnification, but will also magnify any movement. They require faster shutter speeds to ensure sharp images. The age-old rule of thumb is to use a shutter speed that is equal to 1/focal length. If you have a 200mm lens, you should use a shutter speed of 1/200s. A 500mm lens will need 1/500s, but a 15mm lens will only need 1/15s.

Other factors may apply as well. Many cameras or lenses will have a stabilization system that may compensate for handheld movement and allow handheld use 2–5 stops slower that the standard rule of thumb. Cameras with smaller sensors or crop sensors magnify the image more than full-frame cameras, and thus magnify movement. Finally, there is the unique way that each of us holds a camera. Some of us are steadier than others. In the end, a little of trial and error will show the limits of your handholding ability.

Recommended Shutter Speeds

Recommending shutter speeds can be a tricky business because it depends on the motion of the subject, its size in the frame, and the direction of travel. On top of all of this, you must consider the style you prefer in your image. For instance, aviation photographers often like to have a little blur in the propellers of an airplane in flight. How much blur to give it is up to you. Experience will be the best guide, so get out there and test every shutter speed available to see which ones you prefer for the action that you like to capture.

3

APERTURE

CHAPTER 3

The opening of the lens, otherwise known as the aperture, serves as both a technical and artistic control for the photographer. Occasionally, the technical demands of an image require one setting, while your artistic preferences will call for something very different. An understanding of the different aperture openings is critical.

The aperture unit is located in the lens itself, so this part of the camera can be exchanged on all cameras with interchangeable lenses; thus, understanding the aperture is an important element when it comes to choosing a lens. The aperture will have an impact on the size, cost, and capability of any lens, but most importantly, it will impact the options available to you when capturing an image.

12. WHAT IS AN APERTURE?

AN APERTURE IS an opening through which light travels. In a camera, it also describes the mechanical device that adjusts the size of the opening in the lens. This device comprises several lightweight metal blades that can reduce the size of the lens opening to a variety of smaller sizes. Like shutter speeds, this is another way you can control the amount of light being let into your camera.

F-Stops

Each different lens opening is labeled with an f-stop number that reflects how much light is being transmitted through the lens. *F-stop* is derived from the term *focal stop*. The f-stop can be calculated by the focal length of the lens divided by its opening. A lens with a 50mm focal length and with a 50mm opening for the light to pass through would have a maximum f-stop of 1.0 (f/1.0). If that same lens had a 25mm opening, the maximum f-stop would be f/2.

Maximum Aperture

The maximum aperture is a key indicator of a lens's performance. You can find this labeled quite clearly on most lenses (e.g., 1:2.8 or 1:3.5-5.6). The first number and the colon indicate that the number is a fraction. The number before the colon is the top number in the fraction; the number after the colon is the bottom number in the fraction. It's the second number, or set of numbers, that are key. In this example: 2.8 or 3.5-5.6. The lower the number, the more light the lens can let in.

Fast Apertures

Lenses that let in a lot of light are said to be "fast" lenses. This term is in reference to that lens's ability to gather light quickly, giving you the option of pairing it with fast shutter speeds. We could just as correctly call them "low ISO" lenses because they also allow for low ISO settings.

A Fast Aperture Is Relative

The concept of what a fast aperture is depends on what focal length you're talking about. A 50mm f/1.4 lens is considered fast, but with a 300mm lens, f/2.8 is considered fast. Lenses in the normal focal length range (35mm, 50mm, 85mm) are usually the fastest available. As focal lengths move further away from 50mm, the slower they tend to be.

13. THE APERTURE UNIT AND SETTINGS

THE MECHANICAL DEVICE in the lens that changes the size of the aperture comprises several lightweight metal blades arranged in a circular pattern. By default, the unit is fully open, with all blades rotated so that the maximum amount of light can be let through the lens. When you look through the viewfinder, you're seeing what the image looks like with the aperture unit fully open.

If you are using an aperture setting other than the maximum, the unit closes down after you press the shutter release, but before the exposure has begun. The blades move in toward each other, creating a smaller circular opening. The number of blades can be important—the more blades there are, the closer to a perfect circle the opening will be shaped. The shape of the opening can be important when considering flare and regions of the photo that are out of focus. The rounder the opening, the more pleasing the look of the resulting shot will be. Blades may also be shaped with a gentle curve so the opening remains round rather than taking on the shape of a polygon.

The aperture unit has many predetermined settings available. The list of common, full f-stop settings is: 1.0, 1.4, 2.0, 2.8, 4, 5.6, 8, 11, 16, 22, 32. In this sequence, f/1.0 is the largest and f/32 is the smallest. The numbers follow a pattern that describes how much larger or smaller the lens opening must be in order to double or halve the amount of light passing through it.

The f-stops are a number series based on math. The key to understanding the series is knowing the square root of 2, which is 1.4. However, it may be easier to remember the f-stop series if you can remember just two numbers: 1 and 1.4. The series follows a pattern in which the next number in the series is equal to double the previous number. To determine what comes after f/1.4, look to the previous f-stop (f/1.0) and double it (f/2.0). To determine the next number, double f/1.4 to get f/2.8. This results in the series 1.0, 1.4, 2, 2.8, 4, 5.6, 8, 11, 16, 22, 32. Additional settings can be determined using this formula for either higher or lower aperture settings.

Variable Aperture

A basic zoom lens supplied with an entry-level camera might have a maximum aperture of f/3.5-5.6. This is a variable aperture lens, which means the maximum opening changes as the zoom lens focal length is adjusted. The most common variety, an 18-55mm, will have a maximum aperture of f/3.5 at the 18mm setting, and f/5.6 at the 55mm setting. You'll still have the ability to stop the aperture down to smaller settings like f/8, f/11, and f/16 at all zoom settings, but the maximum opening will be different depending on whether you are at the 18mm or 55mm setting.

Apertures for Depth of Field

When you change the size of the aperture opening, you are not only changing the amount of light being let through the lens, you are also altering the path that light travels. The path the light takes alters the way it strikes the sensor and, as a result, changes how much of the scene will be rendered sharp and in focus. This in-focus area is defined as the depth of field. The lens can only be focused on one point at a certain distance from the camera; but by altering the depth of field, we can vary the amount of space, both in front of and behind this focus point, that also appears in focus.

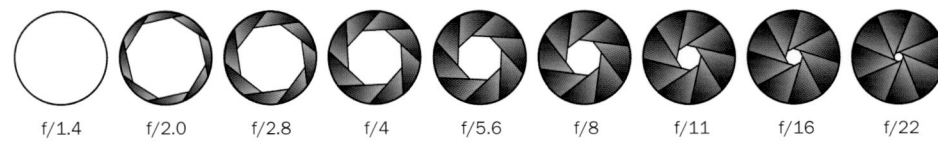

| f/1.4 | f/2.0 | f/2.8 | f/4 | f/5.6 | f/8 | f/11 | f/16 | f/22 |

13.1 Aperture settings for common lenses range from f/1.4 wide open to f/22 closed down.

14. DEPTH OF FIELD

WITH LARGE APERTURES (low numbers, e.g., f/1.4, f/2, f/2.8) you can expect a shallow depth of field. This shallow depth of field will result in a photo that has one area in focus, and regions in front of and behind it that are out of focus with an increasing level of blur the farther they are from the point of focus. At the opposite end of the spectrum, small aperture openings, like f/11, f/16, and f/22, will create images with large depth of field, showing much of the scene in focus.

Depth of Field Is Relative

Depth of field can be a bit tricky to estimate because it's controlled not only by your aperture setting, but also by the focal length of the lens and the focusing distance.

Focal Length Controls Depth of Field

The focal length of a lens will affect the amount of depth of field exhibited at a given aperture. Wide lenses tend to have great depth of field. Telephoto lenses tend to have shallow depth of field. Using an aperture of f/5.6 will result in great depth of field with a wide lens, whereas it will be quite shallow when used with a telephoto lens.

Focusing Distance Controls Depth of Field

The distance that your lens is focused at will also impact the depth of field. Focusing on a subject far away will result in an image with lots of depth of field. Focus at a close distance and your image will result in very shallow depth of field. This can readily be seen with a macro lens or any lens that can focus on subjects at very close range.

Try it out: Set your lens to focus on an object two feet away (0.6 meters) and you'll likely notice that your scene has very shallow depth of field. Use that same lens to focus on something far away, and you will see greater depth of field.

14.1 Depth of field depends on a number of factors. The easiest of these factors to control is the size of the aperture. This series of images shows how results change by adjusting the aperture setting.

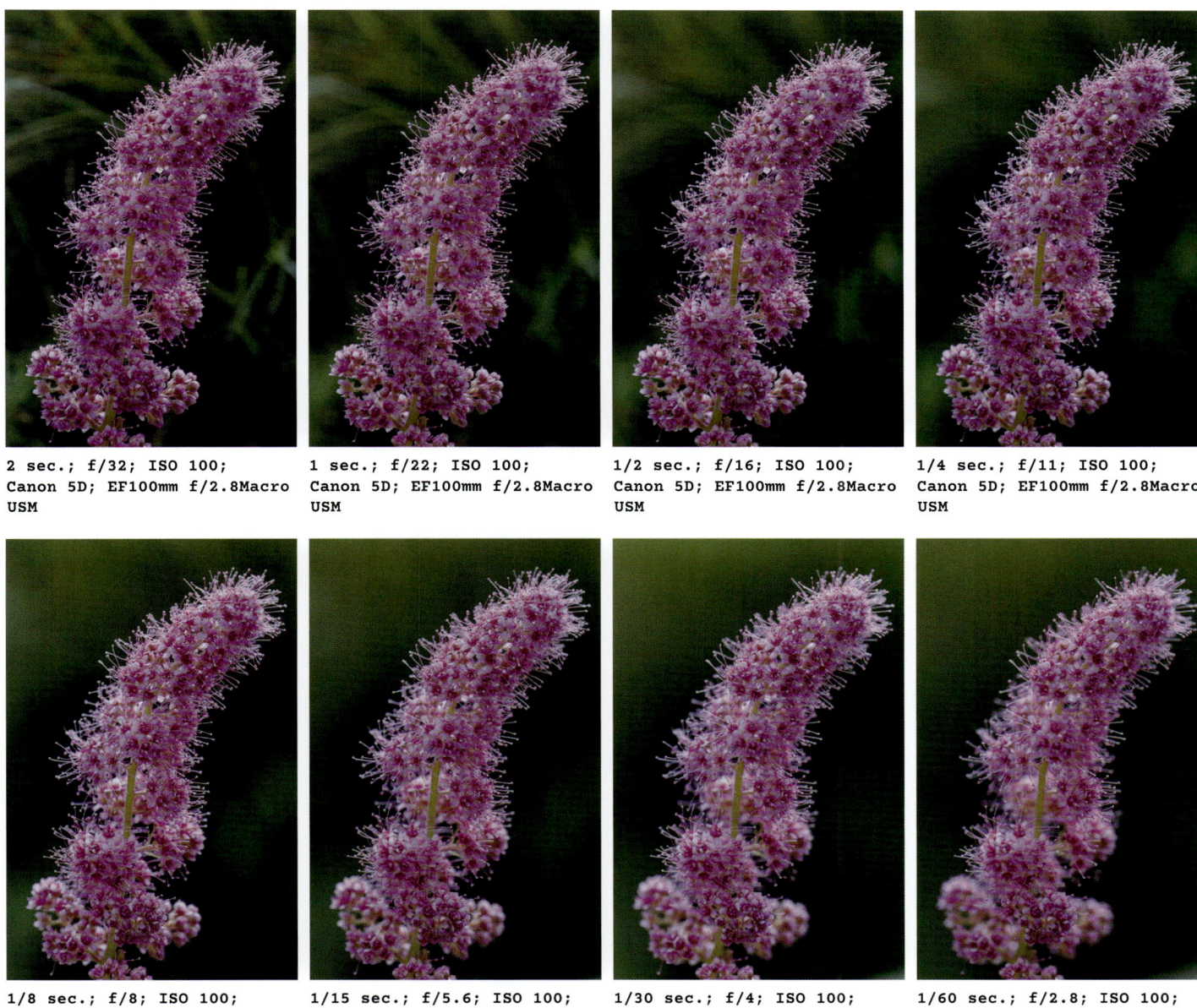

2 sec.; f/32; ISO 100;
Canon 5D; EF100mm f/2.8Macro
USM

1 sec.; f/22; ISO 100;
Canon 5D; EF100mm f/2.8Macro
USM

1/2 sec.; f/16; ISO 100;
Canon 5D; EF100mm f/2.8Macro
USM

1/4 sec.; f/11; ISO 100;
Canon 5D; EF100mm f/2.8Macro
USM

1/8 sec.; f/8; ISO 100;
Canon 5D; EF100mm f/2.8Macro
USM

1/15 sec.; f/5.6; ISO 100;
Canon 5D; EF100mm f/2.8Macro
USM

1/30 sec.; f/4; ISO 100;
Canon 5D; EF100mm f/2.8Macro
USM

1/60 sec.; f/2.8; ISO 100;
Canon 5D; EF100mm f/2.8Macro
USM

15. GREAT DEPTH OF FIELD

IN SOME PHOTOGRAPHS you may want everything to be in focus so that the viewer can discover and enjoy all the details that the image has to offer. Landscape and scenic images are frequently captured using this technique. The entire scene is important, so why not keep it in focus so that it can be enjoyed in the same way you might experience it in the real world.

These great depth-of-field images are often captured with wide-angle lenses that are stopped down to f/11, f/16, and f/22. This combination of wide-angle lens and stopped-down aperture is quite common to the landscape photographer. You might even call it a recipe: find a great landscape, use a wide-angle lens, and set the aperture to f/16—it works all the time.

To shoot these great depth-of-field images, you'll likely need a tripod. When setting the aperture to such a small opening, like f/11, f/16, or f/22, you'll need to compensate for the small amount of light passing through the aperture by using a much longer shutter speed. In all but the brightest situations you'll end up with shutter speeds well below the limitations of handheld shots. You could increase the ISO, but that adds noise and reduces the quality of the image. The ISO should only be increased in cases where you need a faster shutter speed. In a case where you need greater depth of field and faster shutters, raising the ISO would likely be a necessary step. If you don't need a faster shutter speed in your great depth-of-field image, you should use a tripod to support your camera.

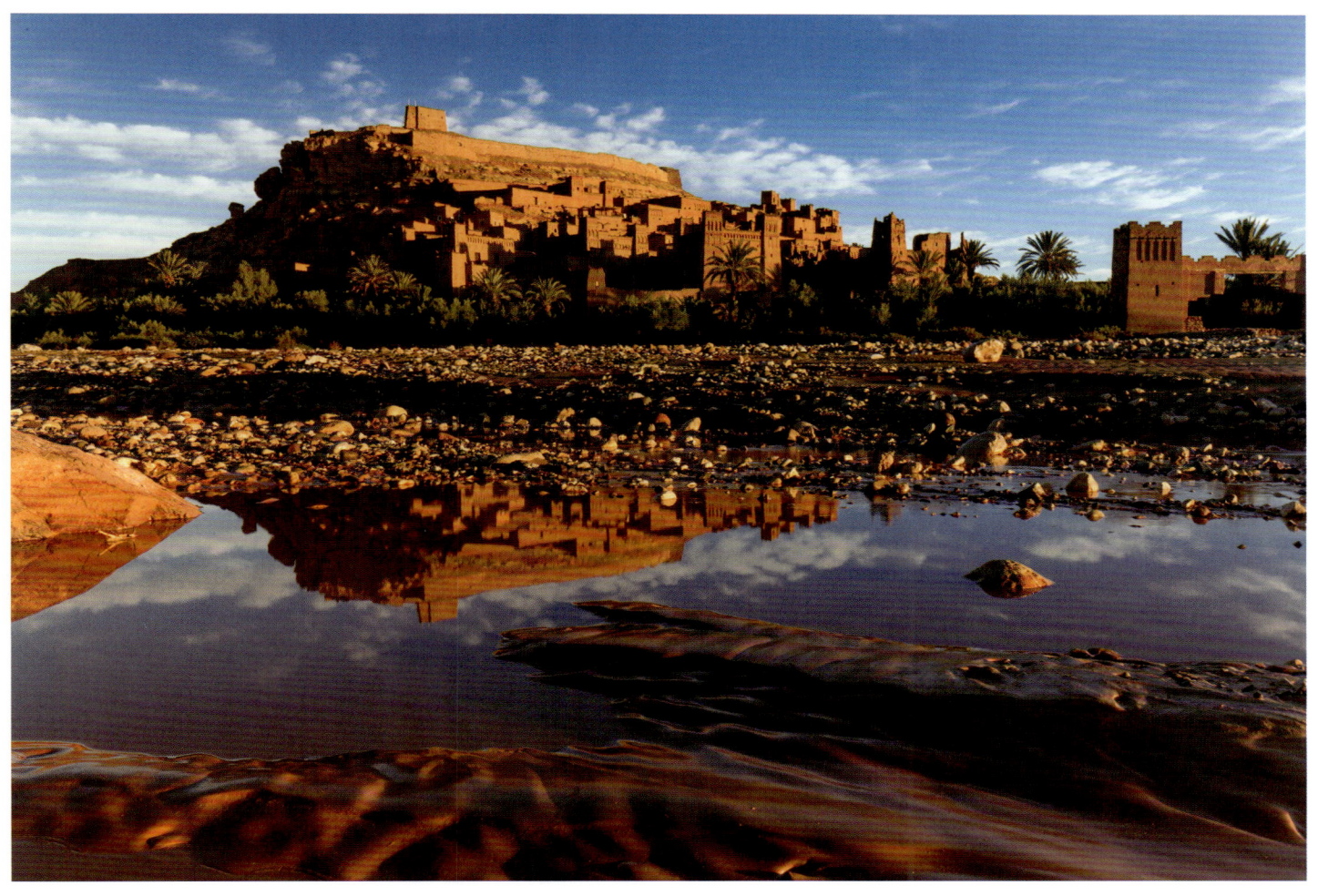

15.1 To capture images with great depth of field, you will need a small aperture opening. An aperture of f/16 was used in this case.
1/2 sec.; f/16; ISO 100; 30mm lens; Canon 5D III; EF16-70mm f/4L IS USM @ 30mm

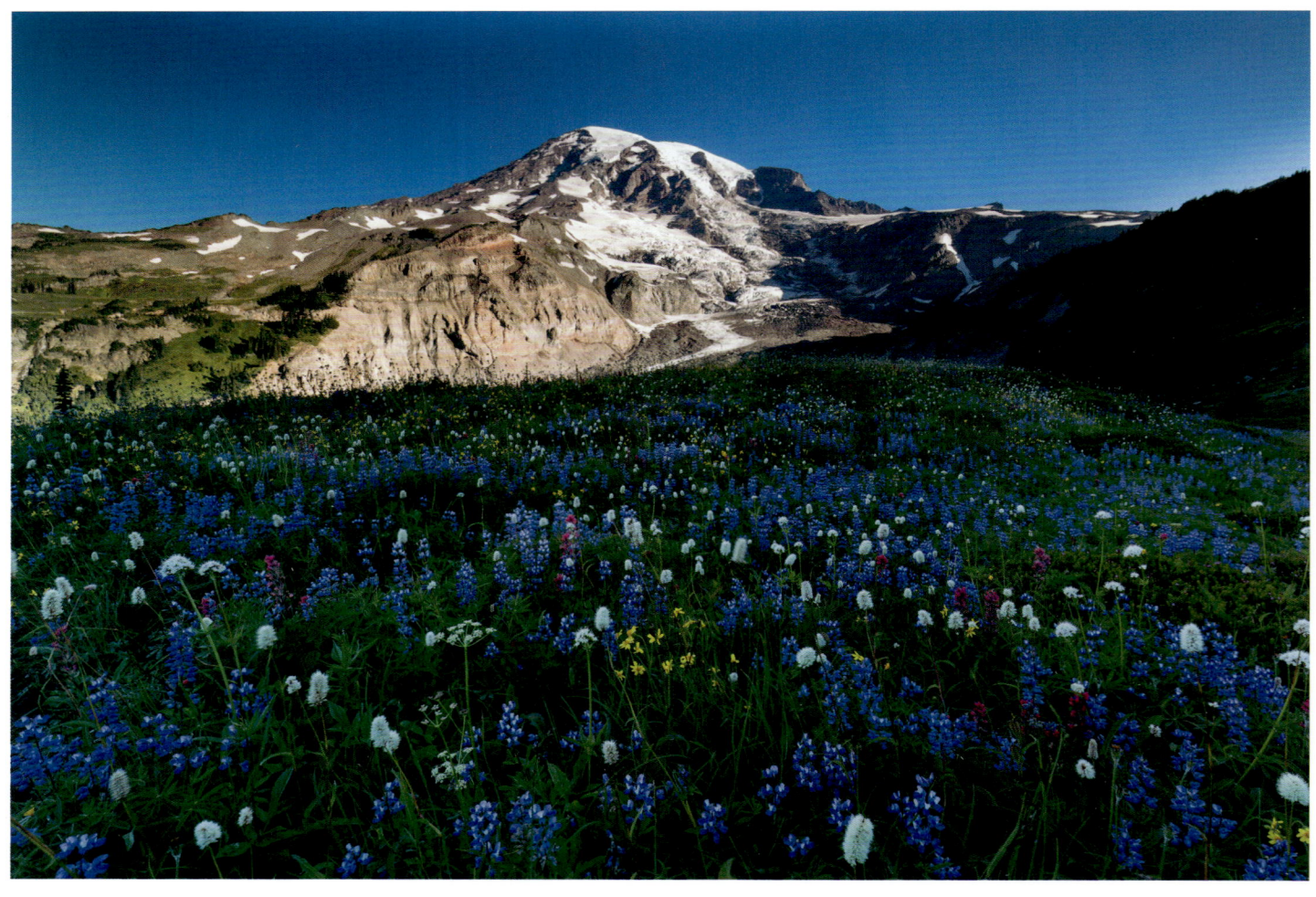

15.2 A tripod will be a handy tool when capturing images with great depth
of field (like this one at f/22) since the necessary shutter speeds are
frequently quite slow (1/2s for this image).
1/2 sec.; f/22; ISO 100; 16mm lens; Canon 5D III; EF16-70mm f/4L IS USM @ 16mm

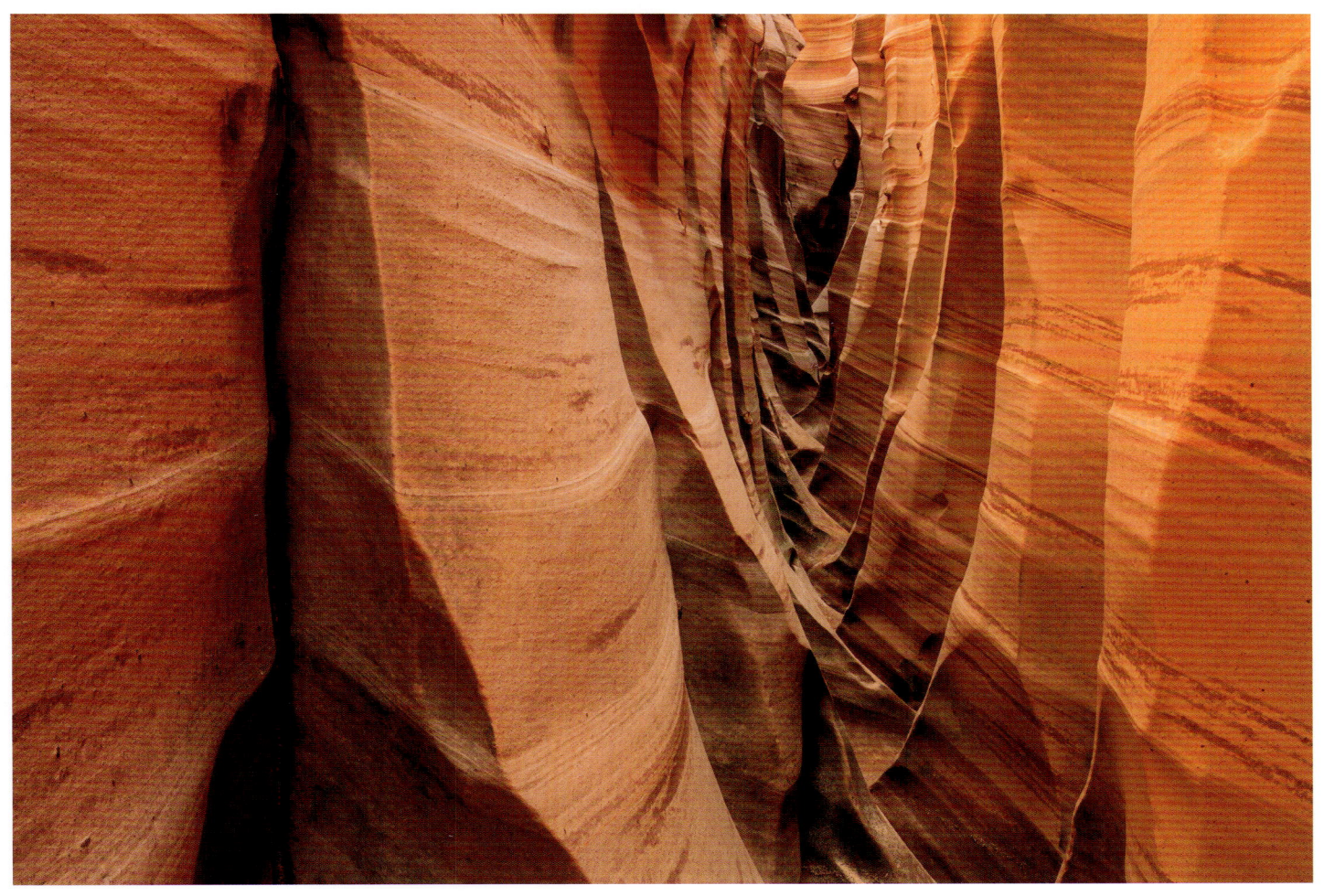

15.3 Capturing every last bit of detail from the foreground to the distance
will require closing the aperture down, in this case all the way to f/22.
1"; f/22; ISO 100; Canon 5D Mark III; EF24-70mm f/2.8L II USM @ 33mm

16. SHALLOW DEPTH OF FIELD

PORTRAIT PHOTOGRAPHERS OFTEN want to draw attention to the face or eyes of their subject. One way to direct attention to those areas is to have a narrow area of focus on a subject's face or eyes. With the rest of the scene rendered into a soft blur, your eyes can't help but be drawn to the area of sharp focus.

This technique works for not only portrait photographers, but anyone that wants to direct attention to a particular area of a photo. It gives the photographer directorial control over the content of the image. It allows you to include elements important to the narrative of the photograph while also emphasizing the most important aspect of the photo. Shallow depth of field is a great technique for directing attention to where you want it to be.

Focus Options

In order to harness this technique you'll want to be very familiar with your camera's focusing system. The main techniques for doing this are Focus Lock and selecting an individual focus point.

Focus Lock

When you have your camera in the standard focusing mode (AF-Single, One Shot) the camera will focus with a halfway press of the shutter release. When the camera achieves focus, you may hear a beep-beep or see an in-focus confirmation light. This means your camera has determined proper focus and the lens in now locked in at this position. The focus will stay locked in as long as your finger maintains the halfway press of the shutter release. With the focus locked in, you are free to recompose the image. When you've settled on the composition that looks good to you, press the shutter release all the way down to take the photo. This focus-lock technique allows you to independently control both the focus and the composition.

Focus Points

A different way to focus on a point away from the center of the frame is to select a specific focus point. Most cameras have a large number of focusing points to choose from. By default, most cameras come from the factory with all focus points simultaneously activated. In this case, the default point is on the subject closest to the camera.

If you want to be precise about where your point of focus will be, you'll need to take control of the focusing system. You can select any individual point within the area you want in sharp focus. The technique for adjusting the focus points is different from camera to camera, so you may need to consult your manual for specific information. When you select a focus point, you can simply press the shutter release halfway to focus and the rest of the way when you are ready to take the photo.

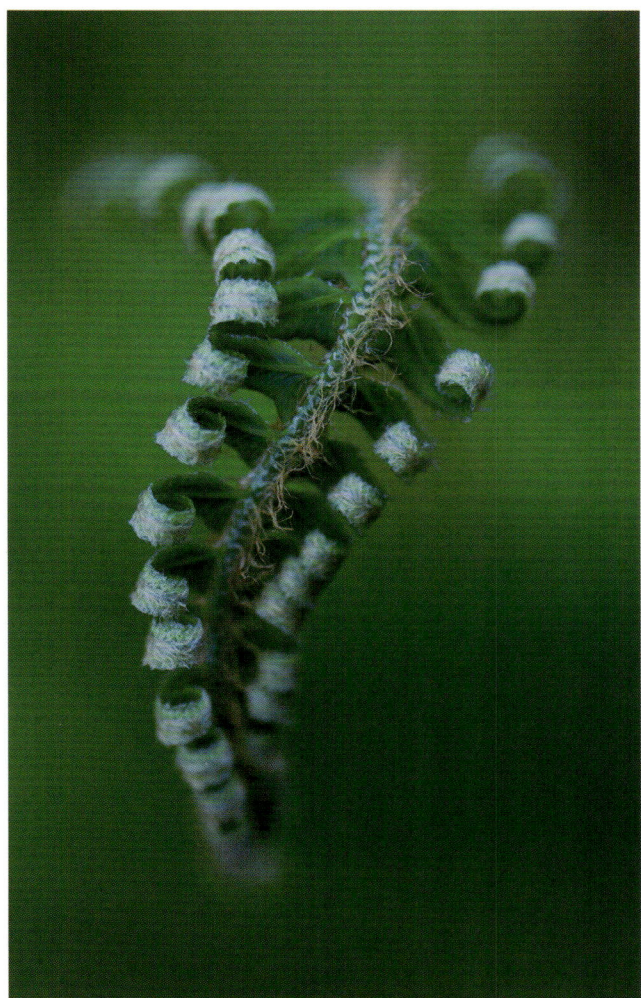

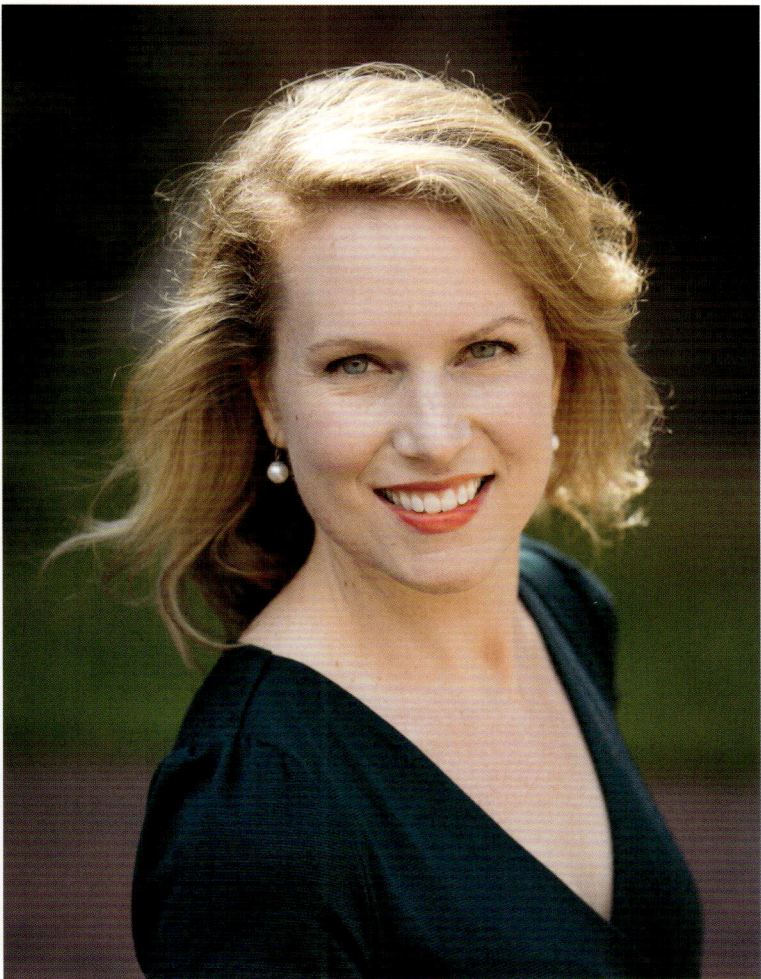

16.1 Shallow depth of field is greatly enhanced by being very close to your subject. In this macro shot, the background of the scene has gone completely out of focus, creating a smooth backdrop for the main subject.
1/4 sec.; f/2.8; ISO 200; Canon 5D Mark III; EF100mm f/2.8 Macro USM

16.2 Portraits are a great time to use shallow depth of field. The out-of-focus background lets your subject stand out. Additional tip: many macro lenses make great portrait lenses because they are the right focal length, relatively fast, and easy to handhold.
1/500 sec.; f/2.8; ISO 100; Canon 5D Mark III; EF100mm f/2.8 Macro USM

17. APERTURE AND LENS CHOICE

THE MAXIMUM APERTURE describes a lens's light-gathering ability when the aperture is fully open. This is a key feature to know when selecting a lens.

It's a sign of how well the lens will perform under low-light conditions. It can also affect the focus performance, size, weight, and price of the lens.

Prime lenses (non-zooms) will have a single number indicating the maximum opening (e.g., f/1.4 or 2.8). Zoom lenses will have either a variable maximum aperture (e.g., f/2.8-4.0) or a fixed maximum aperture (e.g., f/2.8). The lower the number, the better the lens will do in low-light conditions. All lenses will have apertures that can close down, so the minimum aperture isn't nearly as important at the maximum aperture.

Zoom lenses usually have slower apertures (f/2.8 to f/5.6) when compared with fixed or prime lenses (f/1.4 to f/4). Budget zoom lenses will often have the slowest apertures (f/3.5–5.6) and thus a limited ability to shoot images with a shallow depth of field. Faster lenses are available, but typically they are larger, heavier, and more expensive.

How fast a lens do you need? This depends on what you hope to do with your lens and your budget. The standard kit lens, often an f/3.5–5.6 zoom lens, will be perfectly suitable for beginners. For shooting with a shallow depth of field, you'll likely want a faster lens as well as one with a longer focal length. You can get a fast zoom, but their maximum aperture is typically around f/2.8. If you want or need something even faster, you'll need to go with a prime lens, in which the maximum aperture may be as fast as f/2 or f/1.4.

The least expensive and easiest way to shoot with shallow depth of field is with a 50mm f/1.8 or 85mm f/1.8 lens. These lenses are very common and relatively inexpensive. These normal to short telephotos with fast apertures are best known as portrait lenses but they are useful for much more. These are among the most common lenses in use today, and you should be able to easily find new and used options from a variety of manufacturers.

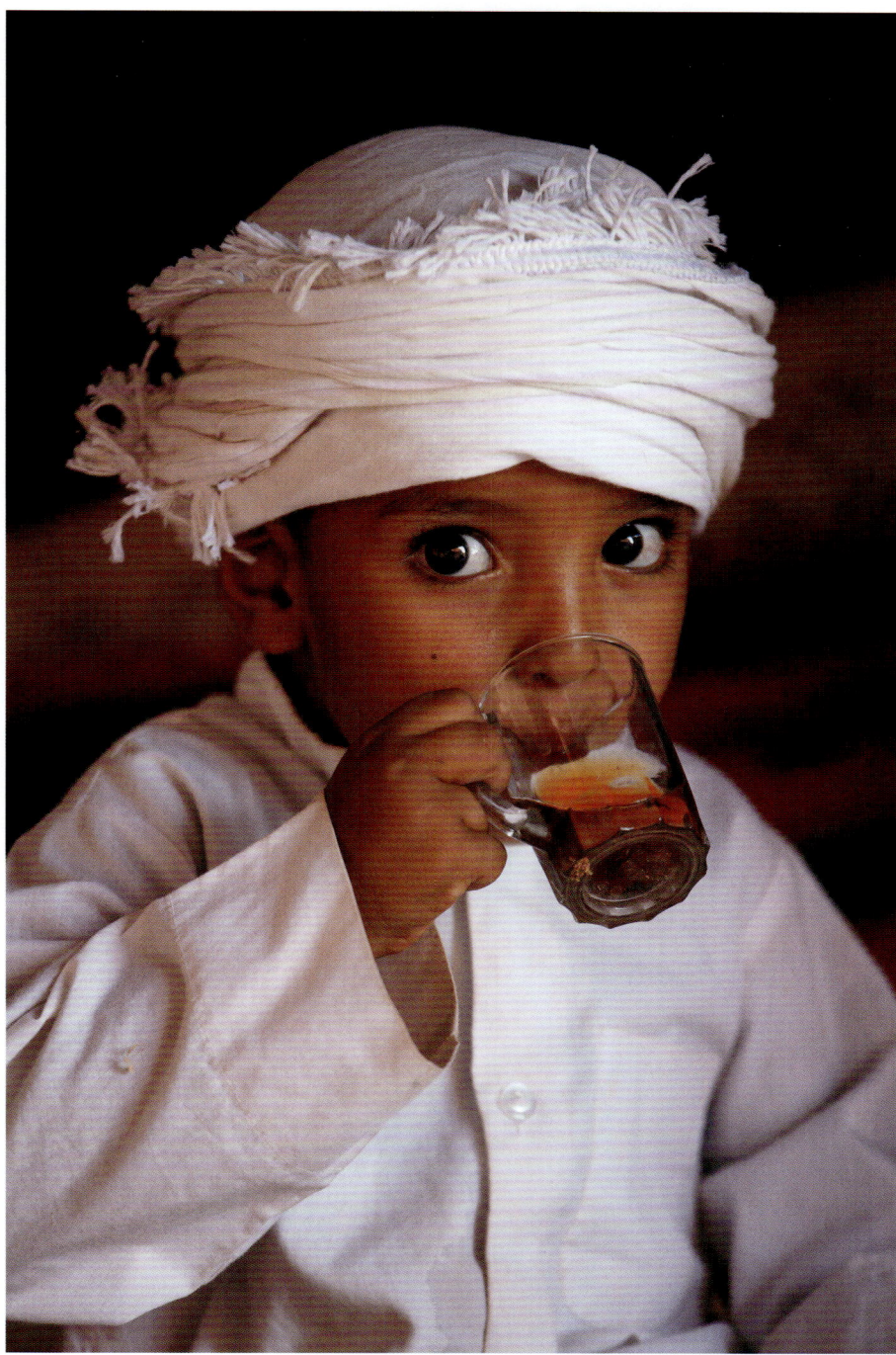

17.1 Images with shallow depth of field are hard to achieve with cameras that have small sensors. This is a unique look best achieved with larger sensors and faster lenses.
1/250 sec.; f/4; ISO 800; Canon 5D Mark II; EF70-200mm f/4L IS USM @ 165mm

4

THE SENSOR

CHAPTER 4

The image sensor is the device that accepts and records the light entering the camera. Cameras used to be known as light-tight boxes for housing film. Image quality was determined primarily by the lens and the film. When digital photography become prevalent, cameras, which were always an important element, became even more critical. Every image sensor has inherent abilities and limitations, which will change the way you capture images. Each new generation of image sensor offers a bit more performance than the last, and this constant improvement results in new procedures and new opportunities for the photographer.

18. ISO

ISO DESCRIBES THE sensitivity rating of your camera's sensor. The sensor records the light that enters through lens, passes through the aperture opening, and moves past the shutter unit. The ISO settings can be adjusted to change the sensitivity.

While the imaging sensor can work with a wide range of light levels, it will achieve maximum performance when exposed to a particular amount of light. This peak performance level is called the *base* or *native* sensitivity.

Base / Native ISO

The *base* or *native* ISO setting is the lowest numbered ISO setting, most frequently ISO 100 or ISO 200. This is the setting that will result in the highest-quality signal, the lowest noise interference, and the greatest dynamic range. When set to a low ISO, the sensor receives just the right amount of light, and the resulting image is free of artifacts and noise. These qualities increase with higher ISO settings.

It's considered best practice to try to use the lowest ISO setting possible for any given situation. The primary reason for selecting a higher ISO is to compensate for a faster shutter speed. For example, if you have a shutter speed of 1/250s and you want to stop the motion of a runner, you should move up to 1/500s to freeze the action. The change of shutter speed will result in less light reaching the sensor, so you'll need to compensate with either a larger aperture or a higher ISO setting. Increasing aperture is a good first move. If you don't have that option, raising the ISO will solve the problem.

As you increase your ISO settings, the image quality will degrade. ISO performance is influenced by the size of the sensor, the size and number of pixels the sensor has, and how the signal is processed. Newer cameras with large sensors and fewer pixels tend to do the best.

Many photographers will test their cameras, checking the results at all ISO settings. As the ISO settings go up, the quality goes down. At a certain point, most find a quality "ceiling" at which point the quality level is unacceptable. For many cameras, the two highest available ISO settings are above this quality ceiling. Test your camera to see how it performs and see how high you can go before hitting your ceiling.

Background Information on ISO

ISO (International Organization for Standardization) is a worldwide independent group that develops voluntary standards. This ISO standard is for recording light. The same standard is used for film. These standards ensure that all cameras will capture a similar image if similar settings are used.

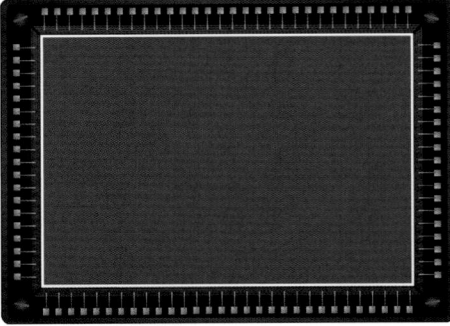

18.1 The sensor

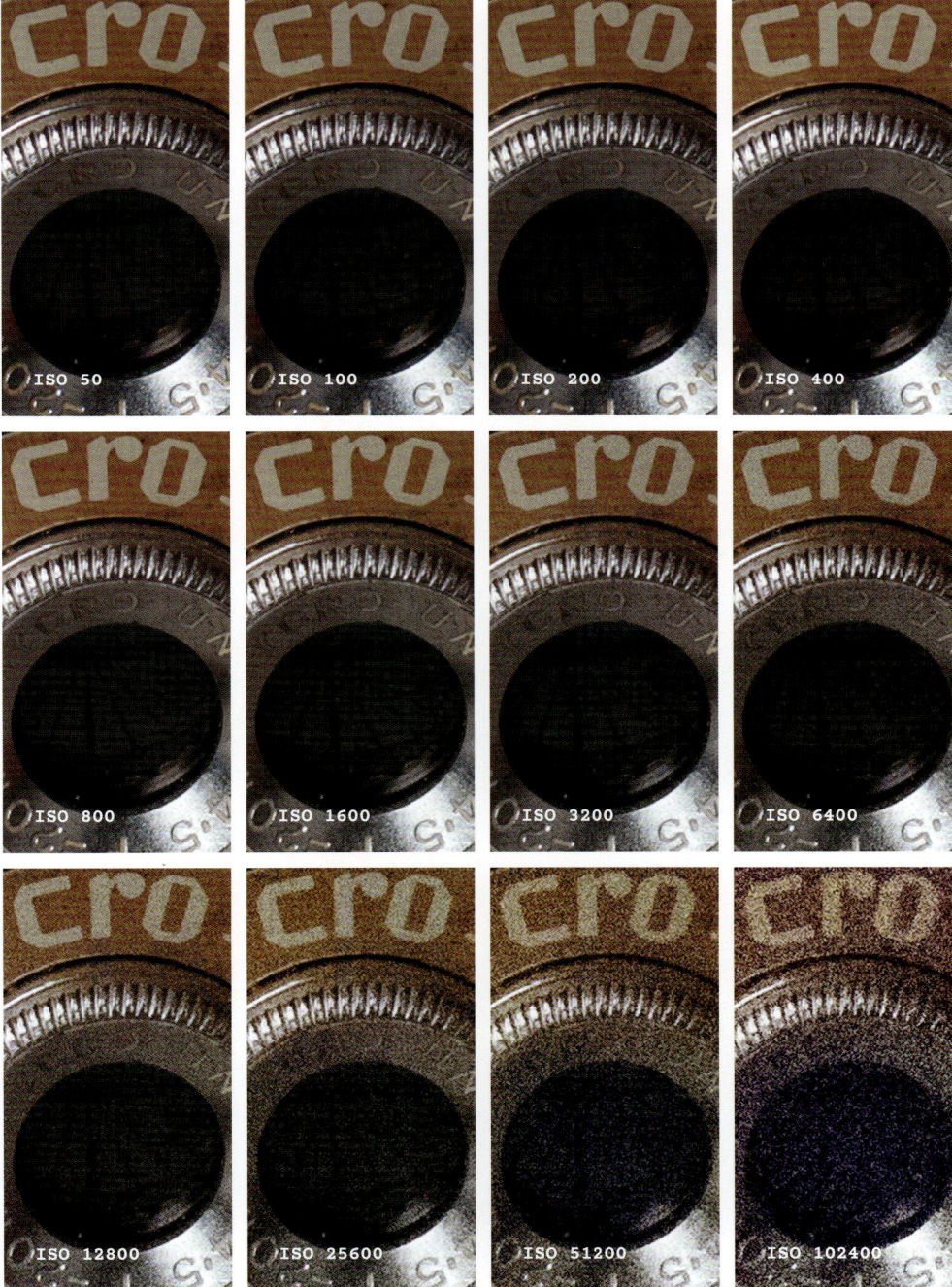

18.2 With higher ISOs come increased noise. The artifacts look somewhat similar to grain seen in film at higher ISO. This series of RAW image crops comes from the Canon 5D Mark IV. At ISO settings of 50-800, the image is very clean; at ISO 1600 the noise becomes visible, and by ISO 25600, the noise is quite heavy.

19. NOISE

WHEN THE ISO is set to a higher number, like ISO 1600 or ISO 3200, the camera will capture an image with less light coming into the camera. This lower light level is then amplified so that the final image is of a normal brightness level. This amplification process produces artifacts; these are most easily seen in the dark regions of the photograph, and areas of low contrast. These artifacts can manifest as errant red and blue pixels that result in a blotchy or grainy look.

Setting an ISO for something higher than the base or native setting (100 or 200) should be done if you need a faster shutter speed that would otherwise not be possible. The need for a faster shutter could arise from a fast-moving subject or to compensate for your movement while handholding the camera.

Using a high ISO setting will result in lower image quality due to the noise, but may be preferable to using a slow shutter speed and getting a blurry image. If you are trying to stop the motion of people dancing at night, you will be faced with the option of a blurry image with little noise (slow shutter speed and low ISO) or a sharp image with some noise (fast shutter speed and high ISO). If an image of a blurry subject is not the objective, you'll need to compromise by setting a higher ISO setting in order to achieve a faster shutter speed. An image with a bit of noise is generally preferable to an image that is blurry.

ISO Setting Process

The best protocol is to set the ISO as low as possible. The time to raise the ISO setting will be when you need a faster shutter speed. Let's say you are taking a photo of action that requires 1/500 of a second with your lens set to its widest aperture, and you set an ISO of 100. If the resulting photo is too dark, you can raise the ISO enough to result in a properly exposed image.

Another example is taking a photo of a city scene at night when you don't have a tripod. First determine the slowest shutter speed that will yield sharp results when you take handheld shots. If you need more light, you should try to open the aperture setting. If the aperture is open to its maximum setting and there still isn't enough light coming in, raise the ISO to a level that will result in a properly exposed image.

High ISOs When It's Dark

Raising the ISO when it gets dark isn't always necessary so long as you have a tripod or other device to keep the camera still. If your scene or subject isn't moving, you can use a low ISO and a longer shutter speed in a low-light situation. High ISO settings shouldn't be associated with dark environments; rather, they are the result of needing faster shutter speeds to overcome subject movement or camera movement.

Hi and Lo ISO Settings

Many cameras will have extensions to the normal ISO range. These settings are often labeled with "Hi" or "High." A setting of "High 1" is one stop higher than the highest numbered setting. If the highest labeled setting is 6400 before going to "High 1," that "High 1" setting is equal to 12,800. Some cameras list these in third stops, like "High 0.3." Some cameras have ISOs that go all the way up to High 5. These high settings tend to yield low-quality shots and should be avoided if possible.

A few cameras have low settings, which work in the same manner as the high ones, but in the opposite direction. A camera may have a low setting of ISO 100 and then a "Lo 1," which is equal to ISO 50 (one stop below the lowest numbered setting). These low settings don't suffer from noise the way the high ones do, but they do have less dynamic range when compared to the camera's native or base ISO settings. These low ISO settings should only be used when you need a longer shutter speed. Suppose you were shooting a photo of a waterfall and wanted a one-second shutter speed in order to blur the water, but after adjusting your camera to the limit of the available settings, you ended up with a shutter speed of 1/2s. You could change your ISO from 100 to Low 1 and then change your shutter to 1 full second. The resulting image will have slightly less dynamic range than the one at 1/2s. You'll have to test your camera's ability at these settings to see which one will result in the best photo.

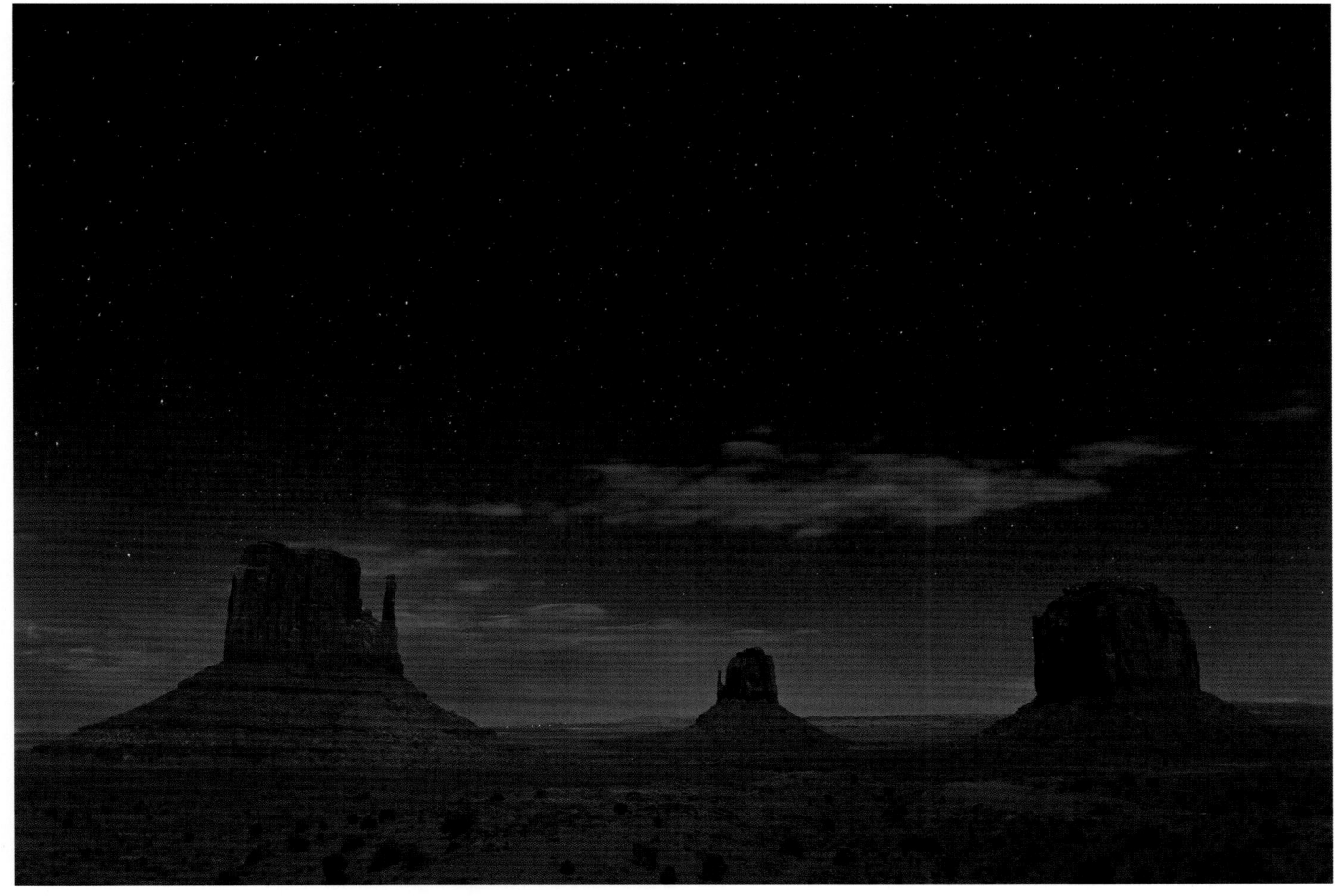

19.1 When it's dark, you won't always need to use a high ISO setting. If you
have a tripod and you can use a longer shutter speed, you can maintain a low
ISO setting to avoid noise in your image.
15 sec.; f/2.0; ISO 640; Canon 5D Mark II; EF24mm f/1.4L II USM

20. AUTO ISO

ALL CAMERAS HAVE an Auto ISO option that will adjust the ISO setting for you. This may prove to be a great convenience for you if you don't want to make the adjustment yourself. It's a bit like automatic drive in a car—a great convenience, but it may be frustrating if it's not done the way you think it should be done.

The way Auto ISO works depends on what exposure mode your camera is in. In Program (full auto) and Aperture Priority mode, in which the camera also has control of the shutter speed, the camera will adjust both the shutter speed and the ISO to get proper exposure. Which setting to change is determined by the shutter speed. When it falls below a certain setting (often 1/60s) it starts setting higher ISOs. This is fine for general handheld shooting, but isn't the best idea if you are working on a tripod and want a slower shutter speeds or if you are capturing a scene that requires a shutter speed faster than 1/60s.

When your camera is set to Auto ISO with Shutter Priority (Time Value) the priority (in most cameras) is to keep the ISO as low as possible for as long as possible. Only when the camera has run out of faster aperture settings will it engage in higher ISO. Once again, this is fine for basic photography, but if you want specific exposure settings, this isn't the best mode.

In the Manual exposure mode, Auto ISO will adjust the ISO so that the resulting image will be properly exposed. Three issues may arise with this system: first the camera may choose an ISO with a setting that is higher than you'd like, resulting in more noise; second, the final exposure will be based on what the camera determines the correct exposure to be, which may be too light or dark for your taste; third, there's a limited number of available ISO settings, and if you're shooting in light that varies quite dramatically, your camera may not have the appropriate setting for the situation.

Controlling ISO

The preprogramed Auto ISO controls don't fit everybody's needs, so many cameras now offer the ability to customize the operation of this feature.

The first and most common setting is the ability to set a maximum ISO.

If you'd prefer that the Auto ISO setting never go above a certain number, you can set a limit to the maximum setting that Auto ISO will use.

Another control for Auto ISO available with some cameras is a setting for the minimum shutter speed. If you have a particular shutter speed that you would like to set as the lowest the camera will choose, you can do that here. This will apply only to the Program mode and Aperture Priority (Time Value) since these modes control the shutter speed.

You can now set the minimum shutter speed your camera will use according to your needs. Perhaps you are photographing wildlife with a 500mm lens and you'd like to keep a minimum shutter speed of 1/500s. Set your camera's minimum Auto ISO shutter speed to 1/500 and whenever your camera needs more light, rather than going to 1/250s or lower, it will adjust to a higher ISO setting. If you shoot with a longer focal length lens or are taking shots that require a faster shutter speed, this is a very beneficial feature.

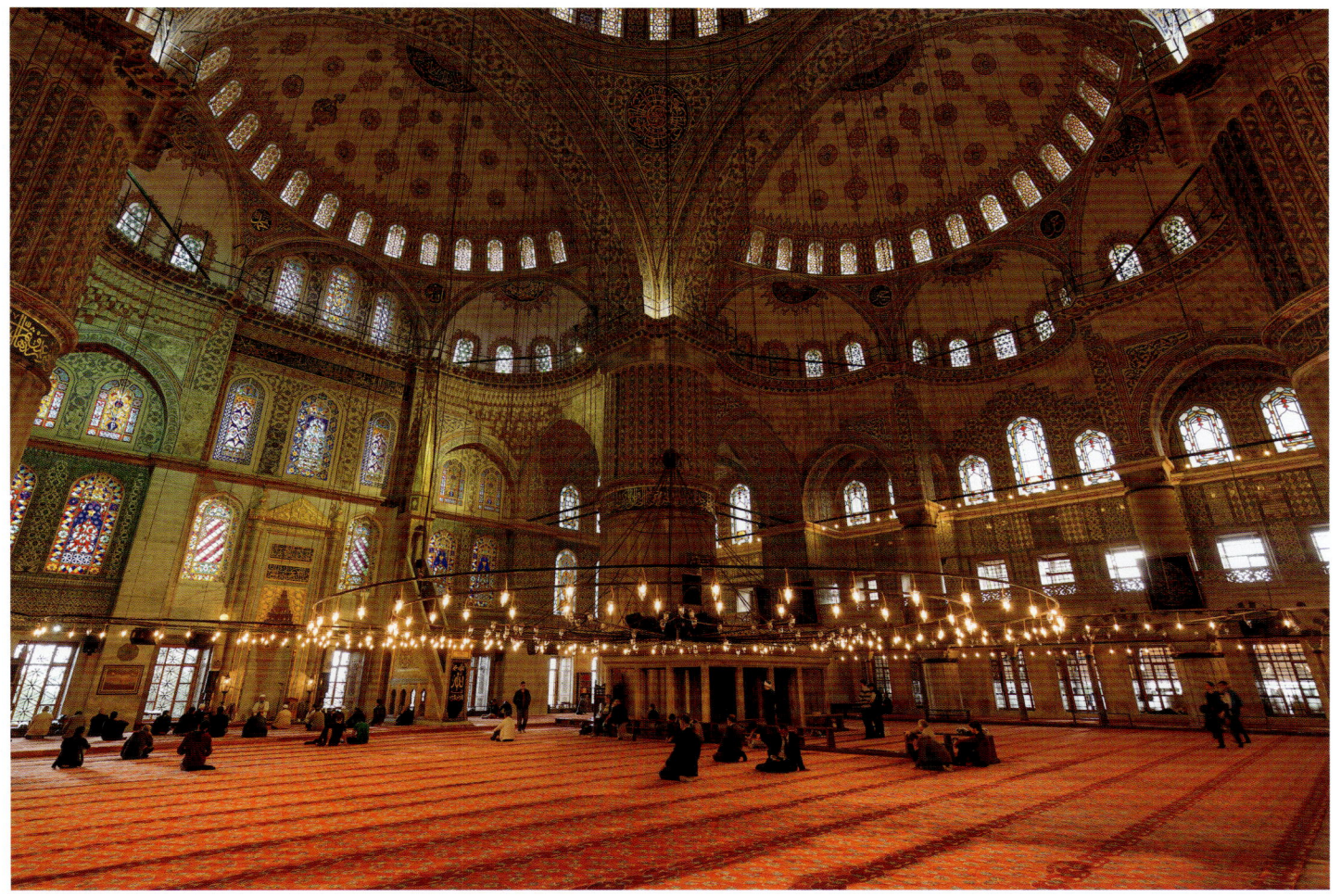

20.1 With the Auto ISO set according to your needs, you can shoot in a variety of environments and the camera will automatically raise and lower the ISO settings according to the available light in the scene and the lens are you using.
1/15 sec.; f/4; ISO 400; Canon 5D Mark III; EF11-24mm f/4L USM @17mm

21. ADVANCED AUTO ISO SETTINGS

SOME CAMERAS NOW offer an advanced level of fine-tuning control over the minimum shutter speed chosen in Auto ISO mode. Rather than setting a specific number, you can set the speed to be chosen based on the focal length of the lens being used. Lenses of longer focal length typically require faster shutter speeds to obtain sharp images due to hand movement that is magnified by the narrower angle of view. The long-standing "reciprocal rule of thumb" for shutter speeds and handholding the camera states that a photographer using a 60mm lens should use a matching shutter speed of 1/60s and a 500mm lens should be used at 1/500s in order to ensure a sharp image.

With the minimum shutter speed set to auto, the camera can recognize the focal length being used and set the reciprocal for the shutter speed. Use a 15mm lens, the camera sets 1/15s; use a 250mm lens, the camera sets 1/250s. This is a great feature and it makes much more sense than using 1/60s for everything.

The auto minimum shutter speed can further be customized according to your needs. For example, if you are a rock-solid, steady camera holder, you may set your camera to -2 (stops) on the minimum shutter speed. This will allow the camera to use a shutter speed two stops slower than it would otherwise with that lens. This means that if you use a 15mm lens, the camera, which would normally allow shutter speeds as slow as 1/15s, will now allow speeds down to 1/4s. If you were to use a 250mm lens, the camera, which would normally set 1/250s, will now allow speeds down to 1/60s. Whatever lens you put on the camera, your minimum shutter would be two stops below the reciprocal of the focal length.

If you have a bit of a tremor in your hand or would like a little extra assurance that you'll be getting sharp photos, you could go the other direction and use a +1 setting. With a 15mm lens you'll have 1/30s as the slowest possible option, and using a 250mm lens will result in 1/500s being the slowest option. The cameras that allow this kind of customization will allow you to go up or down from the auto setting by 2–3 stops. For anyone that shoots in low light with a variety of lenses, this is a great feature.

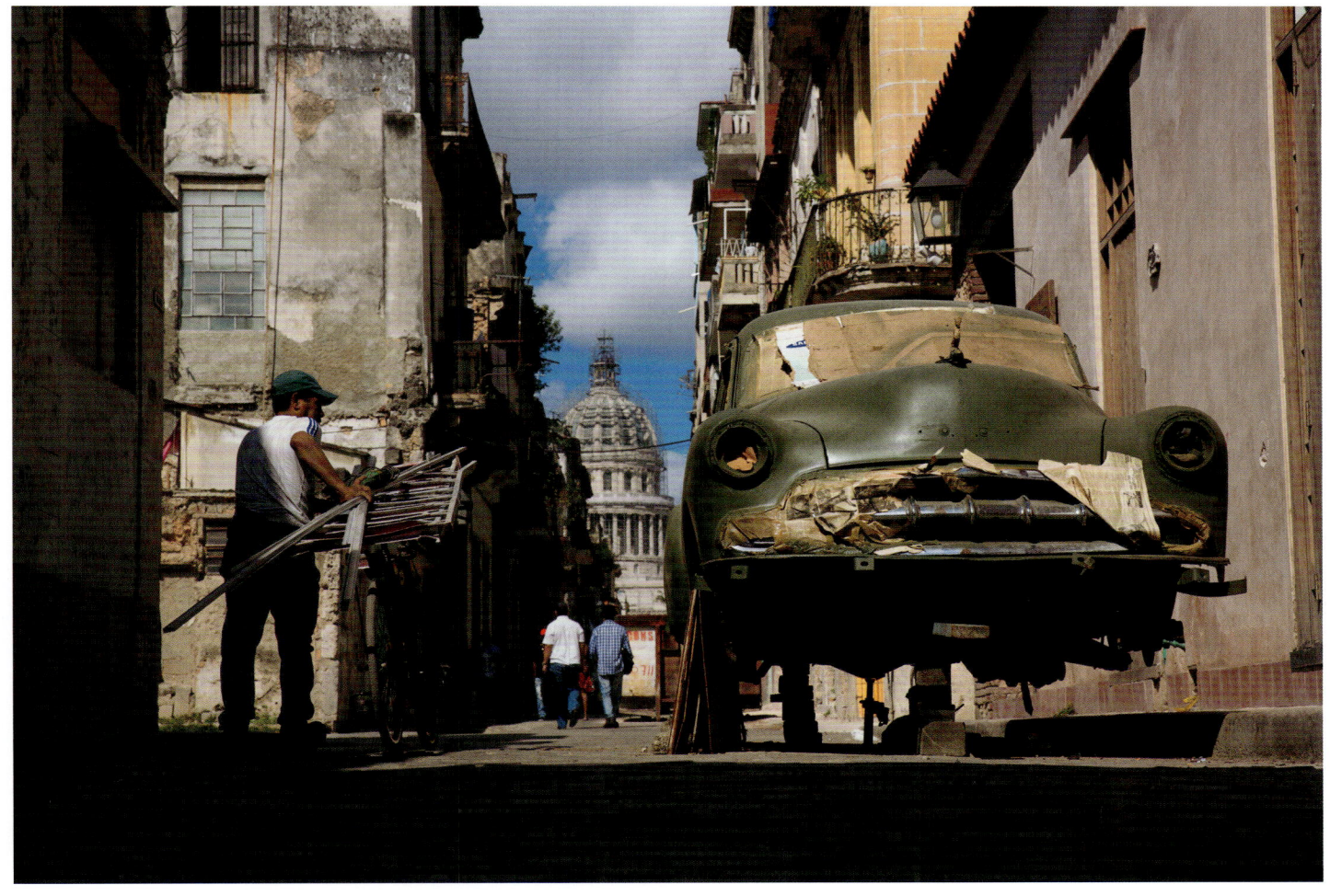

21.1 For tricky lighting situation in which you also need a specific shutter
speed, Auto ISO can be a helpful tool. In the Shutter Priority or Manual
exposure mode, Auto ISO will allow you set a specific shutter speed that will
provide acceptable results in a variety of lighting conditions.
1/160 sec; f/11; ISO 100; Sony A7R Mark II; Canon EF24-70mm f/2.8L II USM @ 70mm

5

EXPOSURE MODES

CHAPTER 5

Every photograph captured will have a specific shutter speed, aperture, and ISO setting. How those settings are chosen is up to you. By choosing an exposure mode, you will be able to tailor the camera to work in a way that you are most comfortable with. The truth is, any photograph could be captured with any of the available exposure modes, but chances are that you'll find that some modes are much easier to work with than others, depending on the situation. Knowing how these exposure modes work will allow you to seamlessly move from one to the next. That way, you can choose which mode will best fit the subject at hand.

22. AUTOMATIC MODES

MOST CAMERAS FEATURE an exposure mode dial with a variety of exposure options—many of which are fully automatic settings. The most ubiquitous is the full auto setting. This is often illustrated with a green camera, a green box, or simply the word "Auto." In this mode, the camera controls every aspect of the camera and will set the shutter speed, aperture, ISO, and a variety of other settings. For the ultimate in simplicity, this is the way to go because everything is done for you.

Full auto is fast and simple, but not without problems. When in this mode, the camera will prevent you from making a large number of manual overrides. Changes to the focus, metering, and the white balance system are usually off limits; options listed in the menu are often grayed out and unavailable to change. There are no overrides to unlock them other than taking the camera out of the auto exposure mode.

Another issue stems from the flash popping up and firing whenever the camera reads the available light as too dark for the settings. The built-in flash is only effective with subjects that are relatively close to the camera—about 10–20 feet (3–6 meters) away. A pop-up flash firing to illuminate a city scene will not do any good—it's too far away. In the full auto mode there is no way of locking the flash down. It will continue to pop up every time you are in a low-light situation and you press the shutter release.

Scene Modes

Many cameras feature scene modes, which tailor the camera for a specific shooting scenario, like landscape, portrait, sports, night, and close-up shots. When set to one of these modes, the camera makes a number of adjustments to improve results for shooting in that specific situation. Since the camera doesn't inherently know what you are shooting, these modes give it a push in the right direction. It's worth noting that the camera isn't doing anything in these scene modes that you can't do on your own. You can do everything the camera does automatically, as long as you know how to set the camera up. If you aren't familiar with how to shoot in a particular situation, the scene modes are the fastest way to get decent results for a particular scenario.

When set to one of the scene modes, be aware that while the camera is adjusting settings for a particular type of photography, it's relatively conservative about its settings. When you set the camera to the sports mode, it doesn't know the difference between a pee-wee baseball game and professional car racing. The camera will definitely choose workable settings, but it may not go far enough to create a look to suit your taste. If the camera doesn't provide results you like, use a manual mode.

22.1 The full automatic modes on most cameras are easily identified. In these modes, all the critical functions are controlled by the camera, including shutter speed, aperture, ISO, focusing, drive, white balance, flash, and more.

22.2 Automated scene modes tailored to specific types of photography will get you closer to the best settings for your shot. These modes will adjust shutter speed, aperture, and several other functions to try to achieve the best results.

23. THE PROGRAM MODE

IN THE PROGRAM mode, the camera will set both the shutter speed and the aperture to achieve the proper exposure. Similar to the Auto and Scene modes, this can be a quick and easy mode for many people. One advantage this has over the Auto and Scene modes is that there are no restrictions on accessing the other features of the camera. Feel free to dive into setting the focus, metering, and other modes according to your needs.

Another good feature is that the pop-up flash, provided you have one, will not fire unless you direct it to do so. If you feel that the photo would benefit from a bit of on-camera flash, simply raise the flash up and let it fire. Most cameras will have the flash set to fire at an automatic level, but you can adjust this if you like.

Note: ISO is an independent setting that can be set to Auto ISO or a specific numeric setting. The following guidelines are given assuming that it is set to a specific number and not in Auto ISO.

In the Program mode, the camera's default system for choosing shutter speeds and apertures is based on achieving a normal exposure without selecting an extreme setting. One priority that's built into the Program mode is the avoidance of slow shutter speeds when possible (below 1/60s). This is perfect for general, handheld shooting. If, however, you want slower shutter speeds, or you're working with a tripod and slow shutter speeds won't result in blurred shots, then this mode isn't the best choice.

Programmed with a Little Control

You will have a bit of control over the settings if your camera allows what is commonly called Program Shift or Flexible Program. With one of your dials or controls, you may be able to adjust both the shutter speeds and apertures simultaneously. This feature maintains a proper exposure but allows you to bias the exposure for faster shutter speeds and wider apertures or slower shutter speeds and smaller apertures. If the light changes, the camera will make minor adjustments to one or both of the settings as needed.

Be aware that some cameras will behave differently once this Program Shift or Flexible Program has been engaged. Some cameras will reset to default exposure settings after the metering system has shut down (6–10 seconds). If this happens, you'll need to adjust the dial and reset your options.

In other cases, cameras stick with your adjustments until you make another. This can result in less-than-optimal settings if you are taking portraits with the aperture open for a shallow depth of field and then later pick the camera up to shoot a landscape. If you neglect to check your settings, your camera might be set incorrectly for what you are about to shoot. Most cameras should reset when turned off.

The AEL Button

If you want to lock in a specific exposure setting while in the Program mode, do so with the Auto Exposure Lock (AEL) button. When you engage this feature it will lock in your shutter speed and aperture settings so they won't change. This feature can be handy if you desire a particular exposure setting but the camera isn't giving you that option when you compose your image. This AEL button will also work with Shutter Priority and Aperture Priority.

Be aware that in Program mode the camera is in control of the overall brightness of your image. In situations that are overly bright or dark, you may need to adjust the Exposure Compensation setting to get the image to the brightness level that you find most pleasing.

24. SHUTTER PRIORITY MODE

WITH THE CAMERA set to Shutter Priority (S or Tv on the exposure mode dial), you control the shutter speed while the camera automatically adjusts the aperture setting. Note: ISO is an independent setting that can be set to Auto ISO or a specific numeric setting. The following guidelines are given assuming that it is set to a specific number and not in Auto ISO.

Shutter priority is a good mode if you are sure about a specific shutter speed setting. If you are photographing a bird in flight that requires a shutter speed of 1/1000s to freeze motion, then set that number and you'll get photos that freeze the action.

With a manual shutter speed selected, the camera adjusts the aperture as needed for the given light in a scene. A problem may arise if you set a shutter speed that is too fast for the available light and aperture options. The camera will try to adjust the aperture to a wider setting, but will eventually run out of options when it reaches the maximum opening. In this case, the camera will alert you with a flashing warning sign in the viewfinder and the resulting photo will be too dark. These blinking warnings can be a bit on the subtle side, so you may need to really look for it. If shooting in a situation like this on a regular basis, you may want to investigate the Auto ISO options on your camera. With Shutter Priority and Auto ISO, your camera will be able to deliver proper results in a far greater range of lighting situations.

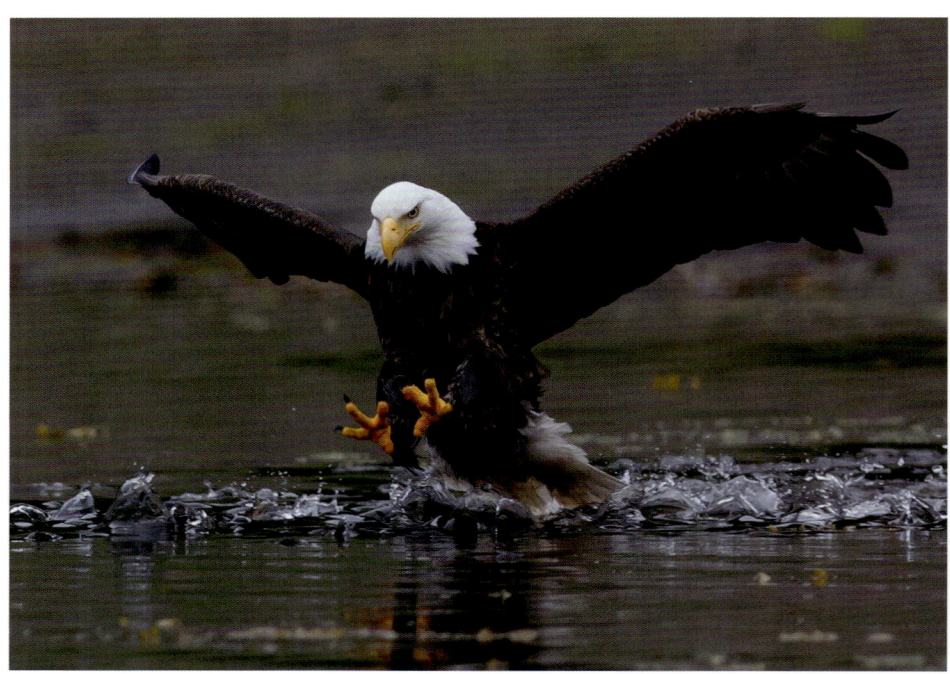

24.1 Fast shutter speeds freeze fast action like this eagle about to pull a fish out of the water in Alaska.
1/2000 sec.; f/2.8; ISO 400; Canon 7D; EF300mm f/2.8L IS USM

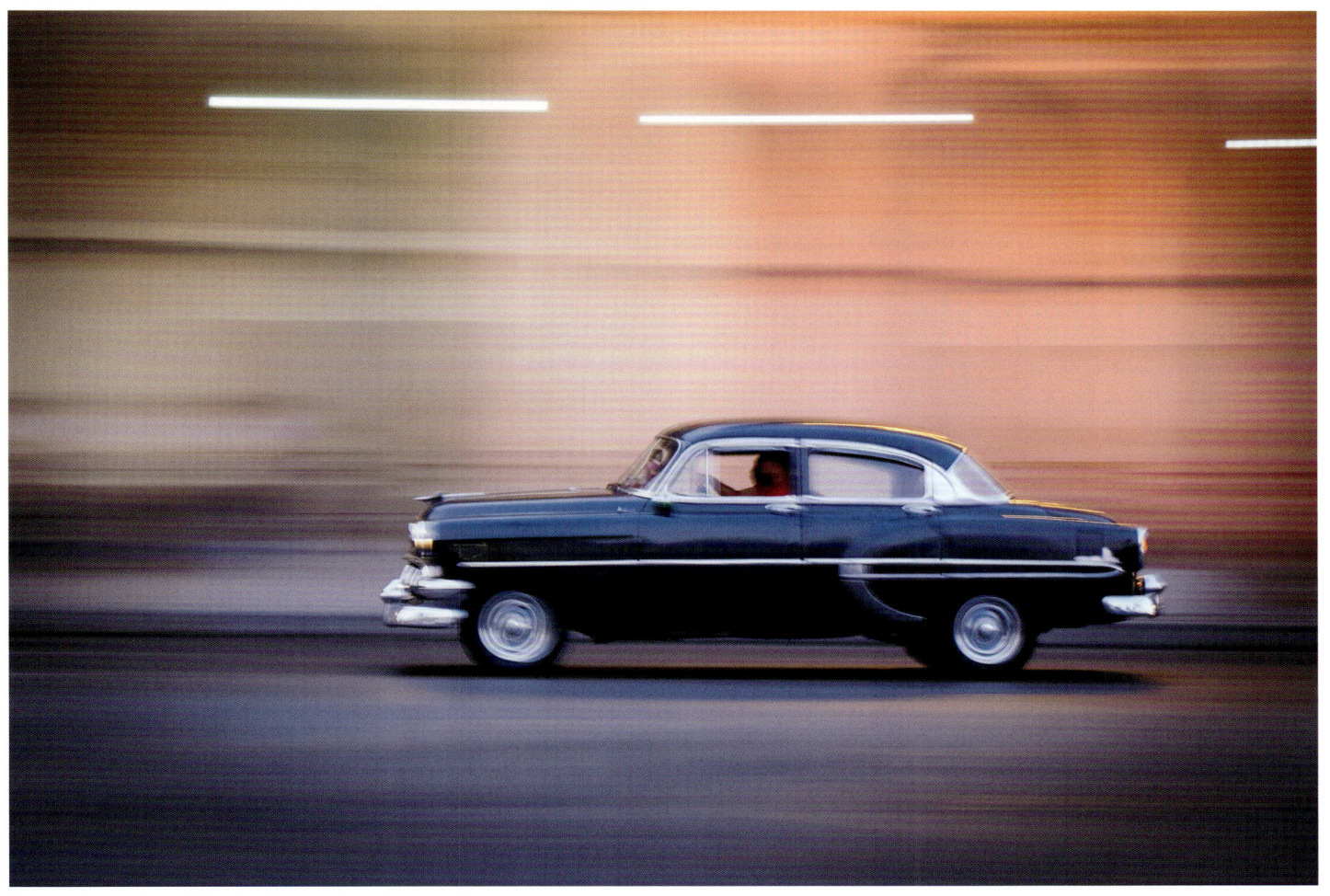

24.2 Using a slow shutter speed while panning the camera with your subject can result in dramatic images with your subject sharp and the background blurry.
1/4 sec.; f/5.6; ISO 400; Fuji X-E2; EF18-55mm f/2.8-4 R LM OIS @ 55mm

25. APERTURE PRIORITY MODE

APERTURE PRIORITY IS one of the most popular modes for photographers looking to have an easy, versatile, and safe exposure system. In this mode, you set the aperture and the camera will then choose a shutter speed that gives you a correct exposure. This system is better than Shutter Priority because there are many more options for the camera to choose from to achieve a correct exposure. Many cameras will have 5-8 different full aperture settings compared to 17-18 full shutter speed options. When you choose an aperture, in most every imaginable case, there will be an appropriate shutter speed for a correct exposure. The reverse cannot be said when in the Shutter Priority mode.

In Aperture Priority you can adjust the aperture for your depth of field needs by turning the appropriate dial on your camera. For greater depth of field, try f/11, f/16, or f/22. If you want shallow depth of field, try f/4, f/2.8, f/2, or f/1.4. If shutter speeds are important, set the aperture appropriately. Want faster shutter speeds? Open the aperture to f/4 or f/2.8. Want slower shutter speeds? Close the aperture down to f/11 or f/16.

A great all-purpose mode is Aperture Priority with an aperture of f/5.6 selected. The f/5.6 setting is in the middle, but it has a slight nod to faster shutter speeds. If something happens quickly, just point and shoot. Your camera will be ready. If you need more depth of field, it's just a few clicks away with the dial that controls your aperture. This is fast and easy, and it will give you good general results with the option for manual adjustments.

Be aware that the camera is in control of the overall brightness of your images. In situations that are overly bright or dark, you may need to adjust the Exposure Compensation setting to get the image to the brightness level that you find most pleasing.

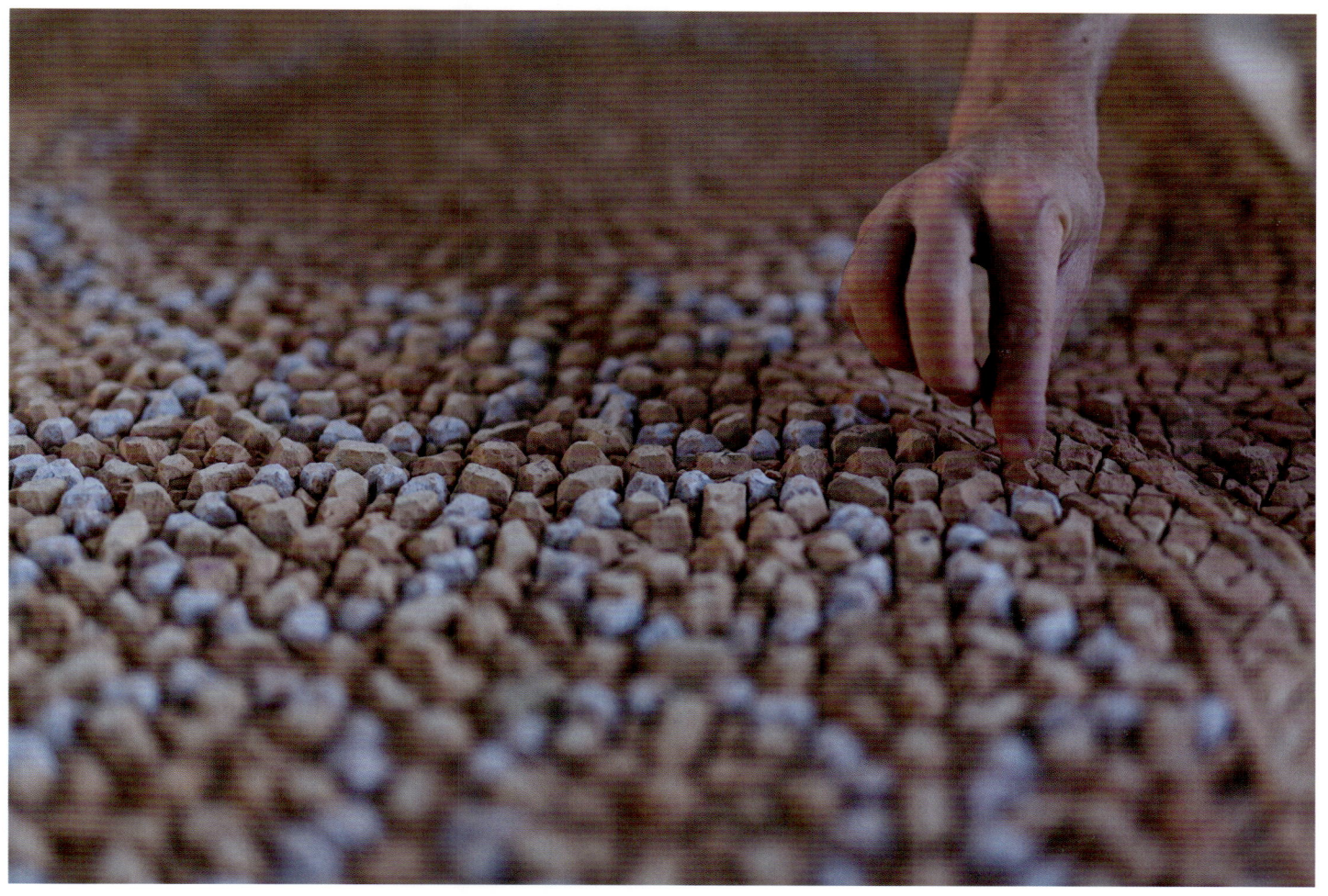

25.1 Using Aperture Priority and a shallow depth of field is an easy way to
quickly shoot while still maintaining manual control.
1/250 sec.; f/1.4; ISO 250; Canon 5D Mark III; Sigma 50mm f/1.4 A

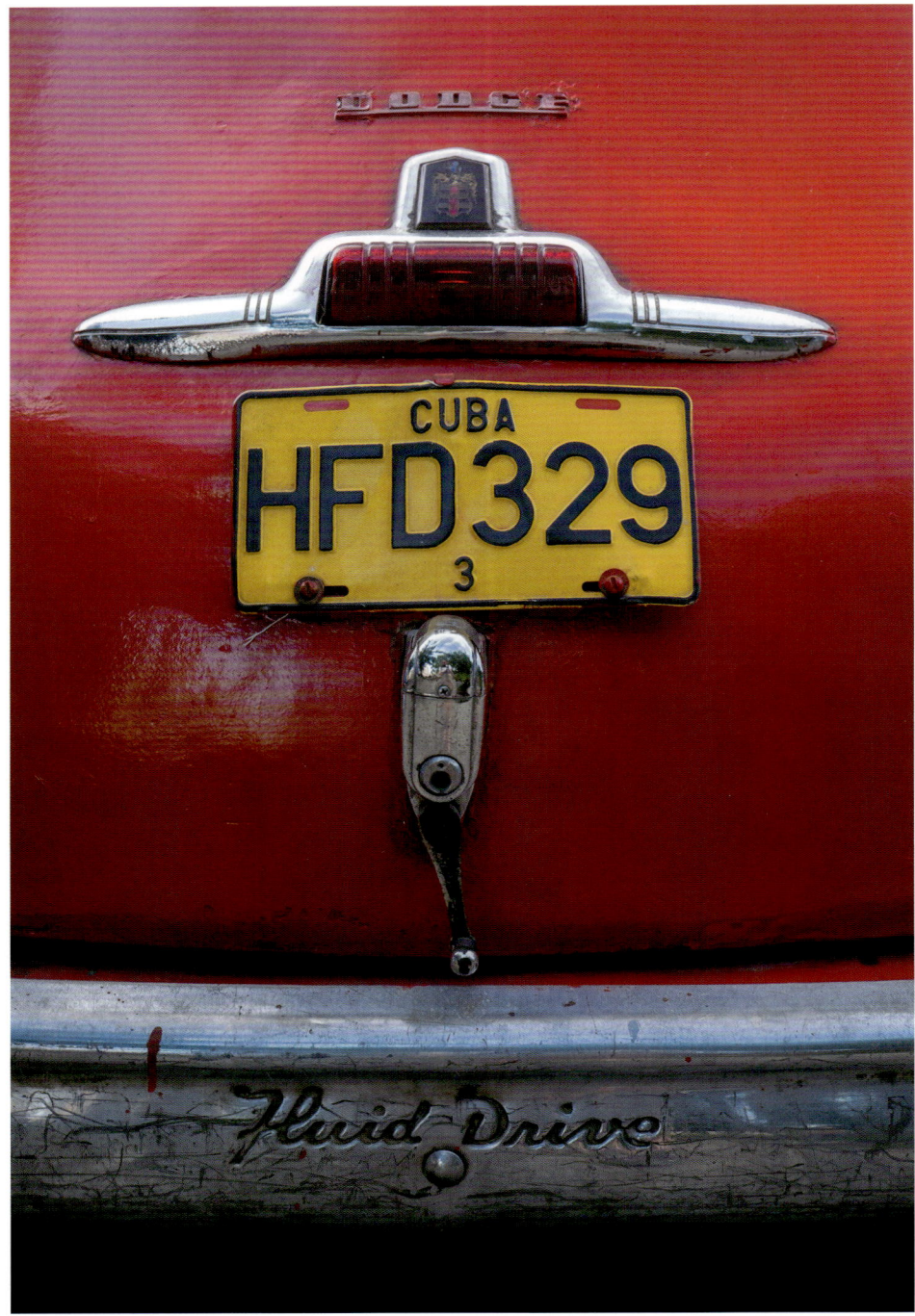

25.2 When using Aperture Priority, it's advisable to keep the aperture in the middle of the maximum sharpness range when you are photographing something that is flat or mostly flat.
1/4 sec.; f/8; ISO 200; Fuji X-E2; EF18-55mm f/2.8-4 R LM OIS @ 30mm

26. MANUAL MODE

IN THE MANUAL exposure mode, you are in full control over shutter speeds and apertures. Knowledge of the effects of the various shutter speed settings and apertures will be key to maximizing this option. In order to get proper exposures, you'll need to monitor your exposure indicator or light meter to check the light levels.

To start, locate the exposure indicator or light meter in your camera. Choose either shutter speed or aperture, and make a setting. Now adjust the other exposure setting so that the light meter's reading is an even exposure (0). Most cameras have an indicator or line below a graphic display with a 0 near the middle, a plus (+) indicator on the right, and a minus (-) indicator on the left. Some cameras will simply have a series of numbers (-2, -1, 0, +1, +2) in which 0 indicates an image that is correctly exposed.

Once the exposure indicator is set to 0, take a photo and review it. Check to see if it's too bright or too dark for your liking. If you aren't happy with the settings or the results, make a change and try it again. If the photo is too dark you could either set a slower shutter speed or a larger aperture opening, depending on what is available and what your preference is. If your image is too bright you can set a faster shutter speed or a small aperture opening.

If you are satisfied with the exposure (brightness) of the image but want to change either the shutter speed or the aperture, you'll need to do some trading. If you make the shutter speed faster, you'll need to open up your aperture. Closing the aperture will require you to use a slower shutter speed. In either case, the light meter will no longer read 0, which in this case is perfectly fine.

A meter reading of 0 simply indicates that the scene has a moderate brightness level that isn't overly dark or bright. In reality, many scenes are brighter or darker than average. In these cases, you'll be shooting photos while your light meter is indicating that you are either over- or under-exposing your image. Don't worry too much about these readings; not all photos have an exposure setting of 0. This is one of the benefits of shooting in the Manual exposure mode—you get to choose the brightness level that seems right to you.

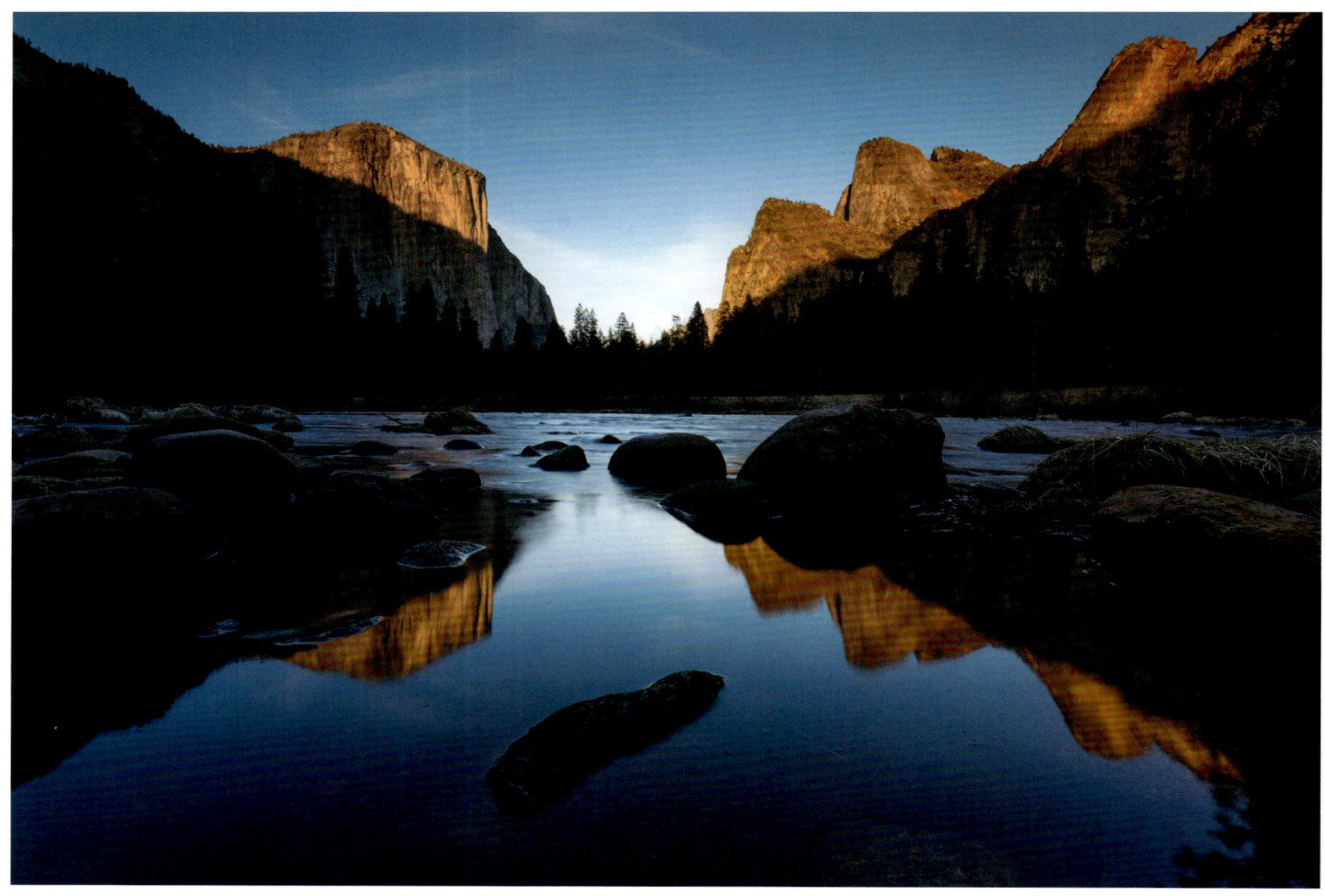

26.1 Manual exposure mode allows you to be very precise about your settings. This precision is helpful in tricky lighting situations where the slightest bit of underexposure or overexposure will ruin the photograph. With scenes like this, you must be careful not to overexpose the sections illuminated by the sun; at the same time, you must allow in enough light to see detail in the shadows.
1/1.3 sec; f/22; ISO 100; Canon 5D Mark III; EF17-40mm f/4L USM @ 17mm

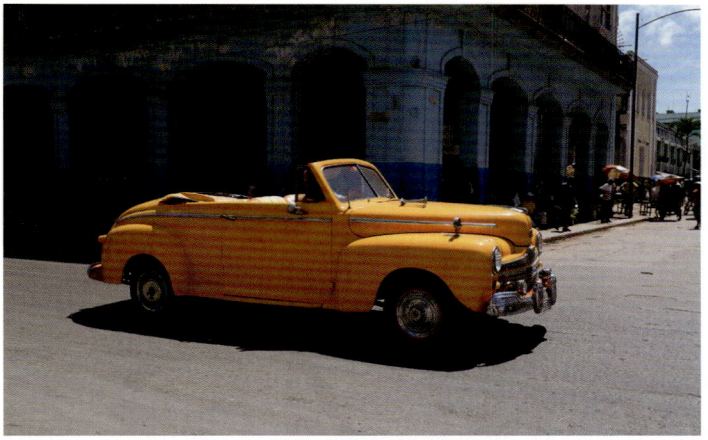

26.2 Full manual exposure is the best choice when the lighting of your subject is consistent. If the brightness of the background or other elements changes during a series of images, your camera will maintain the same settings and record the same light levels in all images. **1/1000 sec.; f/5.6; ISO 250; Fuji X-E2; EF18-55mm f/2.8-4 R LM OIS @ 23mm**

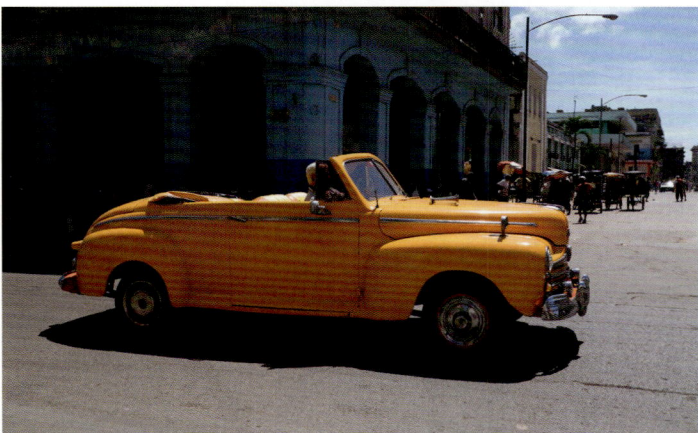

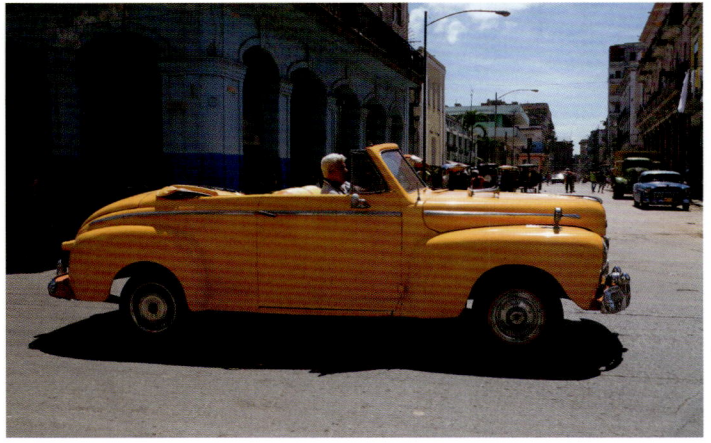

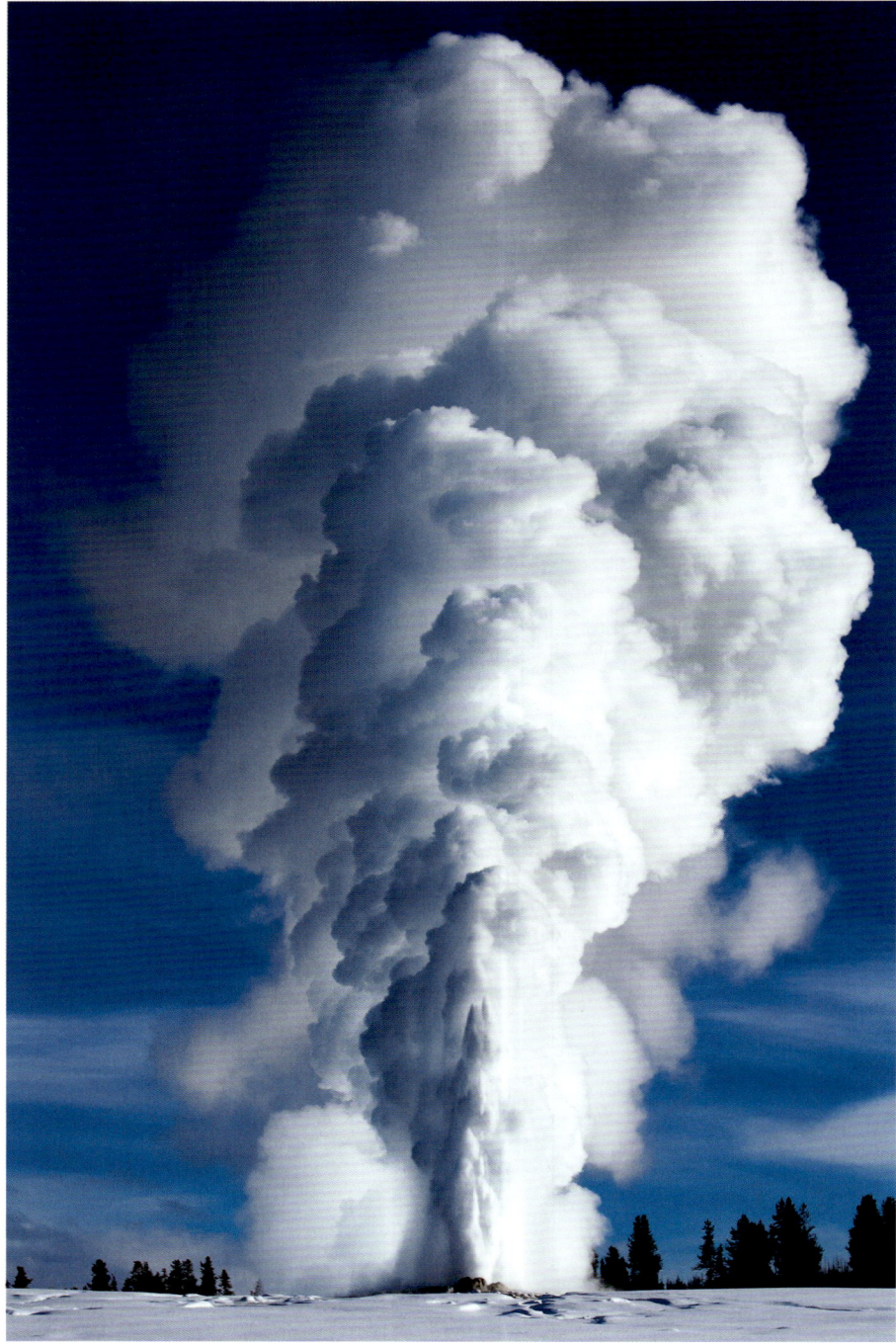

26.2 Manual exposure is great for situations where the lighting isn't changing but your subject or background is.
1/80 sec.; f/16; ISO 200; Canon 5D Mark III; EF70-200mm f/4L IS USM @ 70mm

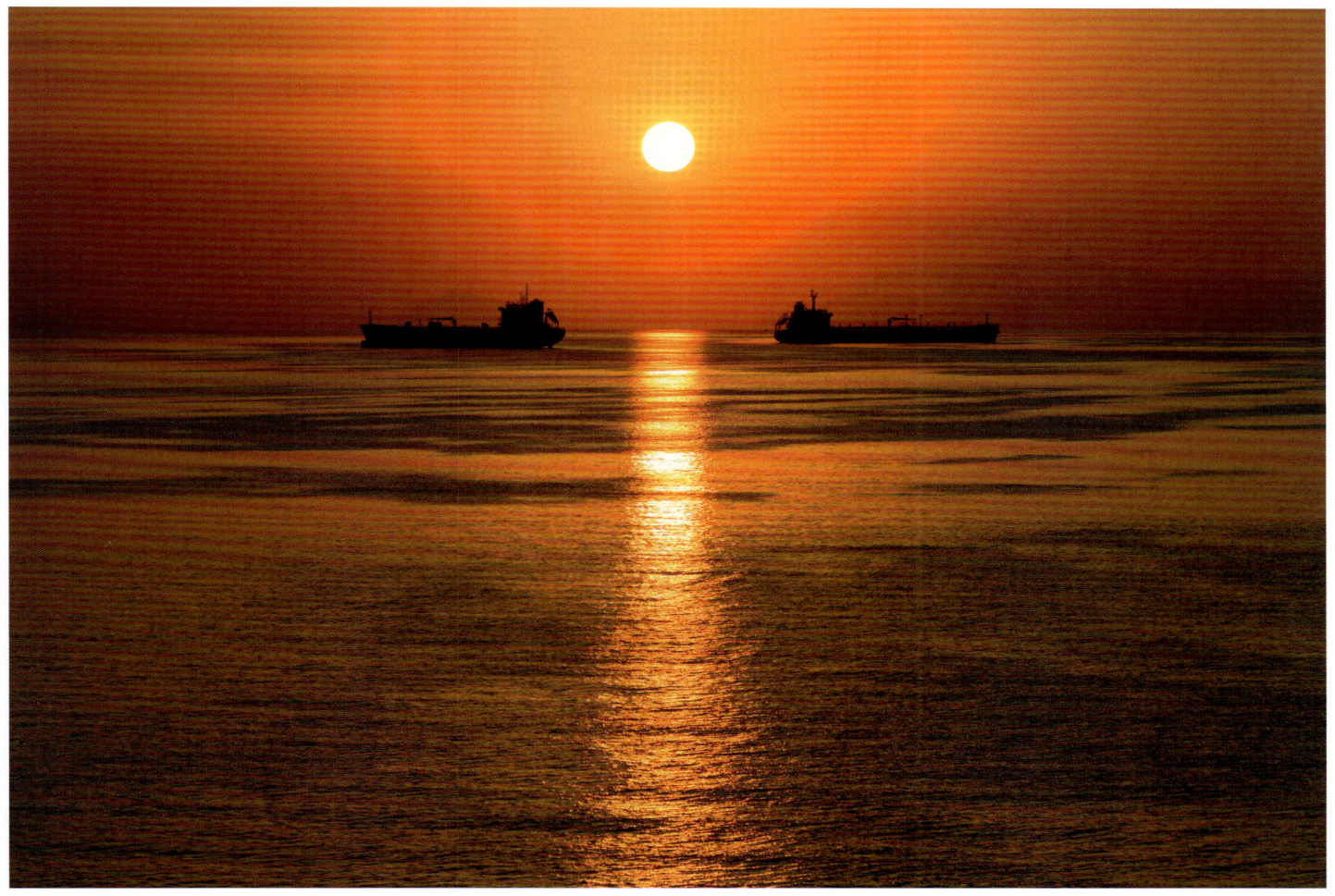

26.3 Pointing the camera directly at the setting sun will cause the camera's light meter to overreact to the brightness of the sun and the resulting exposure will be quite dark. By metering the light with the sun just out of frame, a proper exposure for the scene can be manually dialed in before repositioning the camera for the preferred composition.
1/500 sec.; f/8; ISO 100; Canon 5D Mark III; EF100-400mm f/4.5-5.6L IS II USM

Share Your Best Sunset Shots!

Once you've captured a great sunset shot, share it with the *Enthusiast's Guide* Community! Follow @EnthusiastsGuides and post your image to Instagram using the hashtag #sunset. You can also search that hashtag to see and be inspired by other photographers' shots.

6

EXPOSURE SETTING GUIDELINES

CHAPTER 6

Most successful photographs have been captured using a particular photographic style or technique. This result will ideally be in concert with the subject, story, or intended purpose of the photograph. As photographers, it's our job to identify the important elements in a frame and then apply techniques, including setting the shutter speed and aperture, to achieve the desired result. If you can clearly identify what you want your result to be, you can follow procedure to get as close as your equipment and knowledge will take you.

27. FREEZING MOTION WITH ACTION PHOTOGRAPHY

TO STOP THE motion of a moving subject you will need a fast shutter speed. How fast a shutter speed you will need depends on several variables. You'll recall that in general, the faster the action, the faster the shutter speed necessary to freeze it. And it's not just the speed of the action, but also the appearance of action from the camera's point of view.

The best fast shutter speed is the slowest one that stops the action. What this means is that you shouldn't set overly fast shutter speeds if they're not necessary. For example, let's say you've found that 1/500s thoroughly stops the motion of a typical runner. If you then set a shutter speed of 1/8000s, the runner will look exactly the same, frozen, but the camera will receive less light and will have to compensate by changing either the ISO or the aperture. If you were photographing top-level runners on the track and found that 1/500s did a good job in most cases, but in the faster sprinting events you were noticing some blur, stepping the shutter speed up to 1/1000s would be the right move.

Once the shutter speed has been set, you can turn your attention to the aperture and ISO. You could set the camera to Shutter Priority and turn on Auto ISO, but we want to examine our settings more closely, so let's look at this scenario from a manual exposure point of view. In many cases the same results can be obtained using a more automatic setting, but discussing it and understanding it from a manual perspective will help the process make more sense.

Apertures for Faster Shutter Speeds

Your choice of aperture may serve aesthetic and technical purposes. It's reasonable to focus attention to your subject and away from other areas in the photo, so a shallow depth of field is a logical choice for aesthetic reasons. Fast shutter speeds, which let in very little light, usually need to be matched with larger apertures.

Lower ISO settings result in cleaner images, so that's a good default starting position. Set your camera to its base or native ISO sensitivity, 100 or 200 on most cameras. If you aren't letting in enough light with your chosen shutter speed and aperture, you may need to set a higher ISO to get a proper exposure.

Now it's time to check the light meter. If you have too much light, you could set an even faster shutter speed, which works perfectly well when stopping motion. You could, on the other hand, set a smaller aperture, but this goes against the shallow depth of field technique that draws attention to your primary subject.

In many cases, a fast shutter speed means you're letting in very little light. To achieve a proper exposure you'll likely need to make an adjustment to either the aperture or ISO. First check the aperture and see if it can be opened up any more. If not, raise your ISO until you reach a proper exposure.

If the exposure is the right brightness but you'd like to change some of the settings, you can do some "stop trading" whereby you give a little from one setting to the other. If you'd like a bit more depth of field, you could close your aperture down a stop and raise your ISO a stop. If your ISO is higher than you'd like, you can see if your aperture is able to open any further or if you could reexamine your shutter speed selection to see if you could get away with something slower.

If none of these techniques get you to the exposure combination that you desire, there are other solutions. You could choose to shoot the subject under different conditions when the light is better, or bring in your own lights if that's feasible. You could just set a slower shutter speed and only shoot photos when your subject isn't moving as quickly, if that's an option. If you are photographing dancers, you could avoid shooting when they are jumping or moving quickly and just shoot when they pause or strike a pose.

There's always a solution; it's just a matter of finding the best solution to your problem. When approaching these dilemmas, give yourself a bit of time to work through the problem and shoot test photos to see if your solutions are working.

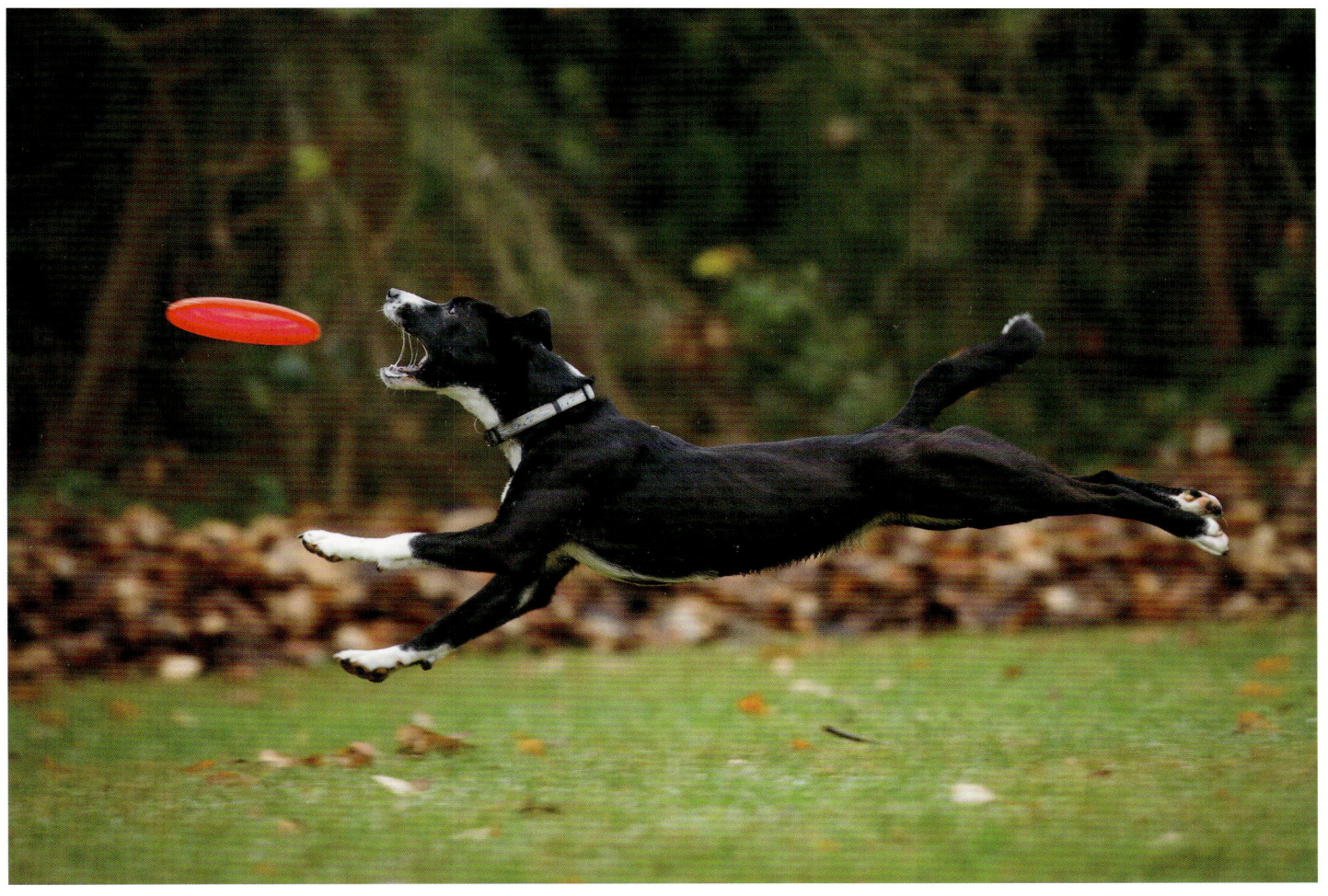

27.1 Fast-moving subjects will usually require a shutter speed of 1/500s
or faster. Fast-moving mammals (that includes humans) will usually require
1/500s for stopping action.
1/640 sec; f/2.8; ISO 1600; Canon 5D Mark III; EF300mm f/2.8L IS II USM

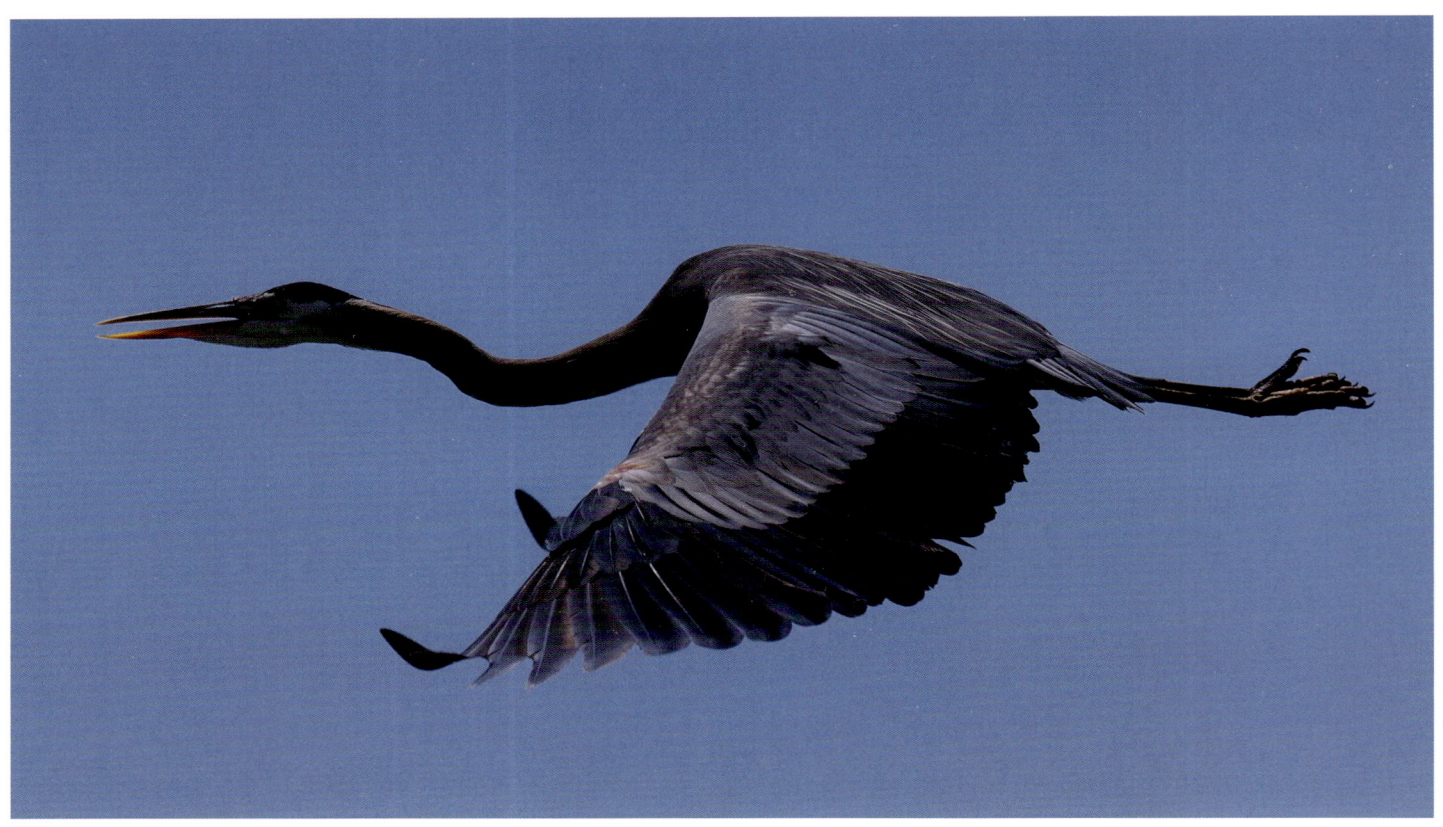

27.2 Birds in flight are among the fastest-moving subjects that many of us will encounter. The smaller the bird, the faster the shutter speed you'll most likely need to stop the action.
1/2000 sec.; f/4.5; ISO 200; Canon 40D; EF70-200mm f/4L IS USM @165mm

28. BLURRING MOTION

AT FIRST IT may seem counterintuitive to want to blur the subject of a photograph, but it's an effective method of illustrating motion. Still photographs by their nature don't show movement, but with the right type of blur, a subject's speed and direction can be illustrated in a dynamic visual manner.

Once you've decided to use a blur technique, the next choice is whether to let the subject move across the frame of the camera or to move the camera with the subject. If you choose to let the subject do the moving, it will result in a streak of blur relative to the length of the shutter speed. Depending on your framing, you may have large parts of the image that are sharply in focus, drawing attention to areas other than the blurred subject.

You'll want to be very careful with the composition and content in these types of images because the eye will wander around the frame. The blurry subject can be either the main subject or a supporting element that's part of a bigger picture. A photo of a city scene with a blurred taxi is helping make the statement that it's a bustling place with lots of activity. The blurred taxi isn't really the main subject, but it does play a critical supporting role.

Panning

A different technique is to move the camera with the moving subject, matching both direction and speed, thus blurring everything in the frame but the subject. This technique is called panning, and it's a very effective way of separating a moving subject from the background. The technique is simple in principle, but challenging to perfect. As your subject moves, keep the subject in the same location when viewed through the viewfinder. The smoother and more consistent the movement of the subject, the easier it will be to follow it when panning the camera. This is a challenging technique for sports and dance performances in which the subject stops and changes direction quickly and erratically. Cars and runners traveling in a straight line, on a predictable path and at a constant speed, will prove much easier targets. It's also helpful if the subject is making repeated passes in front of the camera so that you can practice the technique and dial in the best settings. A track where moving subjects are making repeated loops is an ideal location.

It's common to have a very low success rate with this technique, since getting a sharp subject requires a perfect match of your speed and the speed of the subject. It's the relative speed in relation to the camera position that's important. A subject moving relatively fast and near the camera will be difficult to track smoothly. It's easier to track a subject that is farther away, using a longer focal length lens. The easiest panning setup is from the middle of a circle with a telephoto lens. Panning from the inside of a turn or curve will allow you to easily follow your subject without any change in subject size or distance.

The Right Blur

Achieving the perfect blur is a matter of taste and style. Choosing a shutter speed that isn't slow enough results in a slight blur that can easily be mistaken for sloppy technique. A shutter speed that is too long will result in a blur that is unrecognizable. In most cases you'll need to test a few different shutter speeds to see what looks best. A good place to start is 1/30s. Use increasingly slow shutter speeds until you find the right one for your shot.

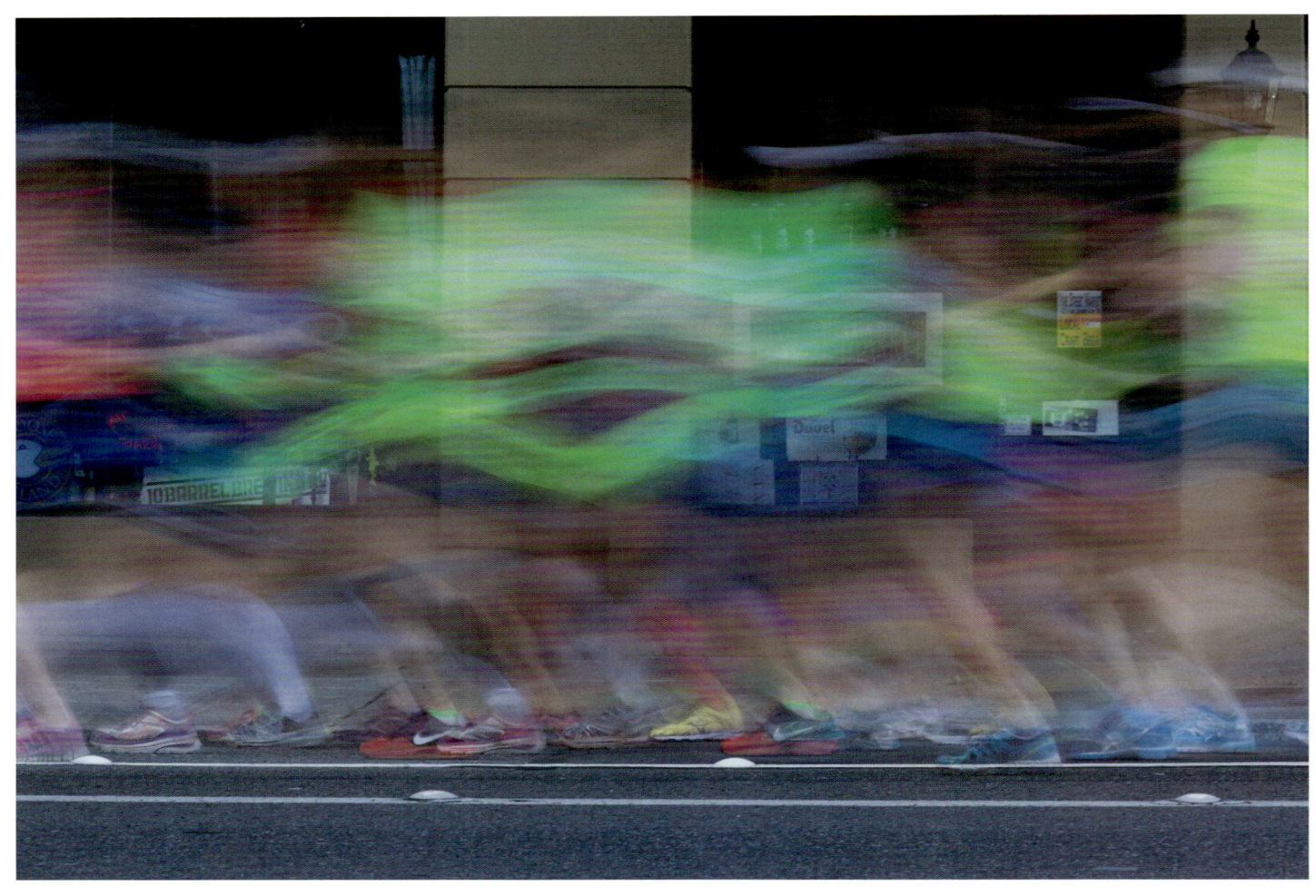

28.1 The marathon runners captured with a shutter speed of 1/2s are a blur, but their feet on the ground are just barely visible.
1/2 sec.; f/16; ISO 100; Canon 5D Mark III; EF70-200mm f/4L IS USM @ 85mm

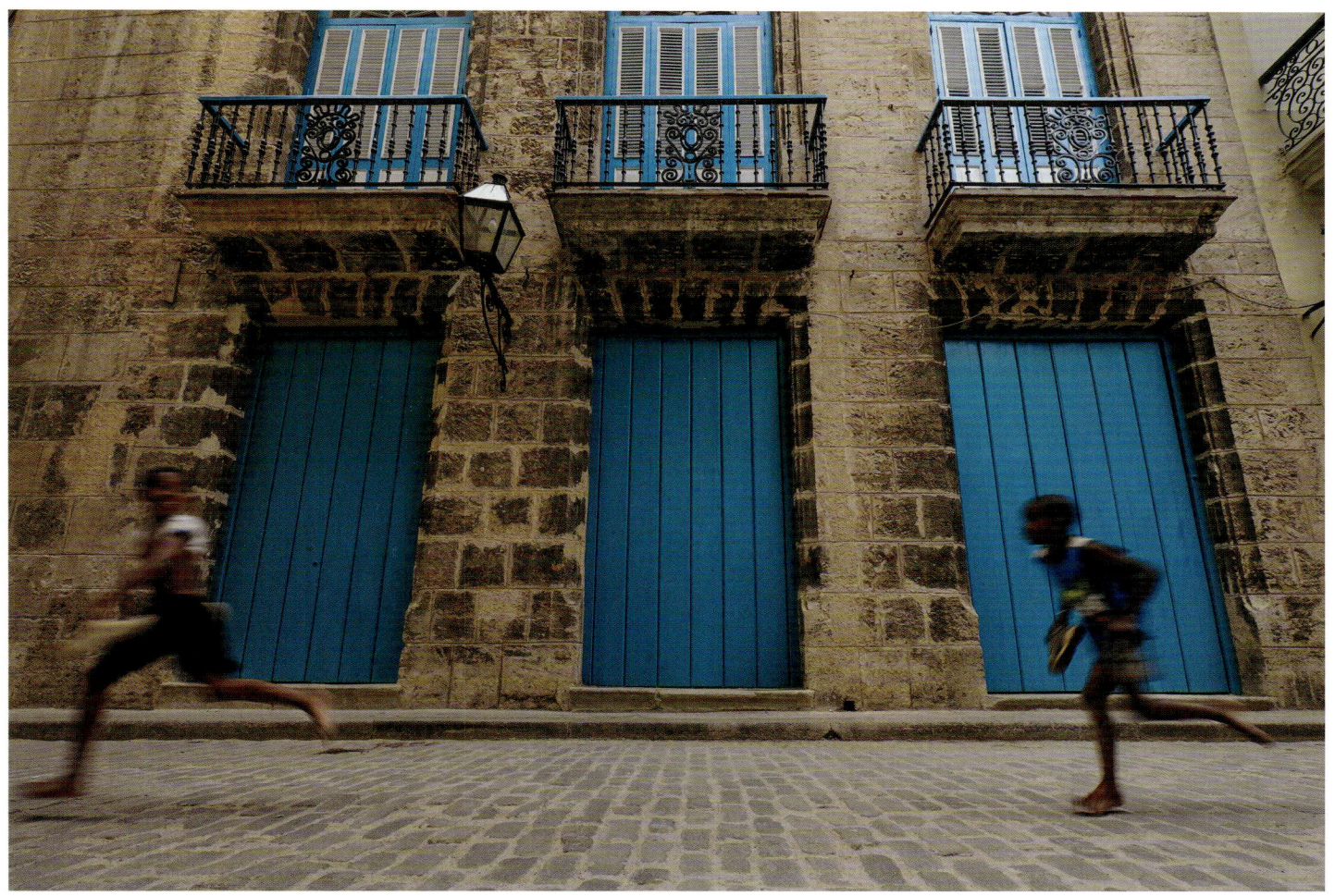

28.2 At 1/60s, fast action will be rendered a blur. Sometimes a blur can be a good thing, like in this photo of a couple of Cuban boys running through the streets. Blur can add a bit of mystery to a photo, and force the viewer to examine the image a bit more closely.
1/60 sec.; f/5.6; ISO 800; Fuji X-E2; 10-24mm f/4 R OIS

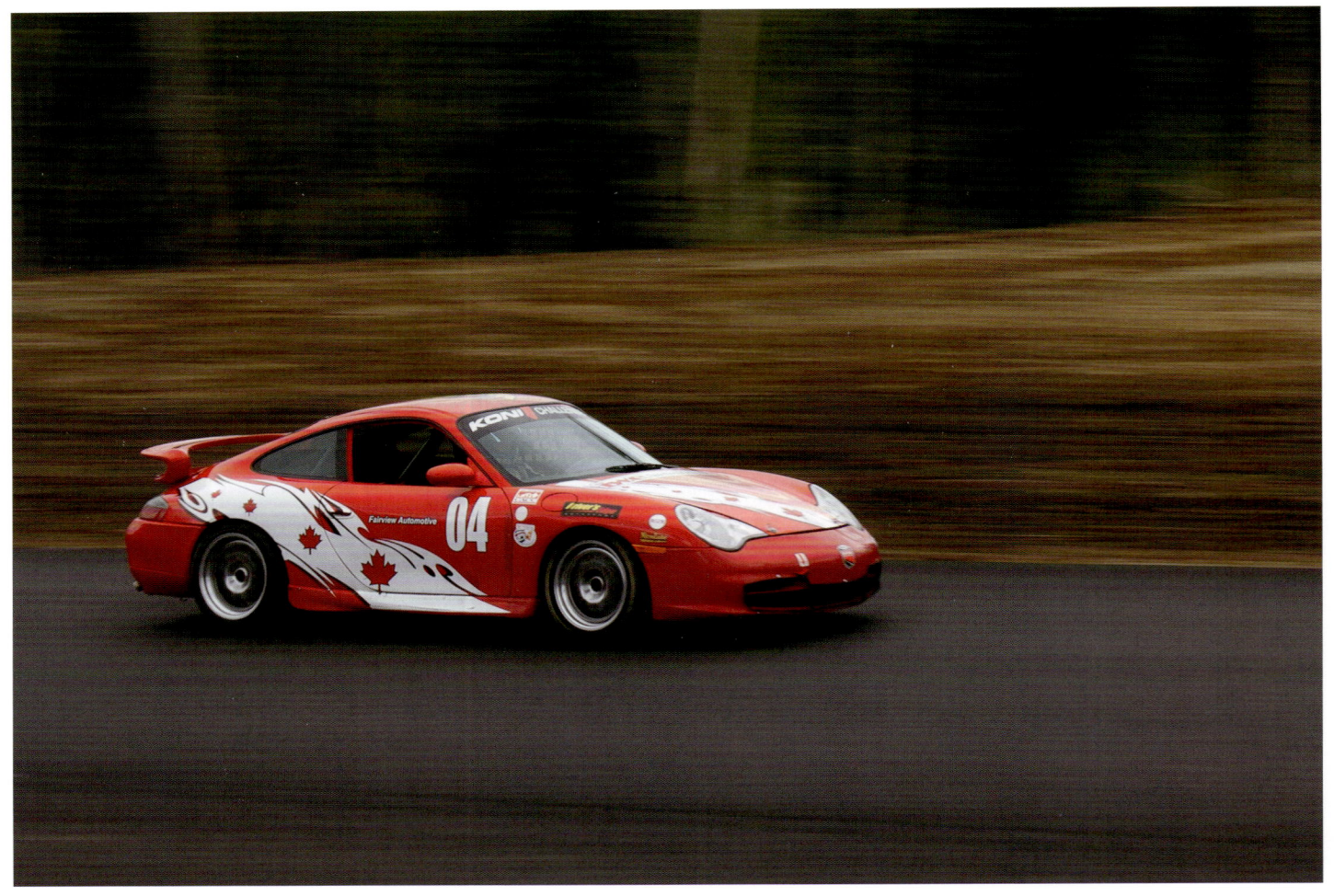

28.3 The best panning speed is usually achieved after a bit of trial and error. Matching the speed of your subject can be difficult because their rate of approach changes as it gets closer.
1/60 sec.; f/8; ISO 100; Canon 7D; EF24-70mm f/2.8L USM

29. MAXIMUM DEPTH OF FIELD FOR LANDSCAPE PHOTOGRAPHY

ACHIEVING MAXIMUM DEPTH of field for a scene is popular among landscape photographers as well as those shooting travel and architectural photography. This technique is quite effective when there is a large, detailed scene that you want the viewer to experience as if they were seeing it with their own eyes. When everything is in focus, the eye is left to wander throughout the large, interesting scene.

For this technique you'll start by setting the aperture. You'll need to assess your scene's depth-of-field requirements and decide what lens you'll be using. The wider the lens is, the more depth of field you will see. A 24mm lens will exhibit greater depth of field than a 50mm lens. In many cases, these maximum depth-of-field images are shot with wide lenses.

Depth of field refers to the region that appears to be in focus between the nearest object and the object farthest away. It's this region, along with how far away the closest subject is relative to the camera, that's important. For instance, the distance from the moon to the stars is huge in terms of actual distance, but relatively speaking, both are near infinity in terms of focusing. With a car parked right in front of your camera, the distance front the front headlight to rear bumper may not be large in the big scheme of things, but it's huge in relative distance. If the front is two feet away from the camera and the back is eight times that distance away, that's a large difference, relatively speaking.

The best technique will be to set an aperture that achieves the depth of field that you need but doesn't go far beyond it. If you need an aperture of f/8, you shouldn't just use f/22 because it has more depth of field. Apertures on the extremes, like f/1.4 and f/22, tend to yield less sharp results than those in the middle of the spectrum. We'll look at this more closely in chapter 31: Maximum Sharpness. Knowing where to set the aperture will come from practice and experience.

A good start would be to set an aperture of f/8, a good middle aperture with a bit of depth of field. A low ISO will yield the cleanest images, so set your camera to its base or native ISO setting (100 or 200 on most cameras). Before setting the shutter speed you should first consider if there is anything in the frame that will be moving and how it might be affected by a slower shutter speed. If you need a particular shutter speed, this is the time to dial that in. If nothing is moving, you are free to use any shutter speed available, so long as you are using a tripod. If you aren't using a tripod, you'll need to set a shutter speed fast enough to ensure you get sharp photos while handholding the camera.

If you do have a tripod, set an aperture of f/8, set the base ISO (100 or 200), and set the shutter speed according to the light meter. Take a photo, examine the results, and make adjustments for lightness or darkness. During playback of the image you may want to zoom in and check focus on the nearest subject and the farthest subject to see if they are both sharp in focus.

If you do not have enough depth of field, there are two items to check and possibly adjust: focus point and depth of field. Achieving the perfect focus point can be a bit challenging. Start by focusing between the nearest and furthest points that you want to appear in focus. If you are shooting a landscape with flowers in the foreground and a mountain in the background, for example, focus on a point between the two with a slight preference for the foreground.

Next, it's time to start closing the aperture down for more depth of field. If you're at f/8 and you don't have enough depth of field, try stopping down to f/11, then f/16, then f/22. The aperture that you need for any particular scene is based on many variables. There are many online resources to help in this calculation, but most seasoned photographers will learn this with a bit of experience.

Once you have closed the aperture down to a small opening, there is a good chance the appropriate shutter speed for a decent exposure will be well below most people's handholding limit. For this reason, the tripod is an indispensable accessory for many photographers. If you don't have a tripod, you'll need to raise your shutter speed to an appropriate setting to prevent any blur. If you do increase your shutter speed, you'll need to make changes to the ISO or aperture, which will compromise the overall quality of the photo, but will make the shot possible from a handheld position. For this reason, photographers wanting to capture maximum depth of field often use tripods.

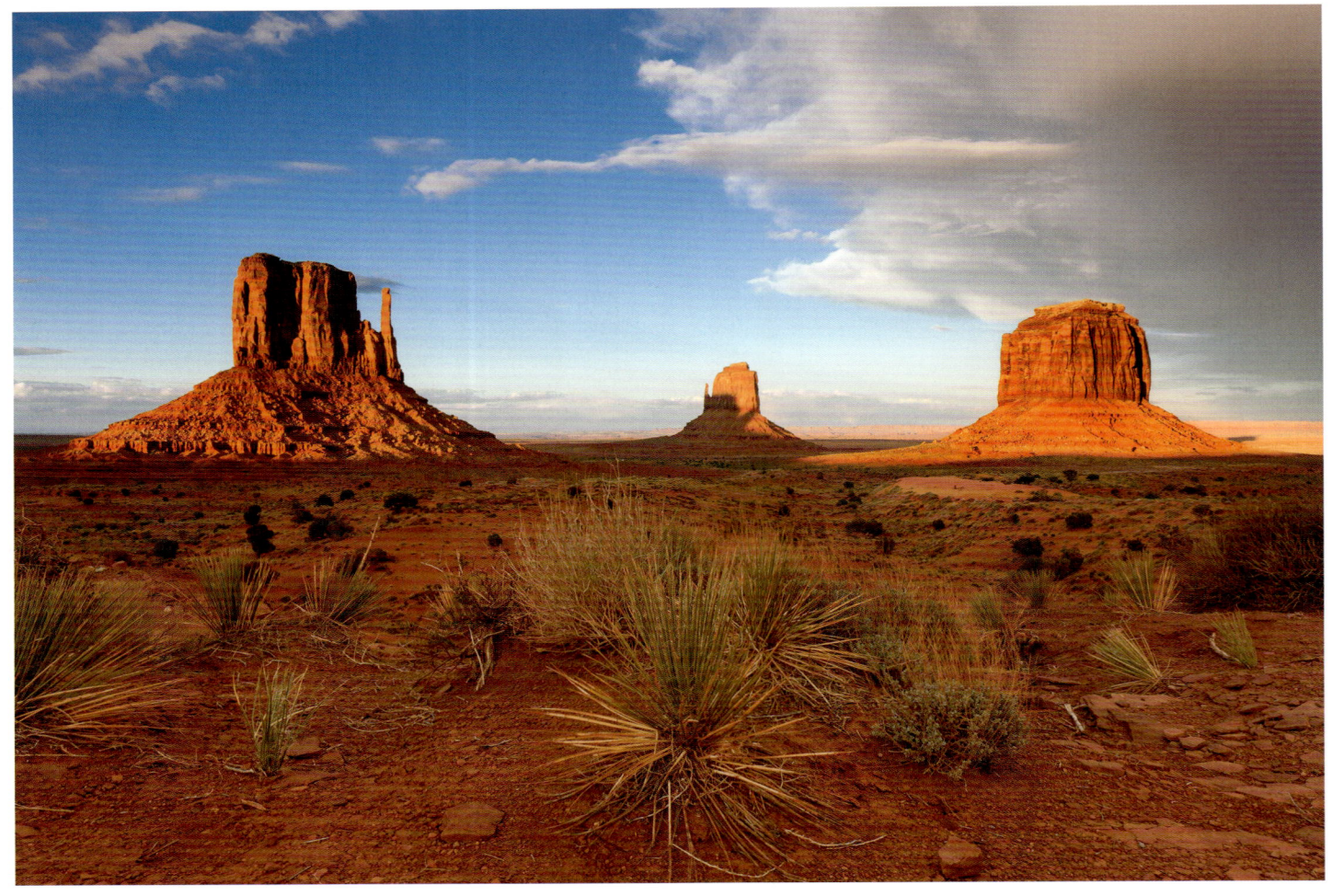

29.1 Holding focus from the foreground to the distance is an important element in landscape photography. Camera placement, aperture, and choosing the right place to focus will all be key elements to achieving maximum depth of field.
1/4 sec.; f/16; ISO 100; Canon 5D Mark II; EF 17-40mm f/4L USM

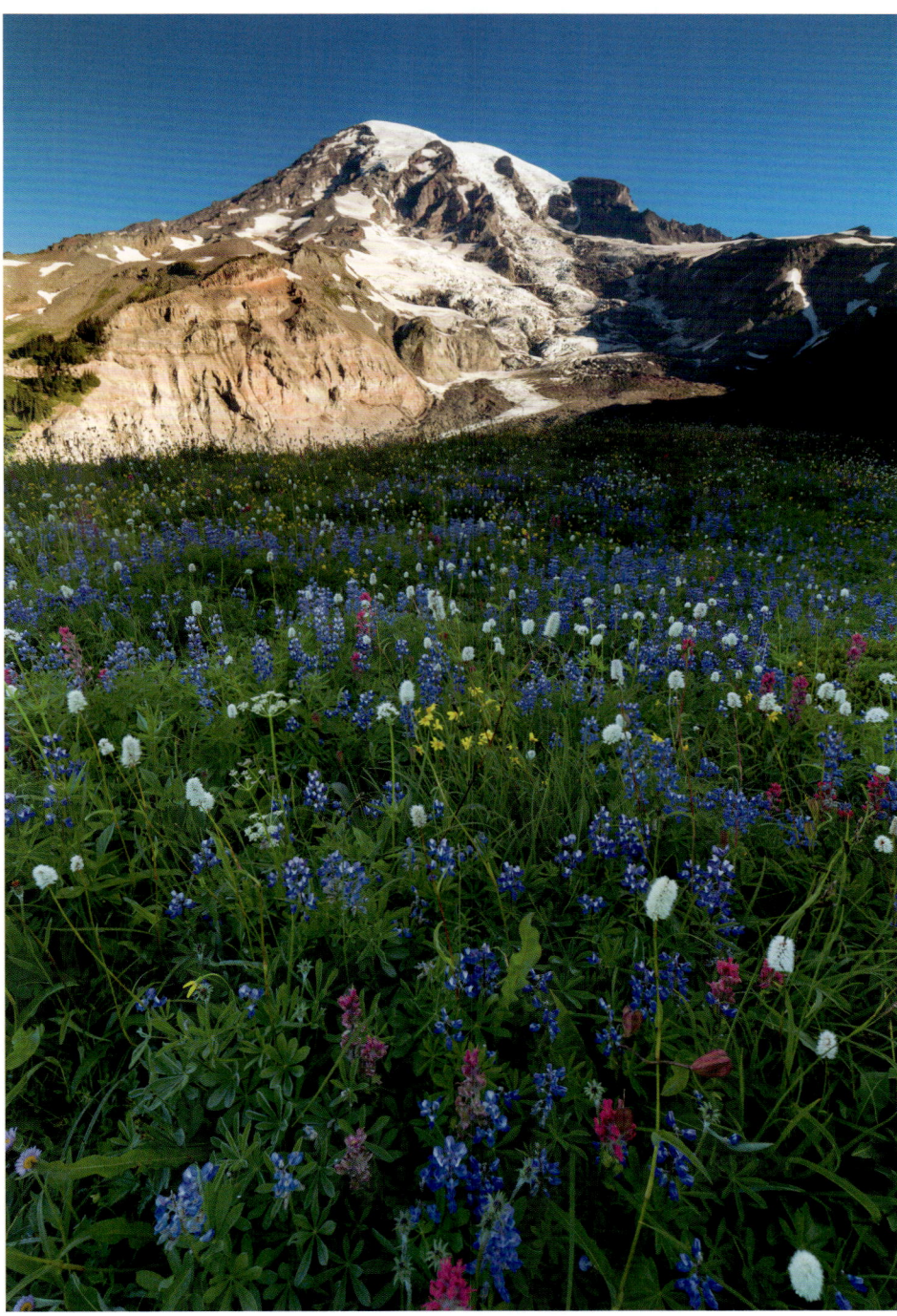

29.2 Having both the foreground and background in sharp focus allows the viewer of your photograph to visually explore the scene in much the same way you did when you took the photograph in person.
1/2 sec.; f/16; ISO 100; Canon 5D Mark III; EF 16-35mm f/4L IS USM

30. CREATING A SHALLOW DEPTH OF FIELD FOR PORTRAITS

PORTRAIT PHOTOGRAPHERS AND those with an eye for details like to draw attention to their chosen subject with sharp focus and let the other elements go softly out of focus. This effect is easy to achieve with the right technique and right equipment. There are three parameters that will help to achieve shallow depth of field: aperture, subject distance, and focal length.

The wider the aperture is, the shallower the depth of field will be. This means that this technique works best with apertures in the f/1.4 – f/4 range. General consumer lenses often have maximum apertures of only f/3.5–5.6, which means they have a limited ability to achieve a very shallow depth of field. Pro zoom lenses that go down to f/2.8 can achieve very nice results.

If you want the shallowest depth of field possible, you'll want to find a lens with a maximum aperture of f/1.4 – f/2. This will usually only be found in a prime or fixed lens.

A second factor in controlling how shallow the depth of field will be is the distance between your camera and your subject. The closer a subject is, the shallower the depth of field will be. If you desire this look, get close to your subject.

The final factor affecting the depth of field is the focal length of the lens. Compare a 50mm lens at f/4 and a 200mm lens at f/4 and you'll find that the longer lens (200mm) will have a shallower depth of field. An interesting trade-off here is that longer focal length lenses are more difficult to build with a fast aperture.

Here are a few of the fastest lenses available today: 85mm f/1.2, 100mm f/1.4, 200mm f/2, and 300mm f/2.8. All these lenses are capable of creating photographs with a very narrow focus. Which one yields the shallowest depth of field is a secondary question as to which lens is right for the subject size, distance, and composition.

Shallow depth of field isn't regulated to a few high-priced lenses; it's achievable with most short telephotos when the subject is relatively close to the camera. Start by setting your aperture either mostly open or all the way open. Next, set your ISO to its base or native sensitivity (ISO 100 or 200). Finally, adjust your shutter speed so that your exposure indicator is showing a proper exposure. Take a test shot to make sure it's the proper brightness. Adjust if necessary. If you end up with a shutter speed that is a bit too slow for handholding the camera, you can use a tripod or raise the shutter speed to an appropriate level and adjust the ISO to compensate. To see the effect most clearly, try focusing on object fairly close (3-6 feet, 1-2 meters) to the camera.

Background

An additional important element in showcasing shallow depth of field is the distance between the subject and the background. The farther the background is from the subject, the greater the blur. If you have a person standing with their back against a brick wall, you will get very little blur on the brick wall because it's so close to your subject. If you shoot your portrait subject at the same distance, but in an open field with a background that's relatively far away, it will be blurred by a much greater degree.

A Special Note for Portrait Photographers

Shallow depth of field can be a lot of fun, and it can separate your photographs from those of people who aren't able to achieve it, but it doesn't have to rule your portraits. Photographers with very fast lenses sometimes choose to stop their lens down to f/4 or f/5.6 for their portraits. With these slightly smaller apertures, more of the face is in focus, which will look more appealing than an image with a large portion of the face out of focus. Use shallow depth of field with care; it's simply a tool for solving a problem.

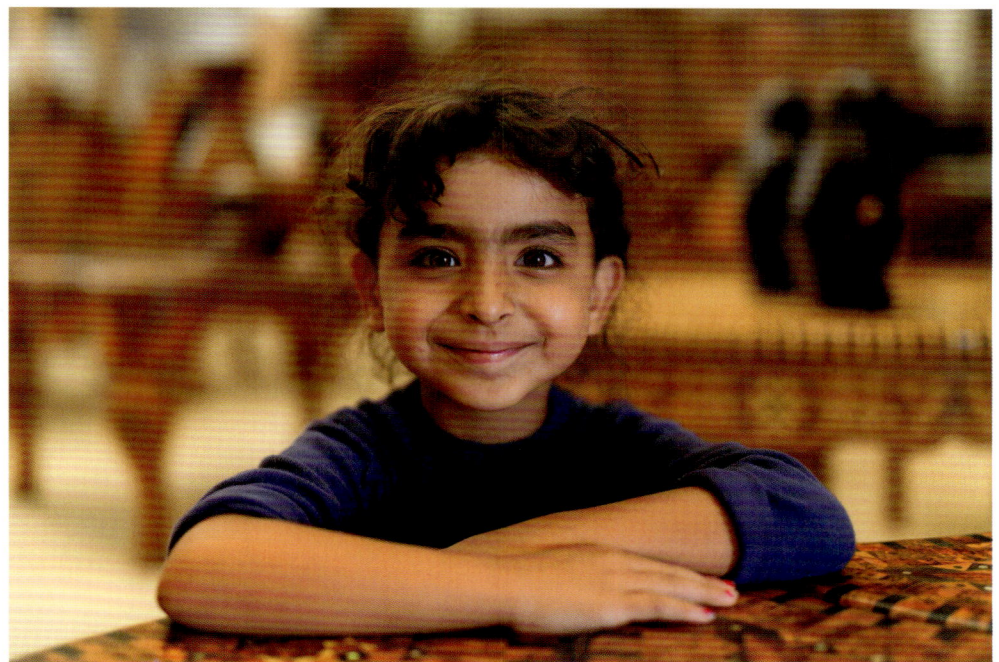

30.1 A shallow depth of field allows your subject to be separated from the background. This wall of blur can be used as a backdrop that you control and can bring with you everywhere you go.
1/60 sec.; f/1.4; ISO 400; Canon 5D Mark III; Sigma 50mm f/1.4 A

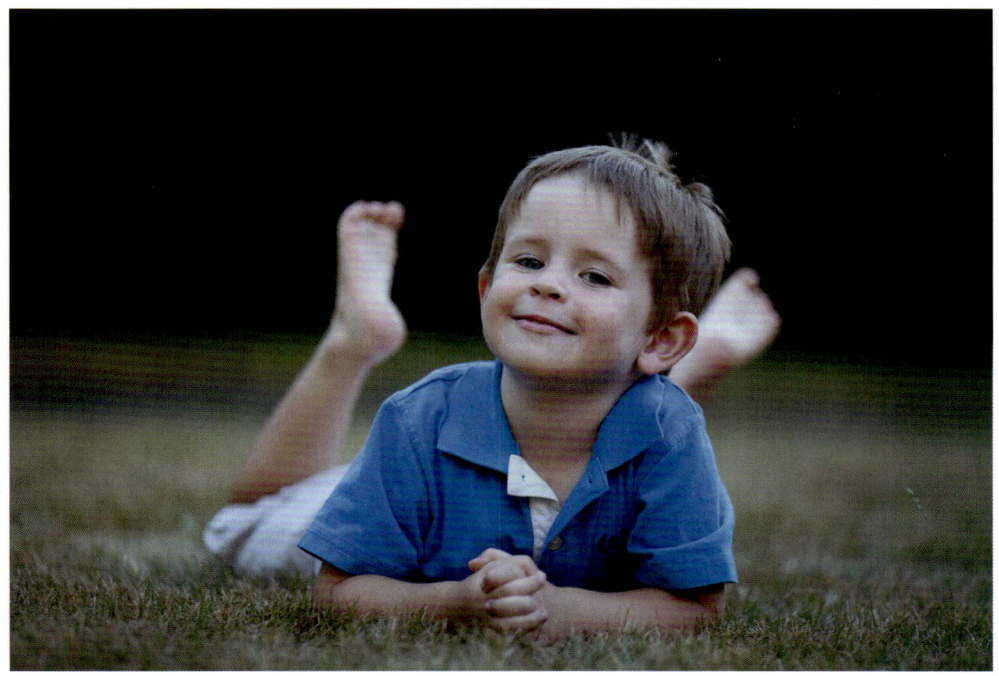

30.2 A shallow depth of field can best be achieved with longer lenses, fast apertures, and subjects not too far away. In this example, the subject was only about 30 feet from the photographer.
1/500 sec.; f/2; ISO 400; Canon 5D Mark II; Canon EF 135mm f/2L USM

31. MAXIMUM SHARPNESS

THE OVERALL SHARPNESS of an image is controlled not only by the quality of the lens and the sensor in the camera, but also by the specific aperture setting. In theory, lenses should be perfect when they are used with a wide-open aperture. But small imperfections can be seen most easily at this setting. When a lens is stopped down from f/2.8 to f/4 to f/5.6, the increase in depth of field disguises and hides those imperfections.

If you continue to stop the aperture down (f/11 to f/16 to f/22), a new problem arises. When forcing all the light through a small opening, some of the light hitting the edge of the aperture scatters, in an effect called diffraction. Small openings have a greater percentage of their light passing through the aperture along the edge and as a result have a greater diffraction rate. Those smaller aperture openings (f/11 to f/16 to f/22) result in an increasing loss of sharpness.

Stopping an aperture down does increase sharpness (and depth of field) until it hits the point where diffraction becomes noticeable and the sharpness then begins to decrease. Where this point is depends on a number of factors, but with full-frame cameras, it will be around f/16; for the APS-C 1.5x cropped frame, it will be around f/11; with the Micro-Four-Thirds system, it will be around f/8. These are very generalized settings that will vary from lens to lens and camera to camera.

As a result of this phenomenon it's often good to start with a middle aperture setting around f/8 for any photo. Ask if you really need an aperture other than that. If so, feel free to set it. While the image quality does decrease as you move away from that middle aperture range, don't let that scare you away from using the extremes of your aperture range. If you need an extreme aperture, use it. For example: if you are photographing a distance scene, where most everything is pretty far off in the distance, you don't need to stop down to f/22—f/8 should be fine for that scenario.

If you'd like to test your camera and lens to see what aperture gives you the sharpest results, it's very simple to do. Use a tripod-mounted camera and focus on a stationary object that has lots of detail. Take a series of photos, making sure to carefully focus on your target, using all available aperture settings. Adjust your settings for proper exposure as you go from one image to the next. You may want to use a cable release or self-timer to make sure that you are not moving the camera in any way when you trigger the shutter. Check the photos for sharpness. You'll likely see that photos from the largest and smallest aperture settings are less sharp than those in the middle. Use this information to determine where you will set your aperture as a default position for the sharpest images.

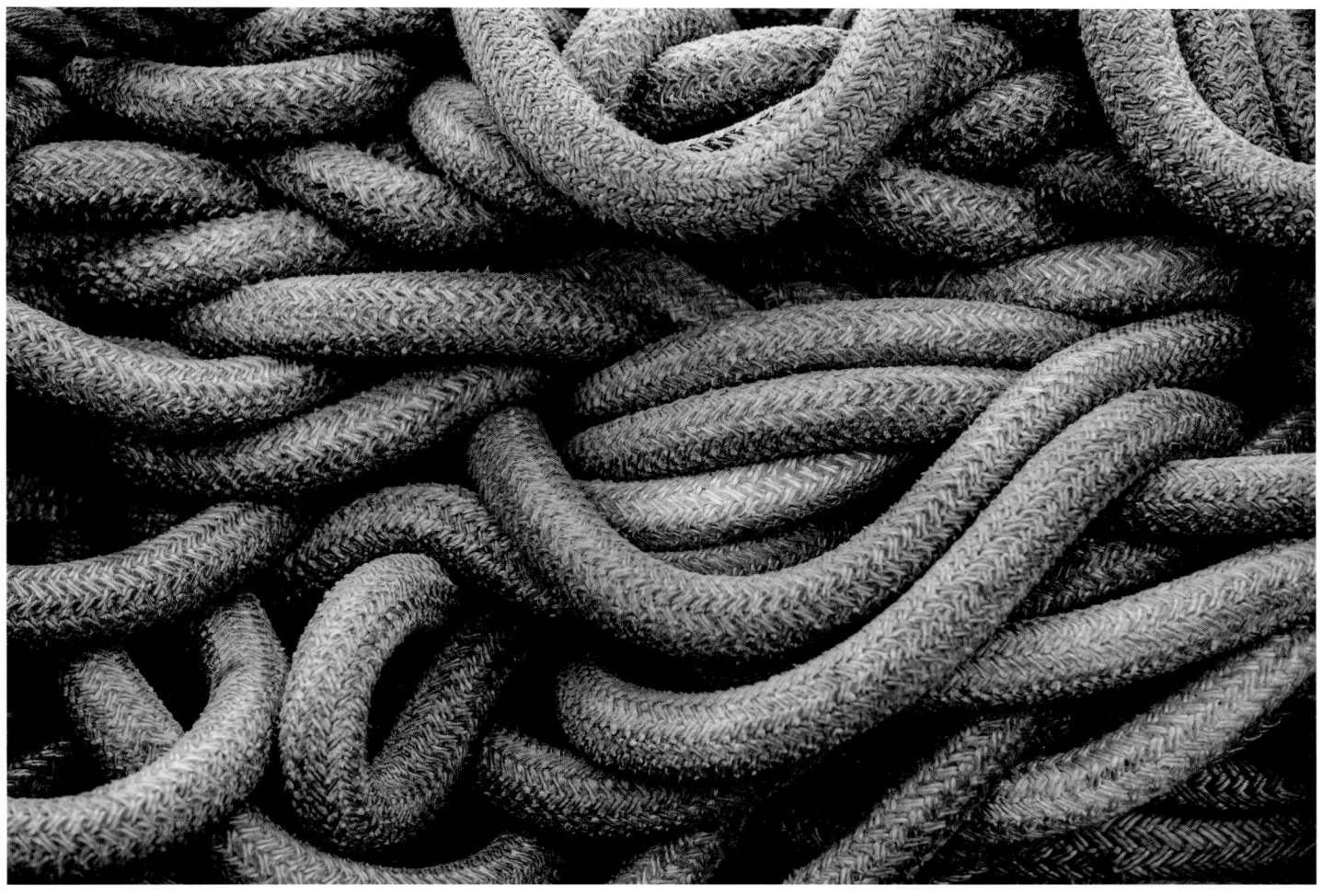

31.1 Flat or nearly flat subjects will allow you to use the middle of your aperture range, which is sharper than either of the aperture's extremes.
1/125 sec.; f/5.6; ISO 200; Canon 5D Mark II; EF 70-200mm f/4L IS USM @135mm

32. HYPERFOCAL DISTANCE

IF YOU HAVE a scene in which you want the nearest element to be in focus as well as the most distant, you'll need to be very careful about what aperture you set and where you set the focus of your lens. When you focus, the camera only focuses on one point at a certain distance from the camera. It can't simultaneously focus on points at two feet away and ten feet away; it must settle on just one point. If we want a great region in focus, we can use a small aperture opening to increase the appearance of the in-focus area. As we close the aperture down, the depth of field increases in front of and behind the focus point. The rate of growth in these two areas is not equal—it tends to grow a bit faster behind the focus point. All of this depends on a number of factors, including focal length and focus distance. In some cases it will be in focus 1/3 in front and 2/3 in back; in other cases it will be 1/2 and 1/2.

When wanting a large area in focus, you neither want to focus on the closest element nor the furthest. There are many apps that can aid you in choosing where to focus, but a simple rule of thumb can do the job in most cases. Focus on a point that is double the distance to your nearest subject. This doesn't tell you what aperture you'll need—you'll need to use the "test-and-check" method to determine that setting. This system works amazingly well with different lenses and different compositions. The only time it won't work is when your nearest subject is extremely close to the camera.

A common setup is shooting a landscape with a 24mm wide-angle lens (on a full-frame camera). The closest flowers are about five feet away, so you focus, either manual or using the autofocus system, on a subject that is about ten feet away. You might try an aperture of f/11. If that doesn't yield the results you're looking for, move to an aperture of f/16 or f/22.

32.1 Finding the hyperfocal distance will allow you to keep every leaf and every cloud in focus. Focus should be set at a point twice the distance to the nearest subject. In this example, focus was set about halfway between the nearest and farthest leaves of the foreground bush.
1/15 sec.; f/16; ISO 200; Fuji X-T1; 10-24mm f/4 R OIS @ 16.6mm

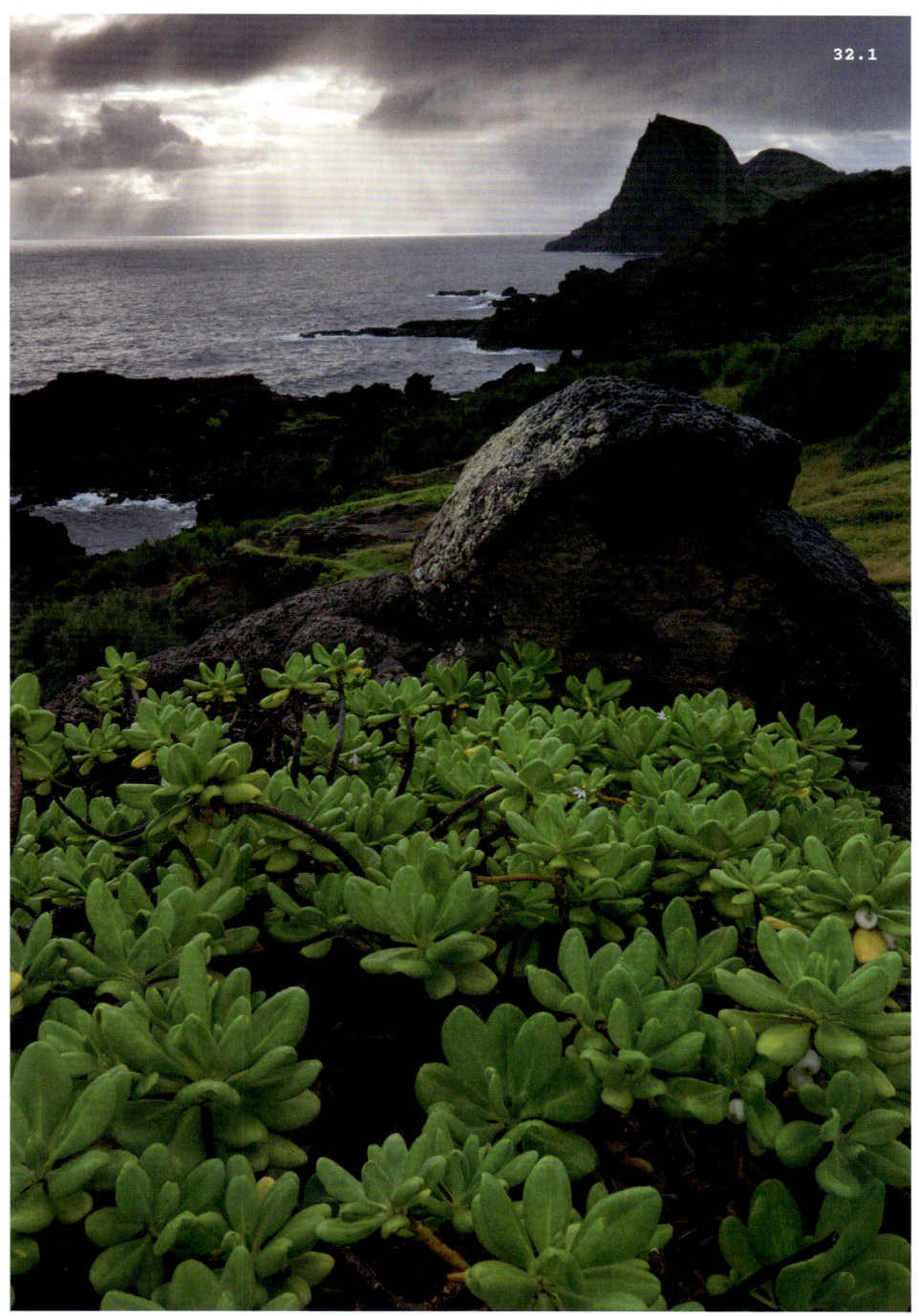

32.1

7

EXPOSURE ADJUSTMENTS

CHAPTER 7

Photographs don't always come out how we hoped they would. Light can be tricky. Cameras and their accompanying light meters, sensors, and advanced technology can't solve all of our exposure problems. From time to time, we must step in and make an adjustment to fix problems. There are often several solutions to any given problem—the one to choose is purely up to you. Knowledge of the options and how to use them will give you the ability to choose the one that best fits your needs. The following techniques can be seen as "tricks up your sleeve." If all goes well, you won't need any of them, but when things aren't coming out right, you'll have a solution ready to go.

33. EXPOSURE COMPENSATION

WHEN USING ANY of the auto exposure modes (P-Program, A-Aperture Priority, S-Shutter Priority), it's the camera that's in control of the brightness of your image. You may have some control over the exposure settings, but it's the camera that's reading the light and determining the brightness of the final image. The light meter in all cameras is calibrated so that all images achieve an average brightness of 18% gray. This is halfway between pure black and pure white.

In reality, some subjects or scenes are dark, some are middle-tone gray, and some are light. The ones that are middle-tone gray will be easy for your camera to get right in terms of exposure. Your light meter won't decipher scenes that are darker or brighter than average quite so well. Your camera can't tell the difference between a light object in a dark environment and a dark object in a bright environment. Using your own eyes, you'll need to recognize the brightness of your subjects and scenes. In situations where the camera may get fooled, you'll need to compensate.

Exposure compensation is a feature that allows you to correct situations in which the light meter misreads the ambient brightness in any of the auto exposure modes (P-Program, A-Aperture Priority, S-Shutter Priority). Cameras have a variety of controls that operate this feature, but it's likely to be displayed with a +/- indicator. You may need to consult your instruction manual to locate this feature. (This is not to be confused with your camera's diopter dial or lever which may also feature a +/- on it. Its purpose is for adjusting the focus of the viewfinder.) Settings with plus (+) will indicate the image is being overexposed and will be brighter than the typical recommendation. Settings with a minus (-) will be darker than average.

If you are in Aperture Priority with an aperture of f/8, the camera will set a shutter speed so the image is of average brightness. If you decide that it should be brighter than the results you are getting, you could set the Exposure Compensation to +1 to make the next exposure one stop brighter. If it needs more, you could set it to +2 or you could go even further if your camera allows for it. In most cameras you'll be able to make these changes in 1/3-stop increments, if you want to be very precise. The resulting image will be brighter than your first.

How did the camera make it brighter? It chose a slower shutter speed. This feature will act in a similar fashion when used in Program or Shutter Priority. To make the exposure adjustment, it simply adjusts whatever setting the camera is controlling.

It's important to note that when Exposure Compensation is set, it doesn't reset back to 0 on its own, even if the camera is turned off. You'll need to remember to reset it back to zero when you are done. If you forget, the subsequent images will continue to be over- or underexposed.

Exposure compensation won't work in manual exposure mode on most cameras because the camera doesn't have control over any of the settings. Some cameras do allow exposure compensation in manual—it forces the light meter to read higher or lower depending on the settings. For these cameras, you'll need to set the exposure compensation setting before looking at the light meter to determine the exposure. If you set it after you've already set your shutter speed and aperture, it won't affect your final image, just the indicator in the light meter.

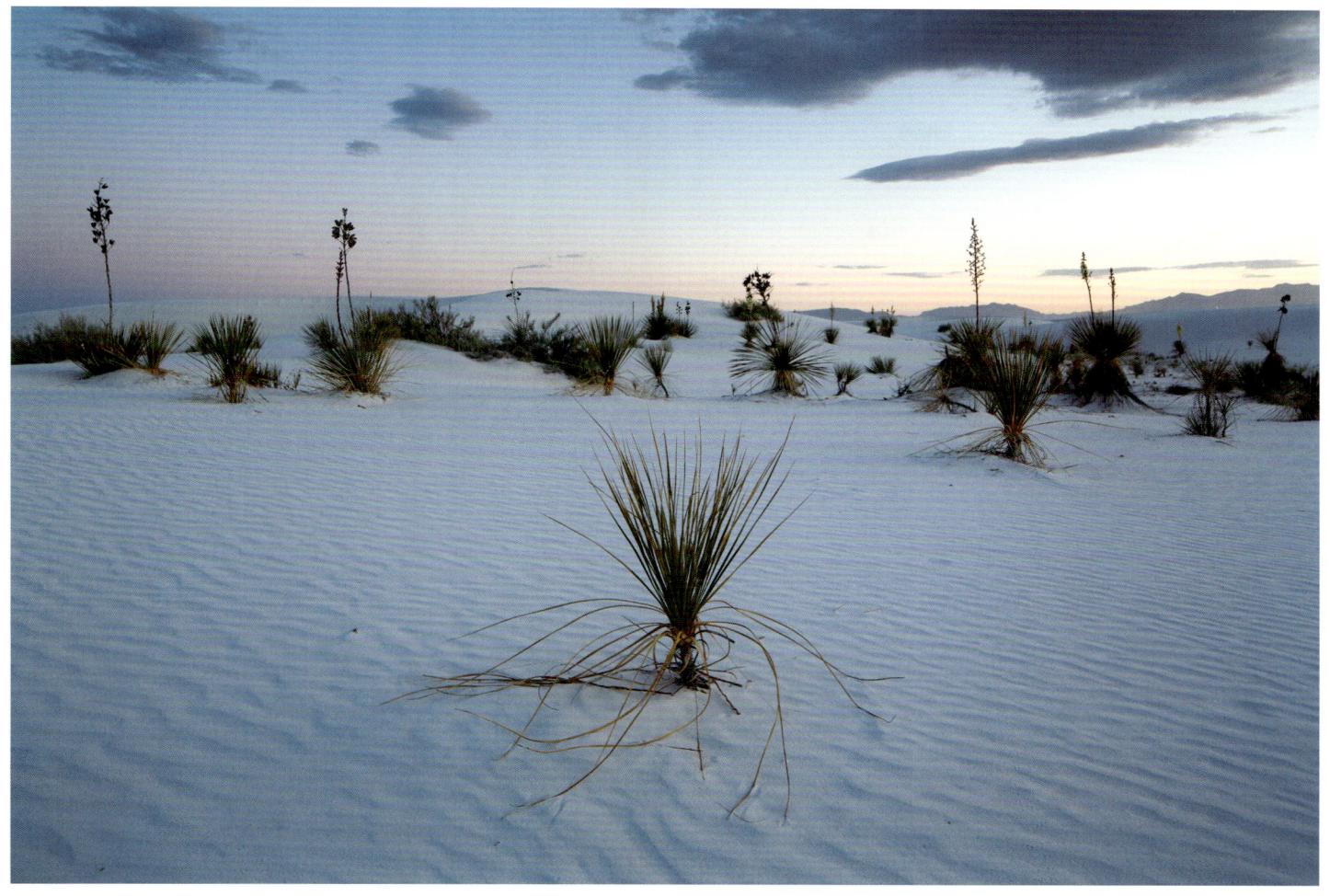

33.1 Any situation that is lighter or darker than average will challenge a camera. Scenes with lots of brightly lit or reflective objects will bounce more light back to the camera, causing the exposure system to respond by darkening the subject to a "normal" brightness level.
1/30 sec.; f/5.6; ISO 400; Canon 5D Mark III; TS-E 24mm f/3.5L II

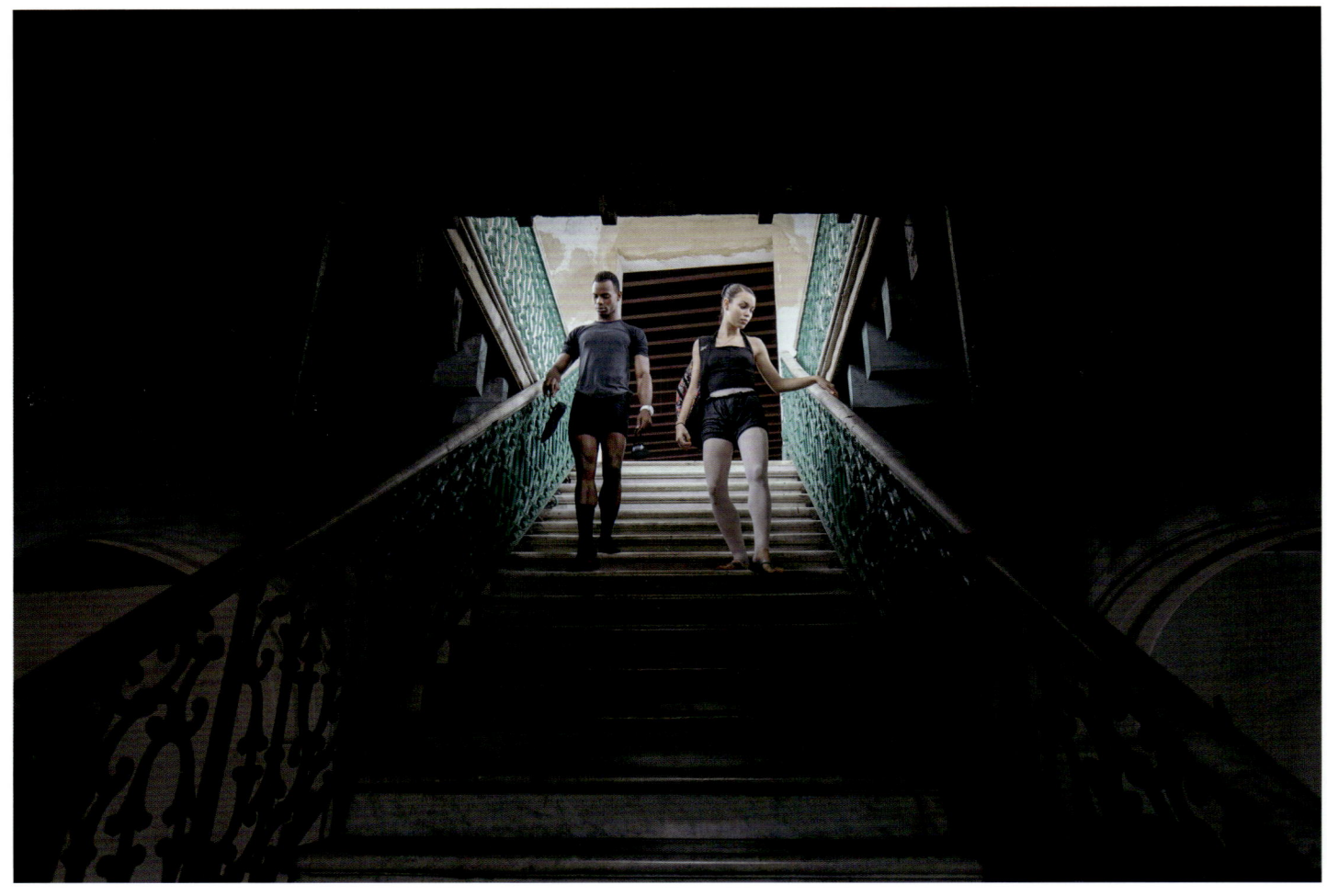

33.2 Cameras want to lighten up scenes that are overly dark, but you'll need to be careful because cameras can't discern the difference between subjects and their surroundings.
1/60 sec.; f/4; ISO 800; Canon 5D Mark IV; EF 16-35mm f/4L IS USM @22mm

34. THE AEL BUTTON

ON THE BACK of most cameras is an AEL (Auto Exposure Lock) button. When pressed, it locks the exposure when you are in any of the three auto exposure modes: P-Program, A-Aperture Priority, S-Shutter Priority.

All of the auto exposure modes allow you some input to the exposure settings, but the final exposure is always determined by the camera.

When you press down halfway on the shutter release, the camera's light meter turns on and your camera will give you a recommended reading for the scene. As you move the camera around, the light meter will adjust for each new scene you point the camera at. When you press on the AEL button, it will lock the current exposure reading.

Imagine photographing a person standing next to a big window with lots of light streaming through it. The camera doesn't know what your subject is; all it sees is a big, bright object and a smaller, darker object next to it. The light meter will read the overall scene as very bright, and the camera will set an exposure to reduce the overall brightness of the scene down to the typical middle-gray average. The resulting photo would be of a window that's darker than it looks in real life, and a subject that is lost in the shadows. The camera reduces the overall brightness of this scene because it doesn't understand overly bright (or dark) situations on

its own. To correct for this, we'll need to give it some guidance.

If we point the camera away from the window and toward our subject in the shadows, we will be able to lock in a more accurate exposure reading. To do this, move the camera so that the window is out of the frame, press the AEL button to lock the exposure reading, then recompose to include the window. Your camera should give you some indication that the AEL button is pressed and that your exposure settings are no longer changing. With the AEL button pressed, you can press the shutter release to take the photo. This version of the photo should have the person properly exposed with the window very bright.

This feature can be handy if you desire a particular exposure setting that the camera won't offer when you compose your shot. There are many situations where the scene you're framing is either too bright or too dark. By moving the camera to an area of average brightness, pressing the AEL button, and recomposing the scene, you will be able to lock in an exposure that is more appropriate for that scene.

Customizing the AEL Button

Most cameras have an AEL button. Some are labeled clearly; some are labeled as function buttons (Fn) that may need to be activated in the custom settings of your camera. With some

cameras the button needs to be pressed for the entire process, while others will "lock in" with a single press. On a number of cameras the AEL button/feature can be combined with a feature called Auto Focus Lock (AFL). The AFL feature locks the focus while the button is pressed. It's a matter of personal preference as to whether you want to combine these features.

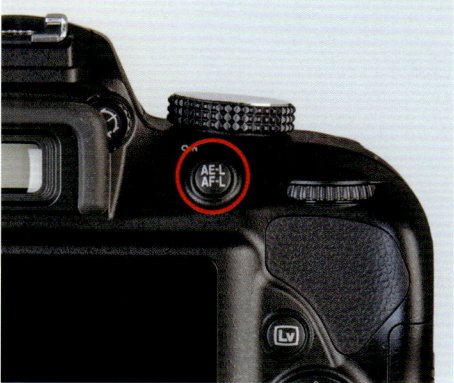

34.1 Found on the back of many cameras, the AEL button will either be labeled or you may find it in the menu and assign it to a button via the custom settings.

35. BRACKETING

BRACKETING IS THE act of taking a number of photos at different exposure levels to ensure that you capture at least one that is at the optimum level.

This can be manually achieved by changing one of the exposure settings or automatically, where the camera changes the settings for you. This technique is valuable when you are unable to determine what the best exposure should be while in the field. This works best for static scenes, since anything that moves will be different in each of the bracketed exposures. An important aspect of this technique is to make sure everything in each of the images is exactly the same (except the exposure). Ideally you should be shooting from a tripod for a bracket series of images.

There are several control factors for this bracket series. First, there is the number of photos in the sequence, traditionally three. The first image is the normal exposure, the second image is underexposed, and the last image is overexposed. Some cameras allow up to 9 images in the series.

The second control is the exposure difference between the images. This will vary from 1/3-stop to three stops. Some cameras will allow further fine-tuning to select the image that's shot first: the normal exposure, the underexposure, or the overexposure.

In most cameras if you have the motor drive set to single, you can take each photo individually. When the camera has the continuous motor drive turned on, one continued press of the shutter release will fire through the entire bracket series and stop when the series is completed.

To shoot a bracket series, first locate the feature, usually in the menu system of your camera, and turn it on. Manual or Aperture Priority mode is recommended when doing a bracket series. In these modes, it's the shutter speed that will be changing to modify the exposures. Since the bracket series is usually shot with a static subject from a tripod, a changing shutter speed will only affect the exposure. In other exposure modes, an aperture change will change the depth of field throughout the series.

If slow shutter speeds are needed, it's recommended that you use a cable release or self timer to activate the camera so you don't cause any vibrations that will result in camera-induced motion blur.

This technique is popular with landscape, architectural, and real estate photographers that are dealing with a wide range of exposure levels within a scene. The goal in using this technique is to cover all the bases by collecting as much data as possible. From the resulting series of photos you can choose the image that is easiest to work with, or you can combine one or more of the exposures into a single image.

By blending the images together, you can create an image that would be impossible to capture in a single exposure. The mixing of two images together can be as simple as using an image-processing program to layer the different exposures together. You can also use software specifically designed for High Dynamic Range (HDR) photography.

35.1 Bracketing involves shooting a series of images at a variety of exposures. Many cameras will offer a bracketing feature that will assist in exposure changes and the firing of the shutter.

-3: Exposure: - 3 stops

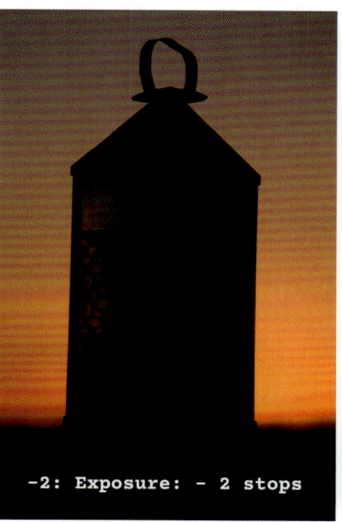
-2: Exposure: - 2 stops

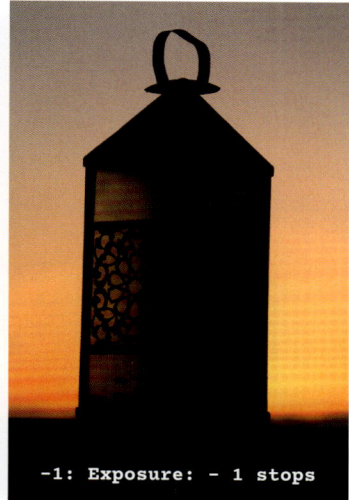
-1: Exposure: - 1 stops

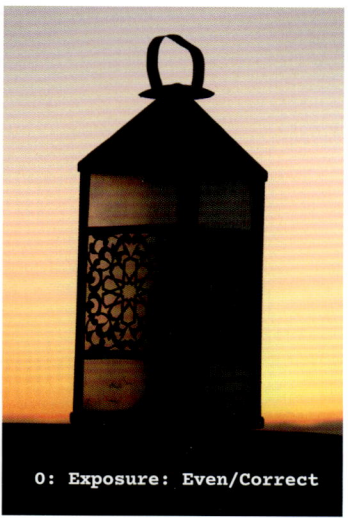
0: Exposure: Even/Correct

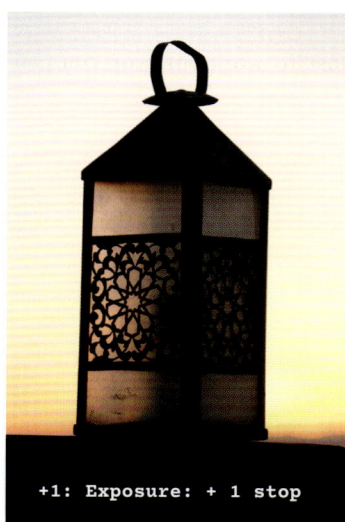
+1: Exposure: + 1 stop

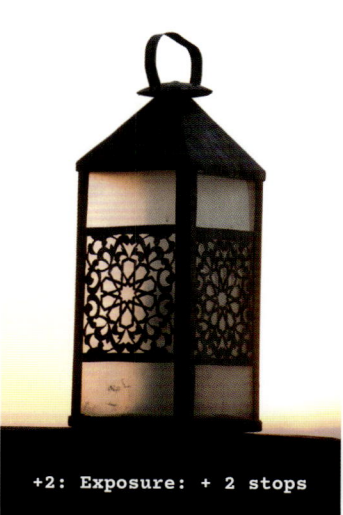
+2: Exposure: + 2 stops

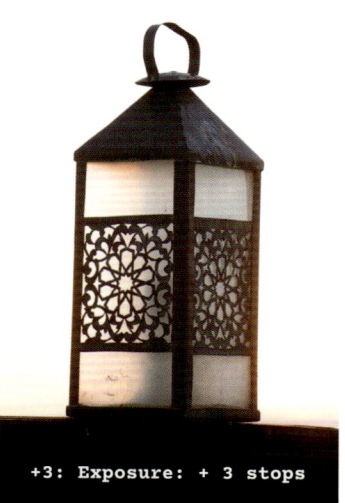
+3: Exposure: + 3 stops

36. FILTERS

THERE ARE MANY different filters available in the world of photography. Two common filters that affect the exposure of a scene are neutral density filters and split neutral density filters.

Neutral Density Filter

The neutral density (ND) filter is a dark gray filter used to reduce the amount of light entering the lens without any change in color. This can become a fourth way of controlling light, after shutter speed, aperture, and ISO. This filter is used for two very different photographic needs.

If you want to take very long exposures in normal daylight, you'd set a low ISO (100 or 200), stop your aperture down to its smallest settings (f/22 or f/32), and use the slowest shutter speed possible. In many cases, this technique might make a 1-second or 4-second exposure possible, but if you wanted to do a 30-second exposure or a 10-minute exposure, you'd be out of luck because your camera would be letting in too much light. To solve this problem use an ND filter to block light entering the lens. An ND filter can come in a variety of densities that will allow it to filter one stop of light to 100 stops of light. For anyone wanting to shoot waterfalls

during the day with really long shutter speeds, the ND filter will make that possible.

These filters are also useful to cinematographers. When shooting video, the shutter speed is often fixed at 1/50s to 1/100s so the frames look consistent. This limits the exposure settings to only aperture and ISO. Shooting at a shallow depth of field may not be possible at certain shutter speeds due to too much light coming into the camera, so the solution is an ND filter to block some of that light. Most cinematographers have an ND filter for each of their lenses, especially if they shoot in sunny conditions on a regular basis.

The Graduated Neutral Density Filter

Landscape and travel photographers face the common exposure problem of an overly bright sky and relatively dark landscape. One solution is to shoot two exposures, one for the sky and one for the land, and then blend them in post-production. For those that want to capture the scene in the camera with one exposure, a great solution is the graduated neutral density filter (Grad ND or Split ND). This filter looks quite different from most filters: it's not of the

round screw-in variety—it's large and rectangular; also, it's dark on the top half and transitions to completely clear on the bottom half.

This filter is either mounted in a bracket or handheld in front of the lens. It's positioned vertically so that the dark top half aligns with the bright sky and the clear bottom is over the darker landscape. These will effectively lower the brightness of the sky by one to three stops of light. The darker sky enables the image to be captured in a single exposure without overexposing any elements.

A variety of Grad ND filters are available with different density levels (1-stop, 2-stop, or 3-stop), different gradations (soft, medium, or hard), and different sizes. Using this filter is better than HDR for subjects that are moving, like trees in the wind or people on the boardwalk. It allows you to get the image right in-camera, which means you'll have less work to do in post-production. The best filter for the job depends on the situation and what you'd like the final image to look like, but if you're looking to get started, I recommend a 2-stop medium-gradation filter.

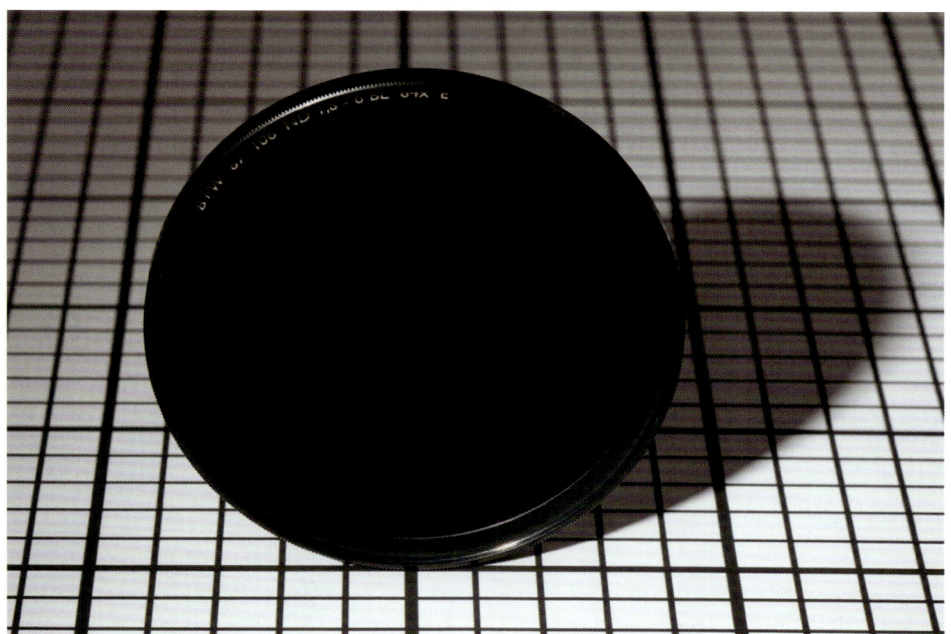

36.1 A neutral density filter is dark and without color. These filters are very helpful as a way of controlling the light that enters the camera.

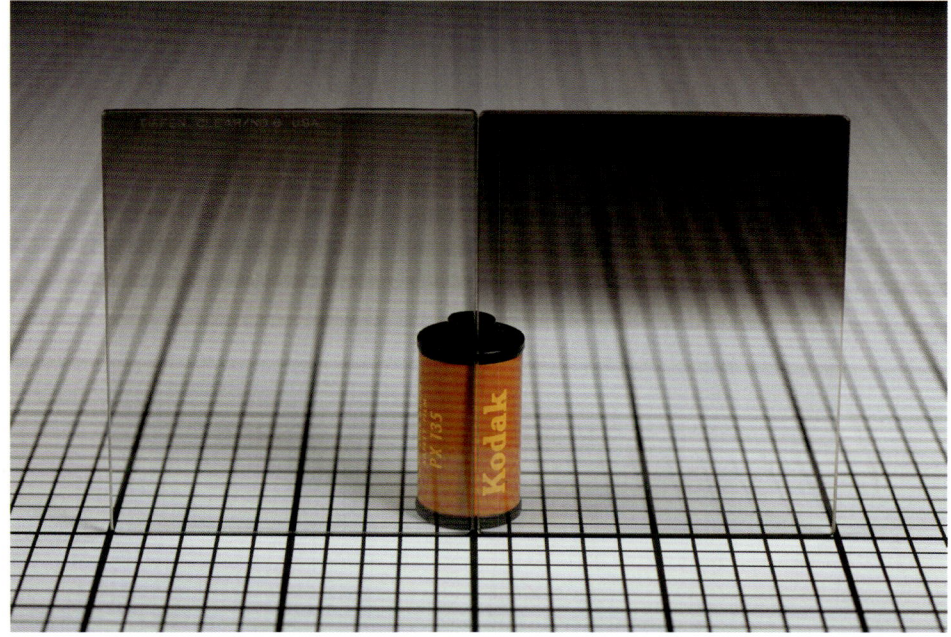

36.2 The graduated neutral density filter is a rectangular filter with a dark top that graduates to clear on the bottom. These filters are very helpful with bright skies in that they lower the brightness so that scenes can be captured that cover a wide dynamic range.

37. HDR

HIGH DYNAMIC RANGE (HDR) is how we describe a scene with a wide range of brightness, often ranging from deep shadow to bright sun. Imagine a scene on a sunny day with sunshine illuminating part of the land, but in part of the image, a large shadow hides a portion of the scene in darkness. Capturing the entire image in one shot, with detail in all areas, would be impossible because the range of brightness is beyond the recording capability of modern sensors. You could try to capture everything in one image by setting an exposure exactly between the two extremes, or you could try to adjust the image in post-production, but this may not be enough to hold detail in both the highlights and shadows.

Recording a scene with intense highlights and deep shadows that keeps detailed information in all areas requires recording multiple images that each capture a different level of brightness. The resulting images are combined into a single HDR image.

To record an HDR image in the field, you'll follow the same procedure described for bracketing. The idea is to take a series of images at different exposure levels. The number of images you take and the exposure difference between each shot will depend on the scene, how you will process the shot, how the final image will be used, and what your final vision for that photo is.

To start, you'll need at least two images of different exposures. Most HDR photographers will shoot at least three, often five, and sometimes as many as nine images. The difference in exposure from one image to the next can vary according to your needs, but a 1-stop EV difference is quite common. A bracket series of three images taken one stop apart would cover a basic scene; five images one stop apart would cover a greater exposure range.

To do the job right, you should use a tripod so that all of your images are perfectly aligned. Some cameras offer a handheld option where the camera crops the image and automatically aligns the resulting images. This technique is less desirable because it changes the angle of view, reduces the resolution, and may introduce handheld blur into the image.

Always make sure there isn't any subject movement. If there is anything moving, whether it's people walking or flowers blowing in the wind, they will likely cause ghosting in the final image. For these reasons, HDR is not a viable solution in many situations.

Processing the images into a completed HDR image can be done several ways. Some cameras can shoot and process images right in the camera, albeit with limited control factors. For the greatest control, you'll want to use one of the many image-processing programs available for processing HDR images. Results can vary from subtle brightening of shadows to fixing overcooked images that look like they came out of a CGI comic strip. The HDR look is a hot topic among photographers, but in the end it's all a mater of taste.

For many photographers, HDR is an indispensable technique. Real estate photographers trying to capture a modern kitchen with beautiful amenities along with the view into the back yard now have an option to capture all of it in one image.

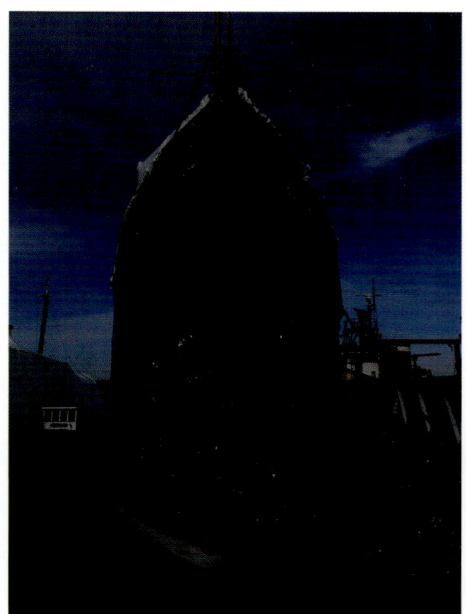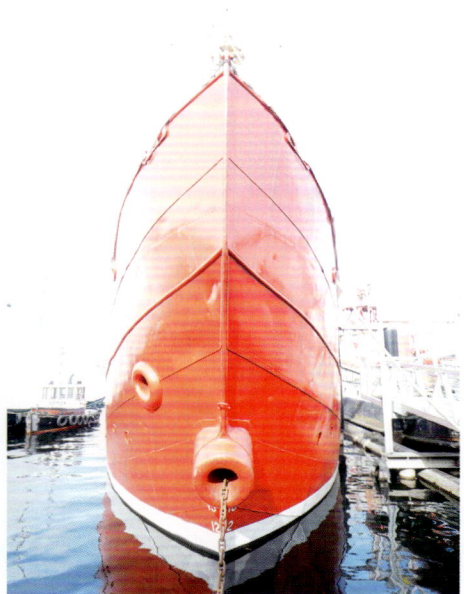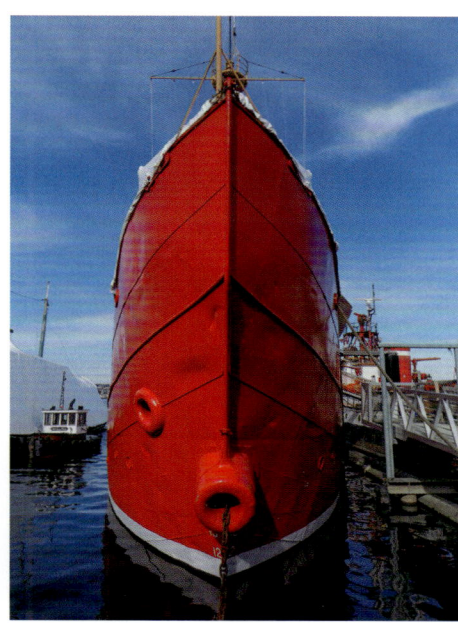

37.1 An HDR series of photos will cover the wide range of light exposure in a certain scene. In-camera or post-processing programs will then combine the images to create a blended image including the most detailed information from all the photos. This series shows how two images, one underexposed (left) and one overexposed (center), can be combined into the final HDR image, which maintains detail in the highlights and the shadows.
Underexposed image (left): 1/640 sec.; f/14; ISO 200; Olympus E-M1; Olympus 12-40mm f/2.8 ED PRO @12mm
Overexposed image (center): 1/60 sec.; f/5.6; ISO 200; Olympus E-M1; Olympus 12-40mm f/2.8 ED PRO @12mm

8

ADDITIONAL EXPOSURE INFORMATION

CHAPTER 8

Beyond setting your shutter speed and aperture, there are a number of elements that also impact the exposure of the photograph. Having the camera set up properly will make everything else easier to handle. As you progress as a photographer, your needs will change, so it's quite likely that the setup that works for you today will be different than what you will be using in five years. It's not that one set of options is more right than others—it's about what settings best fit your needs. Making the best choice will be much easier when you know the implications of the different options, and how they will affect your final shot.

38. SHOOTING JPEG

IMAGES RECORDED IN-CAMERA and saved to the memory card must be saved in a file format, either RAW or JPEG. RAW files are recorded by the image sensor with a bare minimum of processing. JPEG, which stands for Joint Photographic Experts Group, is a lossy compression that results in an image of a much smaller file size and of a more common format. The best analogy for comparing RAW and JPEG is the negative and the print. RAW files contain the maximum amount of data recorded by the camera, while JPEG files are processed images better suited for final use.

JPEG images are popular because they are relatively small and can be read by virtually all computers and devices. This is the easiest form in which to send an image via email or post it on a website.

Processing

There are a number of adjustments that can be applied to an image to improve the look of the photo. Some of the more popular adjustments are color, saturation, contrast, and sharpness. With a JPEG image, the camera will adjust these settings, and maybe others, to achieve a final look that has been determined to be better than the original information from the sensor. This look or style of image is similar to the look of different brands of film from Kodak, Fuji, or Afga. Each company has their own take on what looks best. Many cameras will allow you to select different looks for your images, including standard, landscape, portrait, monochrome, neutral, and a custom option where you choose all the settings yourself.

The problem with processing is that what's good for one image may not be best for another. Once the processing is applied in the camera, changing back can be impossible (photographers sometimes use the phrase "baked in"). This limits the control you have over the final look of your image because all those subtle little adjustments over color, saturation, contrast, and sharpness now have much less range.

Compression

To reduce their file size, JPEG images are compressed using a mathematical algorithm that analyzes the image to determine where information can be discarded without being noticed under normal usage. There are a large number of compression formulas in use, but the general idea is that they look at a group of pixels and disregard certain portions of them in order to reduce the file size. For uses like email, webpage posting, and powerpoints, a compressed image is perfectly acceptable and indistinguishable from the original. The missing information is needed when you want to adjust the photo with an image-processing program or when you want to print it. You'll need to access the full set of data to achieve the highest-quality results in these actions.

39. SHOOTING RAW

THE TERM RAW is not an acronym. It simply means the raw information from the sensor has been recorded into a format that can be read by software. In theory, this is the pure information acquired by the sensor and nothing more, but in fact, there is a small bit of processing necessary to organize the information into a recordable format. Some companies use this opportunity to "fix" problems that may be inherent to the lens or sensor. Generally these tweaks to the raw information are very minimal. The basic RAW file is as good as it's going to get for most of us.

The RAW file doesn't have any adjustments made to the color, saturation, contrast, or sharpness. RAW vs. JPEG is very similar to film vs. print: having the original source file allows you to work with the best and most pure data.

RAW images are only created by cameras. Once a RAW image is opened, adjusted, and saved, it must be saved as a different file type: TIFF, JPEG, PSD, etc. When you open a RAW image, no matter where it's been, it's the original source of information.

One downside to the RAW file format is the large file sizes. The file size of a RAW will be based on the total number of pixels on the camera's sensor. In general, you will get about 1MB of data for each megapixel; thus a 24-megapixel camera will produce a 24MB image (with variance from scene to scene). A typical 24-megapixel RAW image, if recorded as a JPEG, might be only about 5MB of data, depending on the set level of compression.

The second big issue with RAW is the unique file format. Every camera is different. Nikon RAW files (NEF) are very different from Canon RAW files (CR2), which are very different from RAW files from every other manufacturer. This means software programs must have a code for every camera that uses a RAW format. Your camera is supplied with software from the manufacturer that will allow you to see and work with RAW images from that camera (and others of that brand), but many people prefer the more popular software programs like Adobe's Lightroom and Photoshop because they can work with RAW formats from all the manufacturers. The slight catch in this system is that Adobe and other companies may not get official information from the camera manufacturers about the RAW format, so they may need to reverse engineer how to read the RAW files, so these programs may not be as effective at pulling information out of the file as the manufacturer's software. It also means that when a new camera is introduced, it may take a little while before you can use one of the third-party programs to read the RAW image.

For most serious photographers, the RAW image is worth the minor hassles. Having full control over processing the pure data, and having an image that can't be damaged, is a great option. One particularly important advantage to RAW images is their dynamic range. The RAW file isn't compressed like JPEGs are, which makes recovering data from the shadow and highlight areas much easier. Recovering shadow and highlight information from images recorded in JPEG will be impossible if that data has been discarded. If you are ever in a tricky lighting situation, it's recommended that you shoot in RAW, because it will allow you the greatest versatility for adjusting the image in post-production.

This doesn't mean that all serious photographers only use RAW. The JPEG image is a vital part of many photographers' workflows. All photographers work with JPEGs for websites, email, and delivering final digital products. If you have the RAW files, you can create as many JPEGs as you need and have them adjusted perfectly for their final use.

Many photographers shoot JPEG files

in-camera. Sports and wildlife photographers will shoot JPEGs because the reduced file size allows the camera's buffer to shoot through more images before it fills up and causes the motor drive to slow down. The smaller file size makes images faster to transfer for photojournalists on a deadline. Wedding photographers like the smaller file size and usability of the file format for reception photos, where quick, easy-to-read images are more important than large files designed for image manipulation.

Each photographer will have to assess their needs and decide which file format best fits their style and process. Many cameras allow you to record both RAW and JPEG at the same time, should you find that you need both. When your camera is set to this option it will save two images for every one image you take. This is good for anyone that has an immediate need for JPEGs because they will be ready right away. If you don't need a JPEG right away, it would be better to just shoot RAW and make JPEGs later, sized and adjusted according your needs. Shooting and storing RAW+JPEG will use up more space on your memory cards and hard drives.

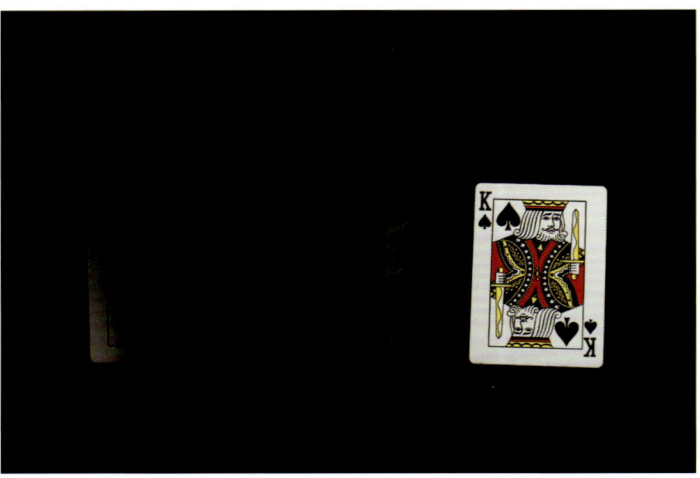

39.1 In this studio example, the playing card on the left is severely underexposed.

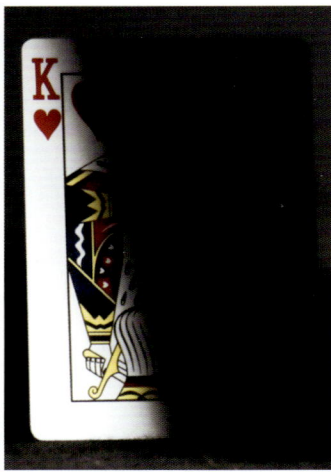

39.2 Because JEPG images are compressed, necessary data may have been discarded. This is the limit to how much shadow recovery is possible for a JPEG.

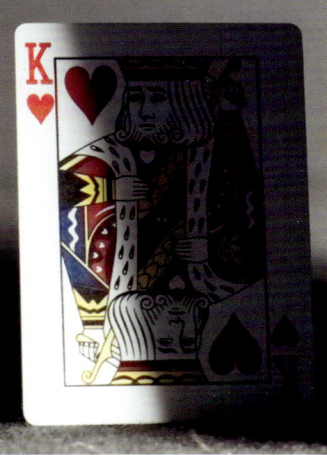

39.3 RAW images are capable of much greater shadow recovery. Despite having information that was barely visible in the original photos, this RAW image maintains an enormous amount of color and detail to be adjusted in post-processing programs.

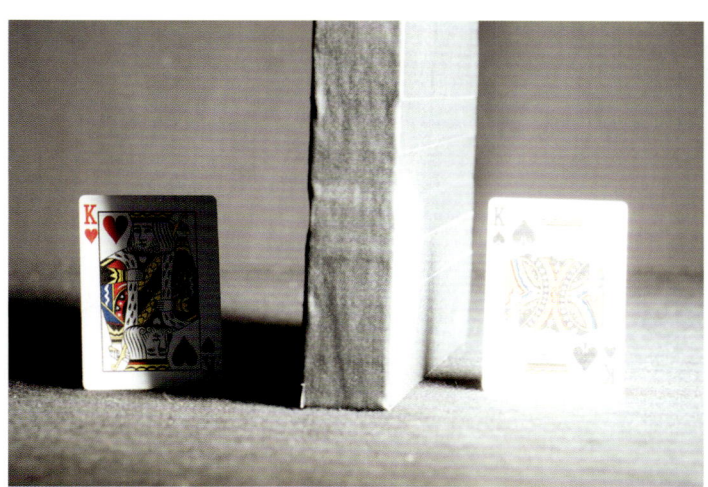

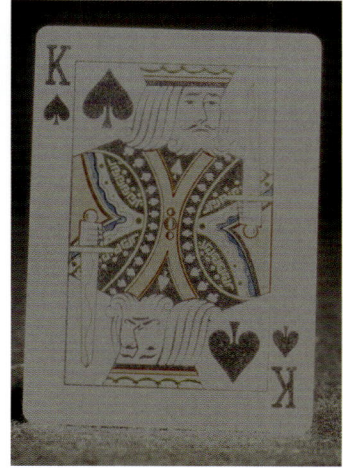

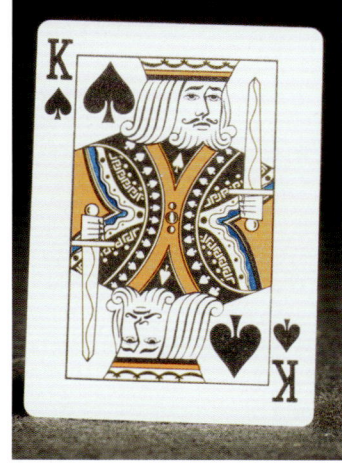

39.4 In this example, we have a correctly exposed card on the left and an overexposed card in the right.

39.5 With a JPEG image, much of the highlight information is thrown away in the compression of the file. Data recovery will only allow a small portion of that information to be recovered.

39.6 The RAW file will allow vastly more information to be pulled from the highlights.

40. SUNNY 16 RULE

IN THE DAYS before digital, before autofocus, before cameras even had light meters, there was a simple rule to help remember what setting would give a proper exposure on a sunny day: the "Sunny 16" rule. This rule states that on a sunny day (middle of the day), with an aperture setting of f/16, you will get a perfect exposure if your shutter speed is set to the same number as your ISO.

So on any sunny day, just set an aperture of f/16. If you are shooting ISO 100, set a shutter speed of 1/125s. Back in the days when this was invented, most cameras didn't have 1/3 stops, so the closest shutter speed at the time was 1/125s. (You could also get good results with f/16, ISO 800, and a shutter speed 1/1000s.)

This rule can be handy whenever you are shooting in sunny conditions and you'd like to double-check what the best exposure settings should be. As we've discussed, the light meter can be fooled in a variety of situations, and it's handy to have a standard that can be relied upon in this common shooting situation. This standard does have a few exceptions: it doesn't work with early morning and late evening sunlight, and it won't work if the sun is being filtered by clouds, smoke, or some other cover. This rule is just for direct middle-of-the-day sunlight. It also doesn't work if there is a significant amount of reflected light, as there might be on a snow-covered mountain, on open water, or in a bright desert environment.

It should be very easy to remember f/16, ISO 100, and a shutter speed of 1/125s. If you need a faster shutter speed of 1/250s, you bump your ISO up to 200. If you need a shutter speed of 1/500s, set the ISO to 400. The ISO and shutter speed numbers don't need to be exactly the same—pretty close will do in this situation. Bumping up the shutter speed and ISO is easy, but when you need a fast shutter speed, you're not likely to need an aperture of f/16, so you may want to look at trading stops of light in a different way. If we take f/16 and open up by three stops, we get f/5.6. If we take 1/125s and go three stops faster, we get 1/1000s. Our sunny 16 (f/16, ISO 100, SS 125) provides the same amount of light as f/5.6 and 1/1000s (f/5.6, ISO 100, SS 1000). This is a good setting to remember because pretty much all lenses have a maximum aperture of at least f/5.6, and 1/1000s should be fast enough to stop most fast-moving subjects.

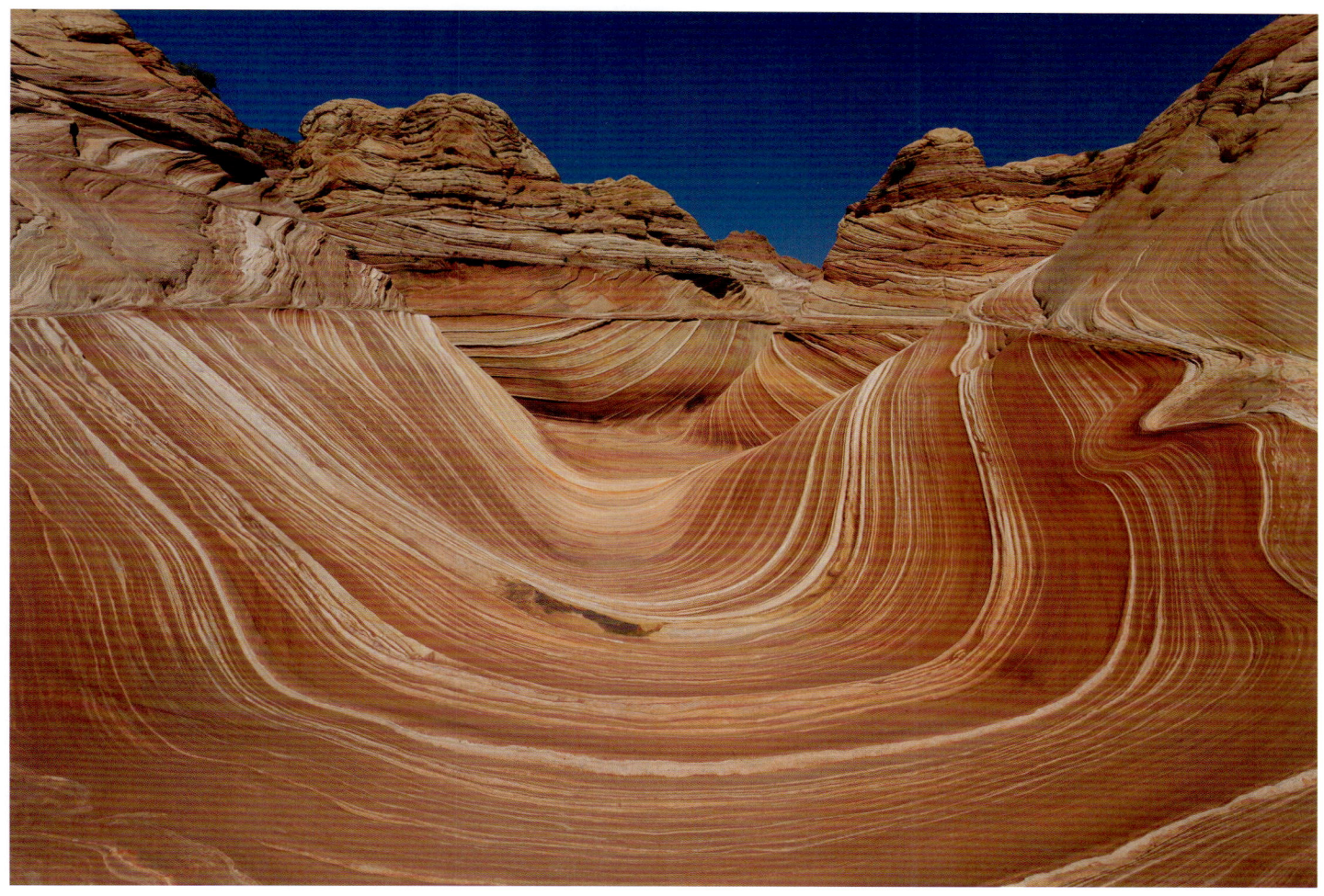

40.1 The Sunny 16 rule is a highly effective rule for achieving a proper exposure on a sunny day.
`1/60 sec.; f/16; ISO 100; Canon 5D Mark II; EF 17-40mm f/4L USM @17mm`

Share Your Best Shots Using the Sunny 16 Rule!

Once you've captured a great shot using the Sunny 16 rule, share it with the *Enthusiast's Guide* Community! Follow @EnthusiastsGuides and post your image to Instagram using the hashtag #sunny16. You can also search that hashtag to see and be inspired by other photographers' shots.

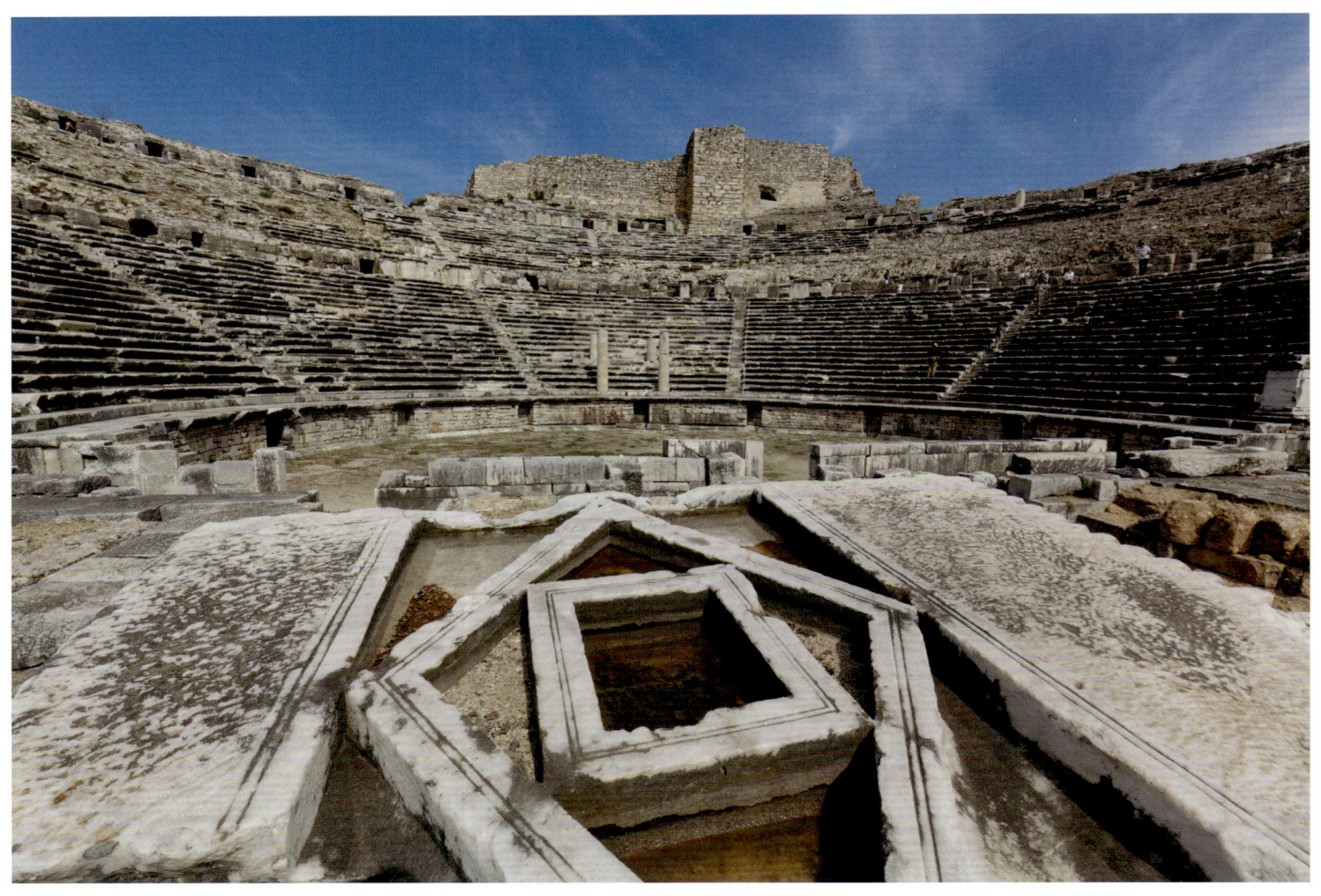

40.2 The Sunny 16 rule states that on a sunny day you should set an aperture of f/16 and a shutter speed the same as your ISO.
1/125 sec.; f/16; ISO 100; Canon 5D Mark III; EF 11-24mm f/4L USM @16mm

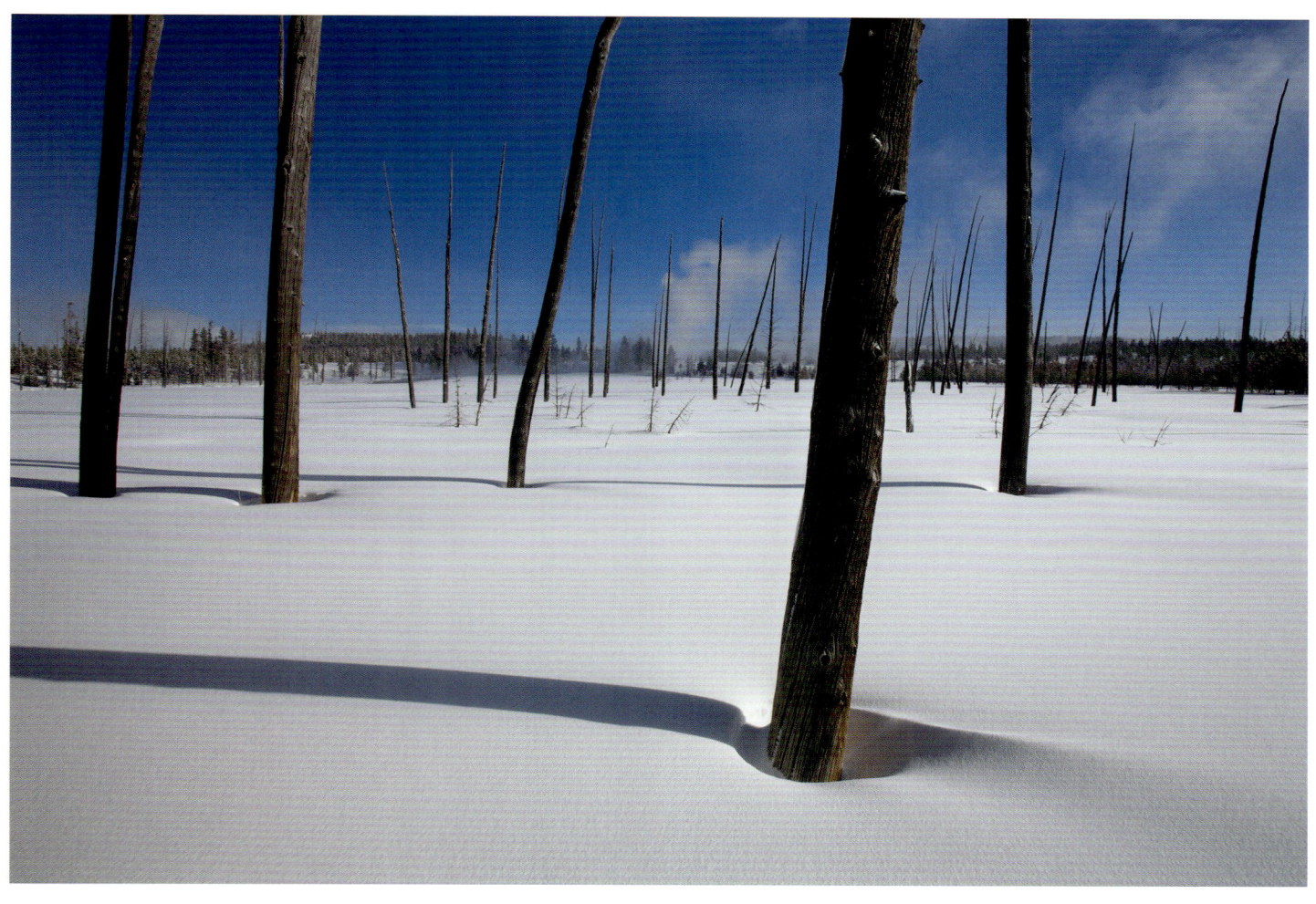

40.3 The Sunny 16 rule in action.
1/60 sec.; f/16; ISO 100; Canon 5D Mark III; EF 17-40mm f/4L USM @17mm

41. WORKING WITH A TRIPOD

TRIPODS HAVE BEEN called the photographer's most important accessory. The tripod, or any other support device, has two main purposes: keep the camera still to allow sharp images to be captured, and hold the camera in a position that would be inconvenient or impossible by hand. Modern image stabilization devices in cameras and lenses have cut down on the need for tripods in marginal lighting situations, but tripods are still useful.

The photographic world can be split into two scenarios: tripod situations and handheld situations. Many photographers resist the idea of becoming a "tripod photographer."

They see tripods as burdensome equipment that will slow them down. Tripods should be seen as a tool, simply a device that helps solve a particular type of photographic problem.

Tripods are a key ingredient for obtaining sharp images of stationary subjects. Capturing that perfect landscape with infinite depth of field often requires an aperture of f/16 or smaller, and likely a matching long shutter speed to let in the required light (1/4s to 2"). You could set a higher ISO, but that will lower the quality of the image. You could compromise on the aperture, but then you'd lose your depth of field. Using a tripod allows you to use the best exposures settings in all cases.

Tripods are also great when handholding isn't a viable option. Beyond the traditional three-legged stands, we can also include all the other mounts that hold cameras to walls, railings, cars, windows, trees, and even photographers themselves. No matter the device, the idea is to capture a unique point of view that helps to tell a story.

Tripods are also quite useful when your equipment is heavy or you'll be using it over a long period of time. Wildlife and bird photographers waiting for hours with long, heavy lenses must be ready to shoot at a moment's notice. A sturdy tripod enables the equipment to be in the ready position for long periods of time.

The most common use of a tripod is for taking a sharp image of a stationary subject. If you have a bit of time and space to set one up, the tripod opens up photographic possibilities. Extra equipment always slows down the photographic process, which can be good in some cases. Chances are you'll be more careful about your composition and exposures, resulting in fewer test shots and mistakes. An out-of-focus image can't be fixed in post-production, so take the time to guarantee a sharp image.

Tripods aren't right for many types of photography. Anytime the photographer needs to be highly mobile or they are photographing in crowds, the tripod invites more problems than it solves. Photojournalists and sports or event photographers don't always have the time or space to work with a tripod. In those dynamic situations, the fast shutter speeds that are needed to stop subject motion will also stop the motion of the handheld camera. A tripod has little benefit, even if it could be used. It might also arouse unwanted attention, even in situations where they are allowed.

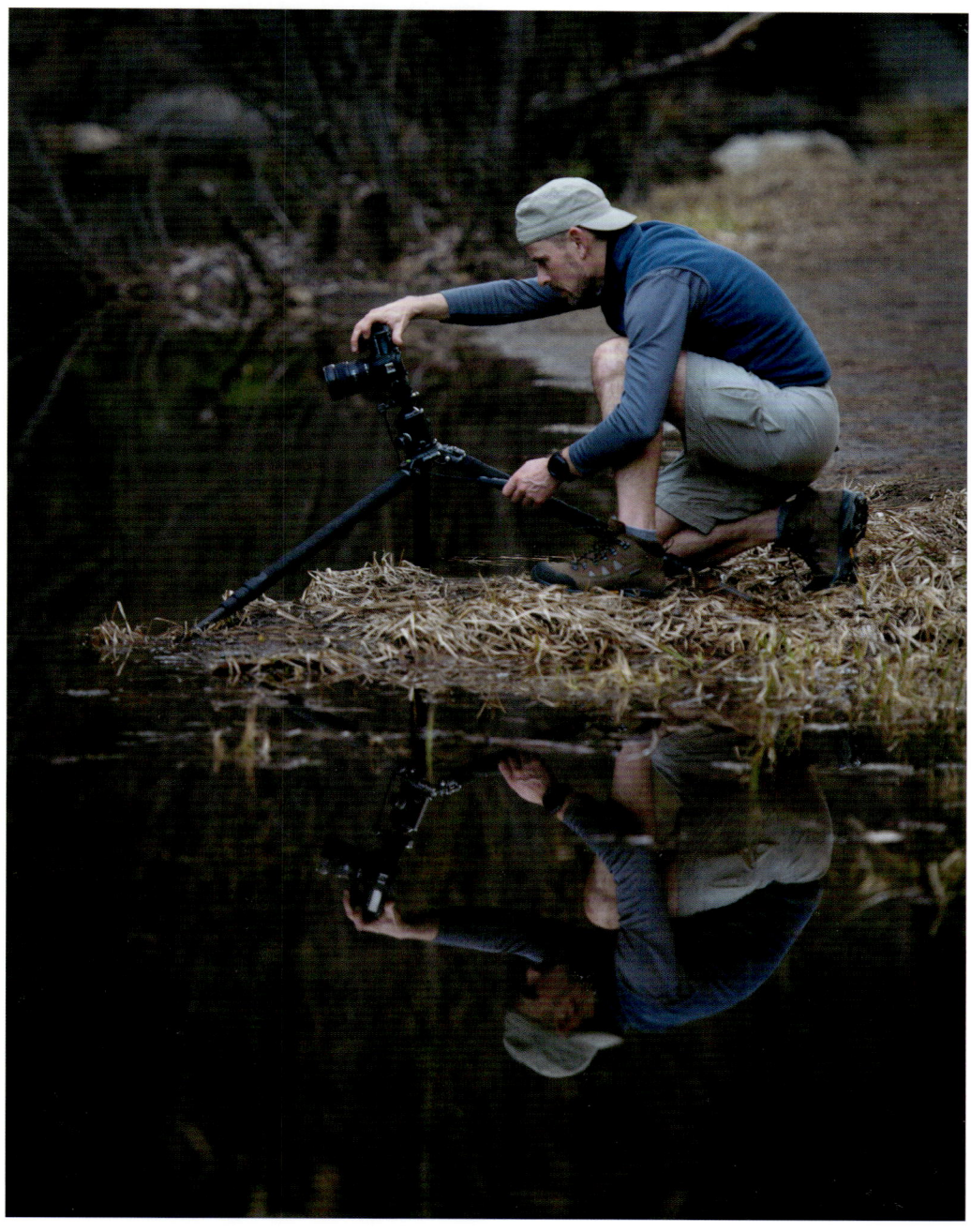

41.1 The tripod will allow you to work with your camera in a comfortable, secure, and highly stable position. Photo credit Jared Rogers.

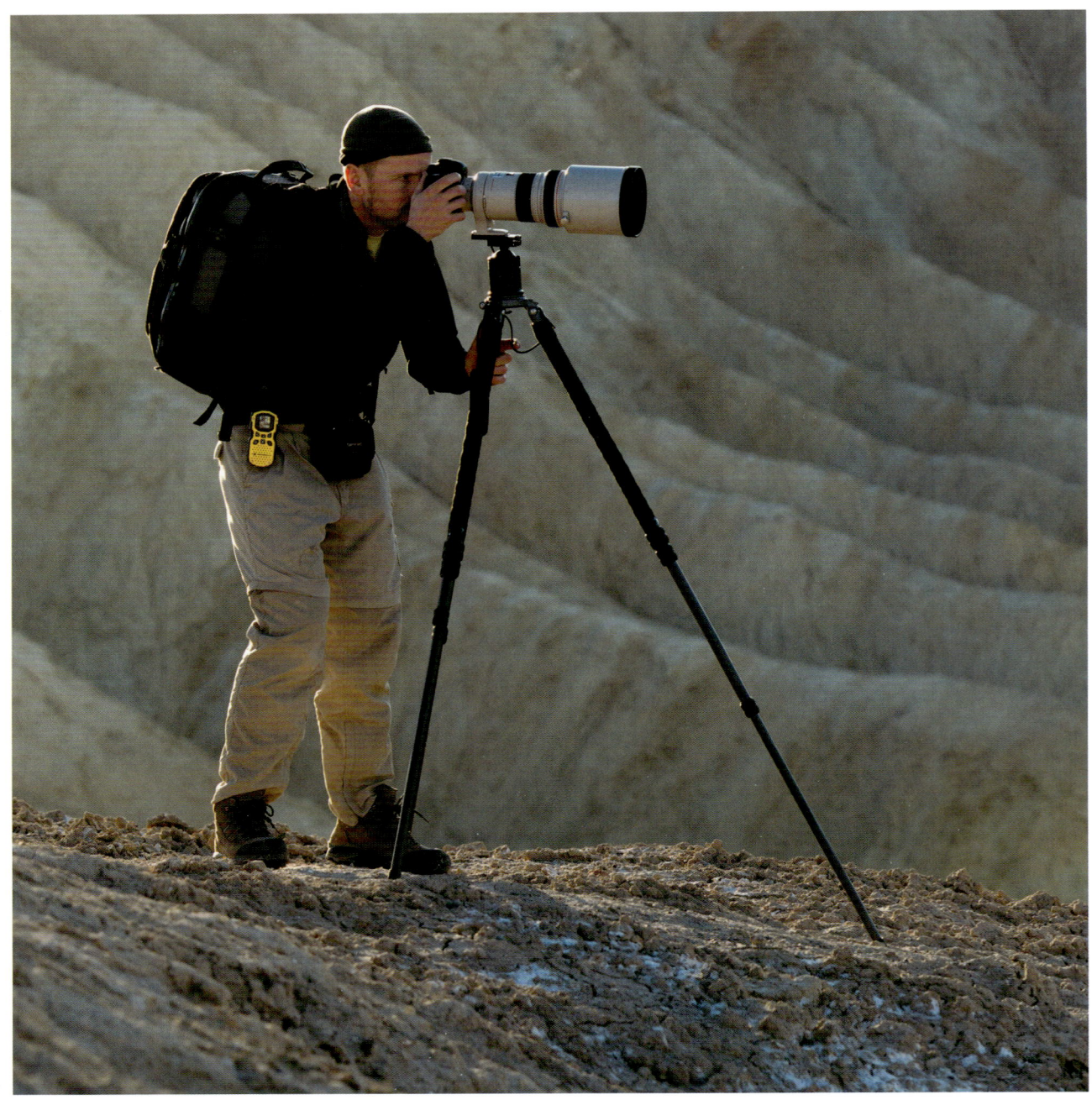

41.2 The tripod is also extremely helpful as a support system to keep you in a shooting position for a longer period of time. Photo credit Jared Rogers.

42. IMAGING SOFTWARE

THERE ARE MANY image-processing programs available, and they are changing in features and operation all the time. Let's look at three different types of programs.

Supplied software from the camera manufacturer that accompanies the camera is one place to start. The good news is that it's free with the purchase of the camera, and is designed to work with the proprietary RAW format from all cameras of that brand. These software programs are known for getting the most out of a RAW file when it comes to detail, sharpness, and color. The downside is that the camera manufacturers aren't necessarily the best software designers, and the resulting programs can be a bit clunky and awkward to use. Another issue is that if you switch to a different brand of camera, you won't be able to use software from one company to read the RAW image from another company. Furthermore, the number of users, developers, and updates are likely to be few when compared to the more popular commercial options.

Next are the free programs supplied with the packaged software on a computer. These are convenient because they are already loaded and ready to go. They work with JPEG images from all manufacturers and will generally be able to work with RAW images as well. They are fine for very casual photographers, but they lack the organization and development tools that a serious photographer will find useful. It's perfectly fine to start with these types of programs, but know that they have limitations and that it's well worth the money to invest in a solid, easy-to-use system that will save time in the long run.

The last category is the commercially available image-processing programs like Adobe Photoshop and Lightroom. These two programs are the choice of the majority of serious photographers for many reasons. These dedicated programs are designed for photographers that shoot lots of photos and who like to do a wide variety of adjustments on them. These programs have lots of tools for solving all types of problems, and they work with all major file types from all major camera manufacturers. In some cases there may be a short lag time after a new camera comes out before these programs will have a software update that allows them to read the new type of RAW file.

You'll find books, videos, and classes for these popular programs wherever you like to learn about photography. Since this is the most popular route, there's lots of help along the way. These moderately priced programs are not free like the first two mentioned, but they are usually well worth their cost considering the problems they solve.

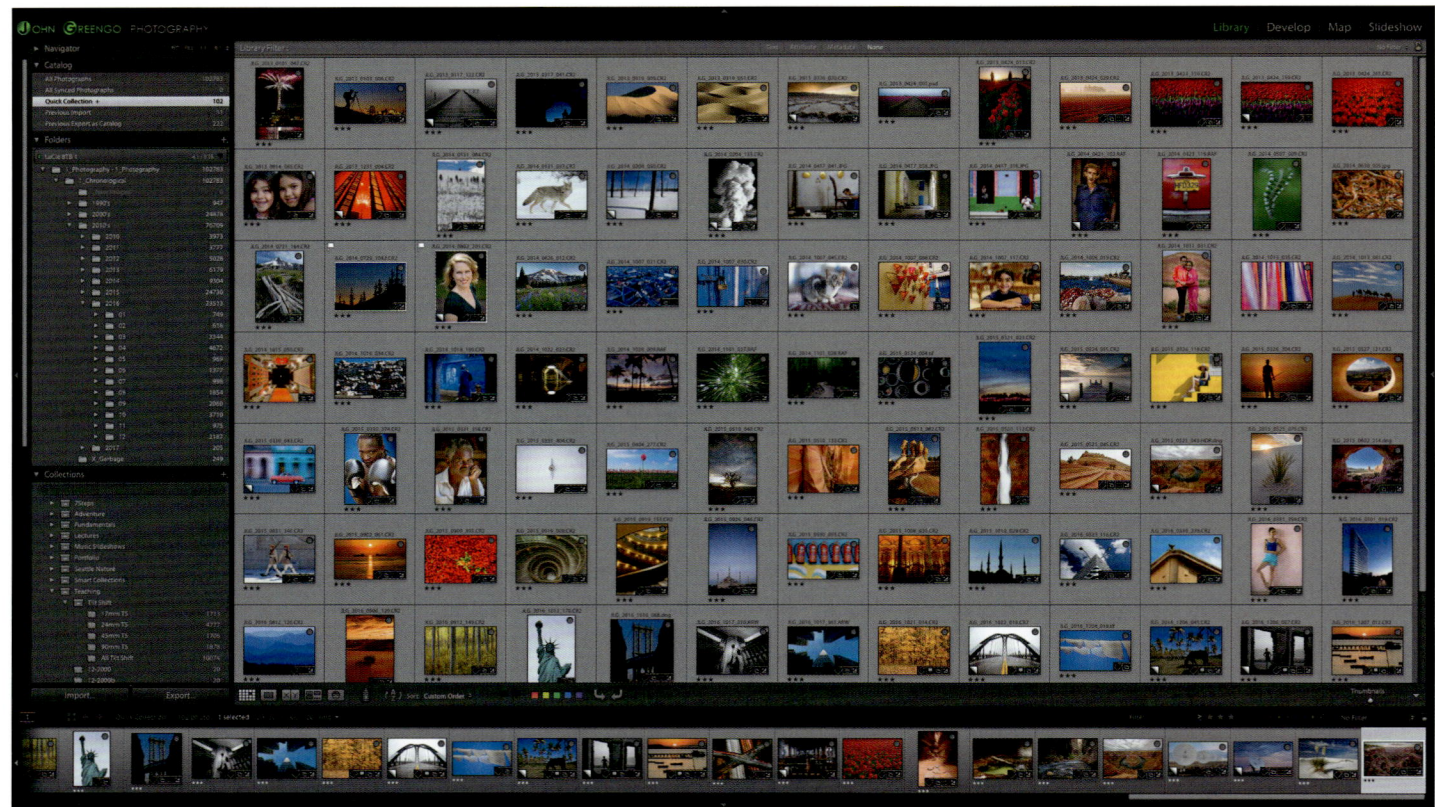

42.1 Adobe Lightroom is a popular photo-editing software because of its organizational and viewing availability, and due to the fact that it works with files from all camera brands. Viewing, comparing, and organizing files are easily accomplished in good-quality post-production software.

43. POST-PRODUCTION

CAPTURING THE PERFECT image is only half the equation. Developing the photograph so it looks and says what you think it should is the next critical step. It's considered good technique to try and capture everything you want in the final image in-camera. No matter how much you do in the field or in the studio, the captured image will still need a bit of help in the world of post-production.

The range of post-production work a photo requires can range from a few seconds spent adjusting minor issues to hours or days of painstaking detail work. How much work needs to be done is determined by whatever the demands of that image are, and the vision of the creator.

JPEG images are processed in-camera, and turn out looking more complete. For full control over post-production of your images, shoot in RAW. RAW images provide the depth of information necessary to make serious and highly detailed adjustments. The RAW file straight out of the camera is flat and lifeless by design. By starting out at a neutral position, a RAW image can easily be processed into a wide variety of styles.

RAW images lack contrast. The contrast slider, while tempting, may not be the best option for adding contrast to the image. It's a bit of a blunt instrument in that it adjusts both the highlights and the shadows the same amount, at the same time. If you have the option to target just one

part of the brightness levels (black, shadows, highlights, or whites), you're better off setting them individually.

Raising the brightness of areas of shadow helps images with people in them because viewers can see faces more clearly. However, most images look better if the darkest pixel is pure black. We often judge the contrast and sharpness of an image based on the darkest visible pixel. Many, but not all, images will benefit by making the darkest pixels a bit darker.

The saturation of a RAW image is also a bit on the lackluster side. Landscape images can be brought to life by increasing saturation (vibrance), but be careful: too much of anything can be a bad thing. If an image is over-processed (too many adjustments), it will no longer look like it was captured on planet Earth, and the realism of photography is lost. You should also be careful when adding saturation to images of people; skin tones don't react well to additional color.

Part of the flatness of RAW images is that they haven't been sharpened yet. Adding a judicious amount of sharpening will help almost every image. Sharpening is really just adding greater contrast to all the edges in the photo. Once again, over-processed images are not well received; in many cases it's better to undercook than overcook.

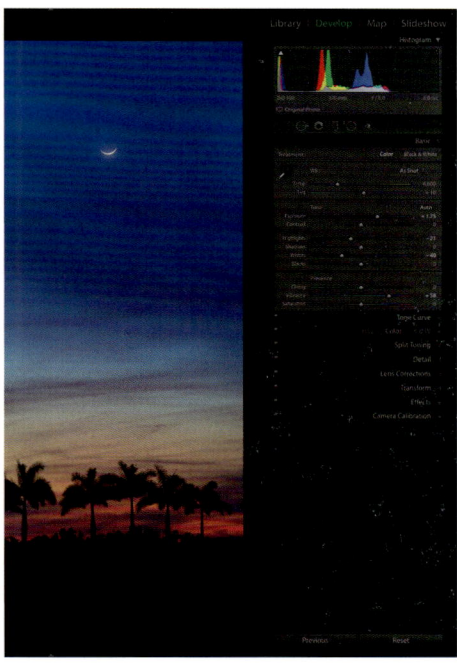

43.1 Post-production of images is a fact of life for the RAW shooter. Small adjustments are normal, but greater action must be taken in some cases.

9

TRICKY LIGHTING SITUATIONS

CHAPTER 9

Light, or the lack of it, can cause some challenging photographic situations. From low-light scenes to high-contrast scenes, not all light is equal. Knowledge of how light works, as well as how best to capture that light with your camera, will offer you numerous solutions to a variety of tricky lighting situations. These types of scenes might be seen as photographic nightmares, but they also provide an opportunity for creating something unique. Great images are a dime a dozen in easy situations, but capturing a great image in a challenging situation will result in an image that truly stands out.

44. LOW LIGHT

WHAT DO YOU do when there isn't enough light to get a decent photograph? Dealing with low-light situations is a common problem for photographers, but there are techniques and equipment that can help you out.

Technique

Start by assessing the scene. Determine potential problems that might arise during the shoot (and their accompanying solution). Perhaps the football team will be playing a midday game next week that will be much easier to shoot than the game tonight. Maybe the band turns on more lights during a particular song. Maybe if you move your portrait subject closer to the window there will be better (and more) light to work with. You could bring more lights into the living room and hide them behind the couch to help illuminate your subject. You want to make things as easy on yourself as possible, which means getting more light on your subject in any way you

can conceive. Be creative, cunning, and smart.

Once you've exhausted the "easy" solutions, you can adjust your settings. First, look at your shutter speed. What is the slowest possible setting you can get away with? You have to get this right—the whole process is pointless if your image isn't sharp. Figure out the lowest shutter speed that will do the job—for both subject movement and to avoid camera shake. If you are photographing dancers on a stage, it would be nice to go with 1/500s but maybe you can get away with 1/250s or even 1/125s if you are careful about your timing.

If your subjects aren't moving, there really isn't a problem. Using a tripod eliminates the low-light problem. What if you don't have a tripod, or using it just isn't an option? Look for another way to support the camera, such as resting it on a table, shelf, rock, or anything that will support its weight. You may need to aim the camera by putting something underneath it, like

a coat or book. You could also use a table-top tripod or a small camera-mounting device.

Now that you've got your shutter speed set, let's look at the rest of the camera settings. If it's really dark, you'll want to open up the aperture all the way to the maximum. Then see what ISO you will need. Use your light meter and adjust your ISO upward until you get a proper exposure, and take a few test shots. One last creative idea: rather than going for sharp, high-ISO images, you could set a low ISO and use a long shutter speed to make a "creative" interpretation of your subject. This won't work for many subjects, but dancers, runners, and race-cars look pretty interesting with a slow shutter and a panning camera. It may be prudent to go for the sharp images first and when you've got enough of them, play around with the slow shutter speeds.

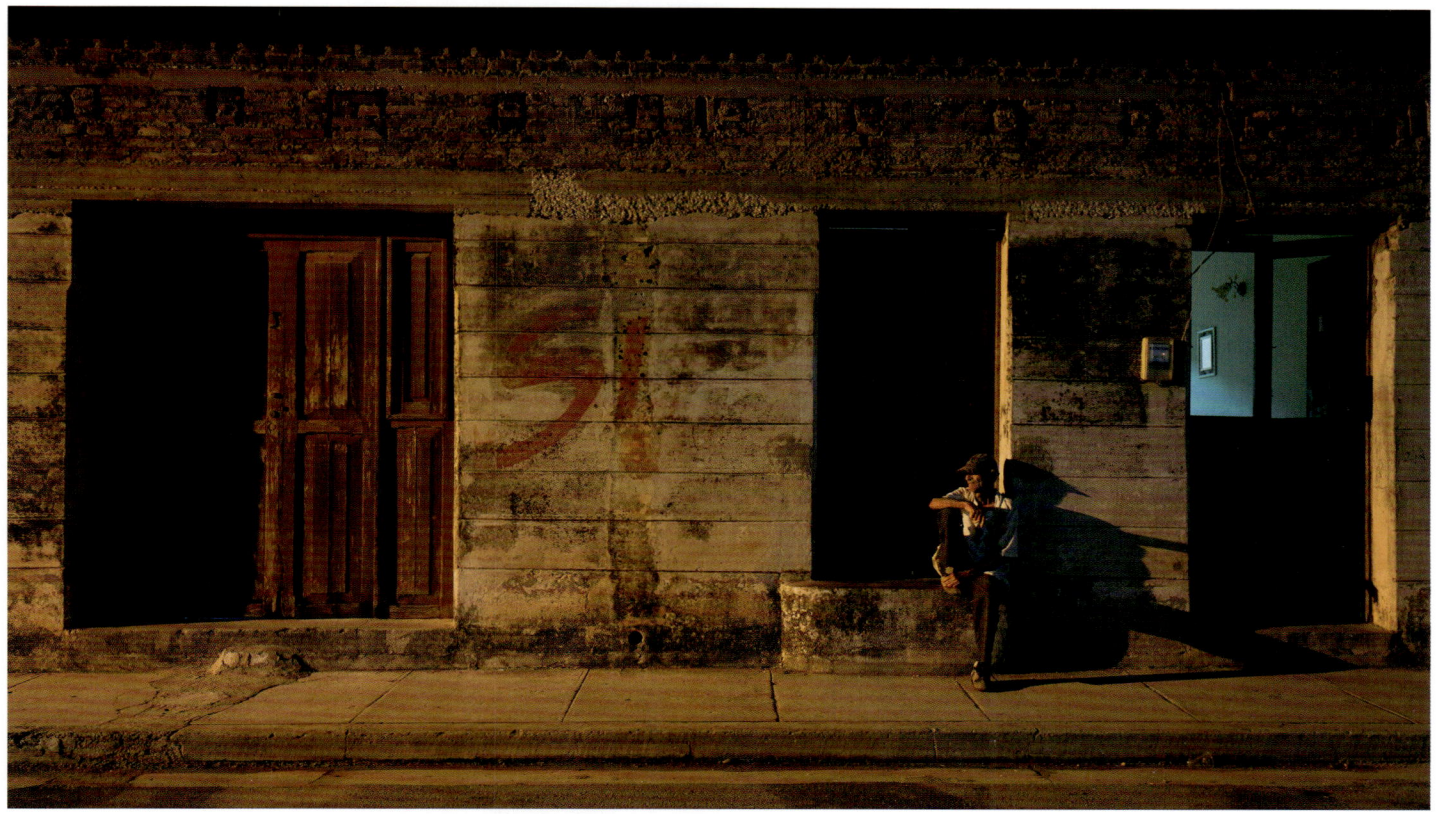

44.1 Low light isn't a reason to put your camera away. Getting good results comes from proper use of the right gear and good technique. A tripod is a good starting point because it will allow photography to occur in dark environments.
1/1.3 sec.; f/5; ISO 100; Canon 5D Mark IV; EF 16-35mm f/4L IS USM @30mm

Share Your Best Low-Light Shots!

Once you've captured a great low-light shot, share it with the *Enthusiast's Guide* Community! Follow @EnthusiastsGuides and post your image to Instagram using the hashtag #lowlight. You can also search that hashtag to see and be inspired by other photographers' shots.

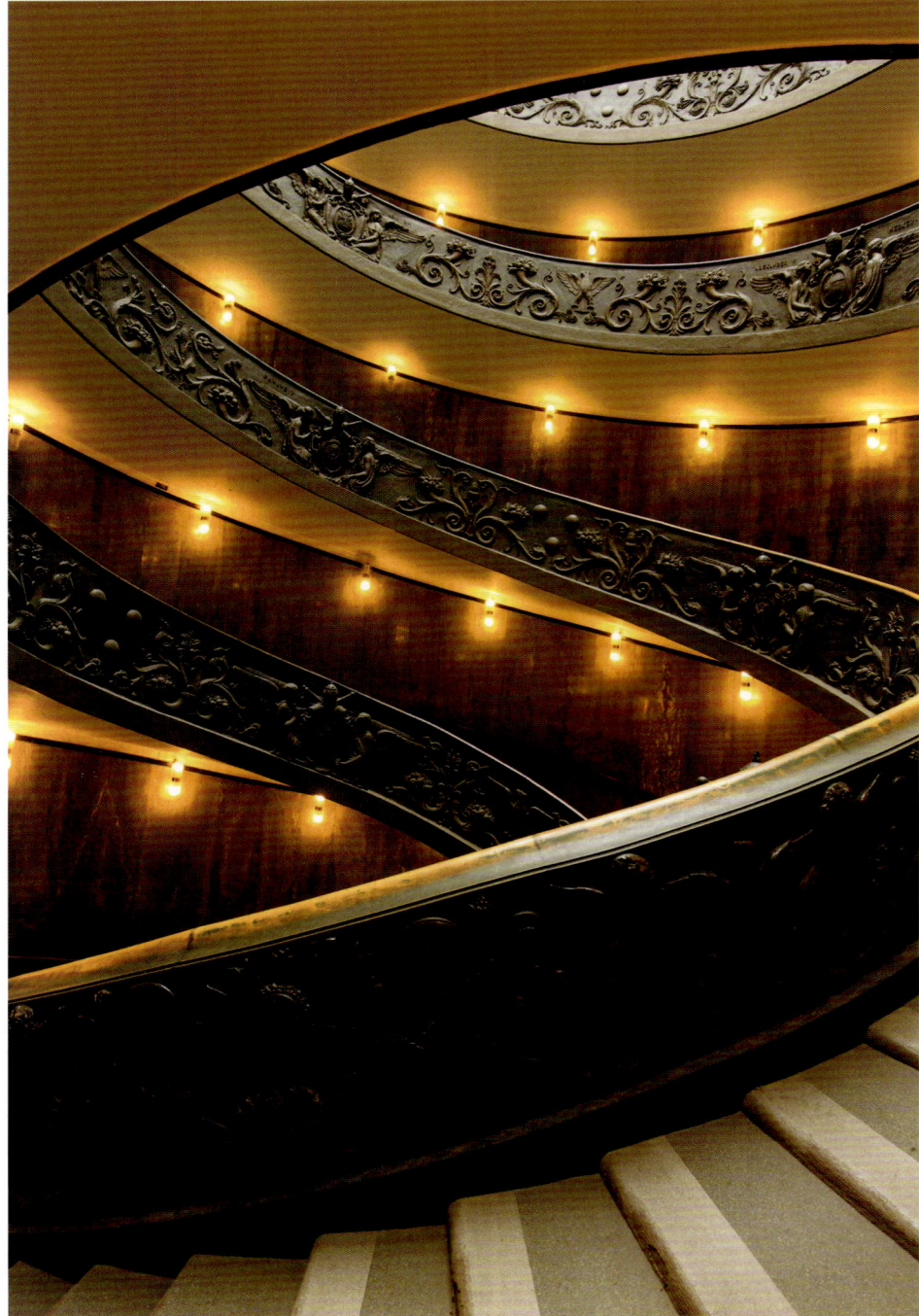

44.2 Proper technique for holding and bracing the camera is of utmost importance when it comes to locations that do not allow the use of tripods. Additional assistance from image stabilization systems will come in handy in these situations as well. **1/20 sec.; f/6.3; ISO 400; Canon 5D Mark III; EF 16-35mm f/4L IS USM @19mm**

Equipment

Now let's turn our attention to solving the problem with equipment. Letting in more light through the lens is one of the best ways of dealing with low light levels. Many consumer cameras come supplied with "slow" 18-55mm f/3.5-5.6 lenses. Trying to use these to shoot a concert, play, or nighttime activity can be very challenging for a number of reasons. The auto-focus system needs a reasonable amount of light to work properly. In dim lighting, your lens will struggle to find focus.

If you still like working with zoom lenses, there are several options for lenses with apertures at a constant f/2.8. Available from the camera manufacturer or from a third-party vendor, these are good long-term options for anyone who expects to regularly shoot under low-light conditions. There are even a few options for zoom lenses with apertures faster than f/2.8, but these are only available for a few systems. All of these faster zoom options will come at a cost of size, weight and money, when compared to the "slow" kit lenses.

The next step is a prime lens with a fast aperture. The maximum aperture that you can get will depend on the focal length of the lens and price you're willing to pay. Lenses near the 50mm focal length will be the most affordable.

As you move away from 50mm, the price gets higher. The least expensive lens in most cases is the 50mm f/1.8—a normal lens for the full-frame user and a short telephoto for the crop-frame user. This is likely the easiest way to get a lens that works well in low light. Depending on your needs, there are many other super-fast and very expensive specialty lenses that can solve problems at different focal lengths.

Cameras for Low Light

Digital cameras have been improving their low-light performance with every new generation. There are three main aspects to look for in a camera with good low-light abilities: a large sensor; a low pixel count; a newer model. The larger the sensor and fewer the pixels, the larger those pixels can be and the better they can absorb light. Full-frame cameras (35mm film frame size) with modest pixel counts are the best performers in high-ISO imaging. High pixel counts grab the headlines as the best cameras, but under low lighting, the camera with the largest pixels will usually do the best. You'll find this information with most camera reviews in their high-ISO test.

Another piece of equipment that might help in a low-light situation is a flash. You'll first need to assess if a flash is appropriate for the situation you want to photograph. There are plenty of situations where a flash can be used without interruption to the subject or others around you. Whether you are using the built-in flash, an on-camera flash, or something fancier, these tools are dedicated to illuminating your subject.

Something to always keep in mind when using flash is subject distance from the camera. Far-off subjects and scenes will be difficult to illuminate with a single on-camera flash. In general terms, you should be within ten feet (three meters) to use a built-in flash, and 30 feet (ten meters) to use an add-on flash. A subject beyond that distance will be very difficult to illuminate. Some flashes have zoom heads that will concentrate the power of the flash into a narrow beam. These can help your flash reach a bit farther. A word of warning: bright flashes in dark environments can be jolting to both subjects and people nearby, so be respectful in the timing and frequency or your flash photography.

As a final note, shooting in the RAW file format will give you the most latitude for lightening your image in post-production software. Some cameras are very tolerant of underexposure and will allow you brighten the shadows along with the entire image without significant image degradation.

45. HIGH CONTRAST

SCENES WITH HIGH contrast can be challenging to correctly expose. It might be a dark forest with bright sunlight streaming through the trees, a bride and groom in a dark church with bright windows in the background, or the interior of a home with windows looking out to a yard bathed in sunlight. In all of these situations, a standard exposure will not be able to show detail in both the shadows and the highlights because they are likely beyond the range that the modern digital sensors can handle.

Most contrast problems are due to the fact that sunlight is so much brighter than the shadows. One way to solve the problem is to shoot only in the sun or shoot only in the shade. This may not always be possible, but it can prove to be a valuable solution if available.

You should assess the situation by determining what you subject is, what any secondary subjects are, where the light is coming from, what's in the shadows, and what's in the highlights. Try to determine if the problems are with the highlights or the shadows. If you have a subject in the shadows and a stray beam of sunlight in the background, then the highlight is the problem. If you're shooting a portrait in the sun and you're getting some unsightly shadows on the face, then the shadows are the problem.

Whether it's the highlights or the shadows, the best way to deal with the problem is to avoid it in the first place. If your lighting problem is with the background, see if you can change your position and your point of view to eliminate it. Maybe shooting the bride and groom from the other side of the church will provide a more evenly illuminated background. Small changes in your shooting position can have a huge impact on the background. The best point of view for any photograph will be a compromise between what is best for the subject and what is best for the image as a whole.

If you can move your subject to a different location, perhaps you could avoid the problem. If it's a portrait you're shooting, perhaps there's an area where the light isn't as contrasty, like the shadow of a building. If you are shooting a car, perhaps take the car to the local park with a large, shaded parking area, or go someplace where the car will be in full sun.

Once you've exhausted your location and point of view options, it's time to look at your timing options. If you are coordinating the shoot, choose the time when the lighting is the best in your location. Rather than photographing a kitchen in the middle of day, wait until dusk when the light outside is about the same brightness level as that on the inside. This is a big key to architectural photography. There is a small window of time, twice a day, when the lighting levels outside are closely matched to the levels inside a building. Anytime you are capturing an inside and outside, make plans to shoot near sunset or sunrise when your lighting levels will be about even.

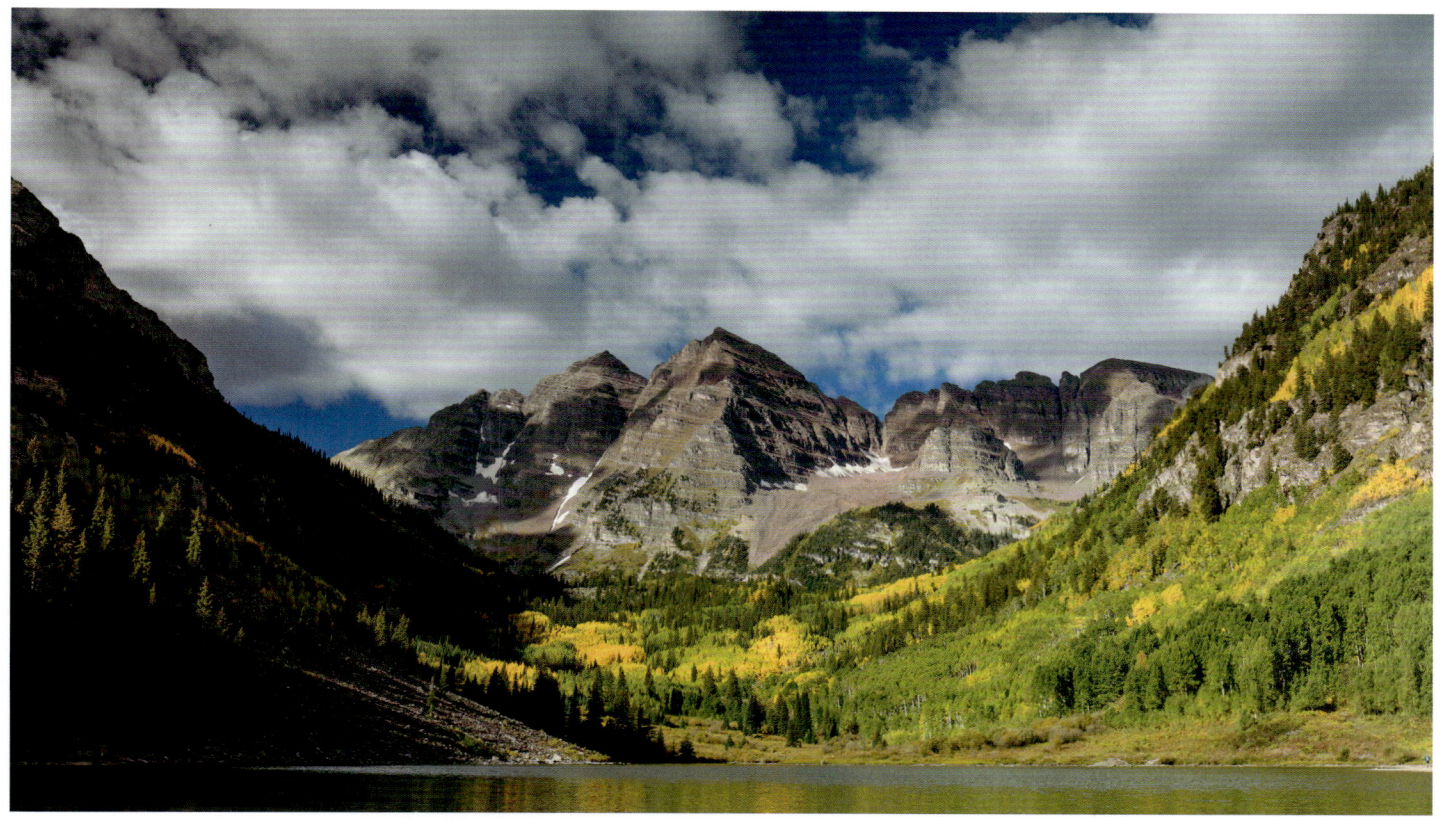

45.1 High-contrast scenes, including those that range from bright sunlight to dark shadows, will be hard to capture with a single exposure.
1/50 sec.; f/11; ISO 100; Canon 5D SR; EF 24-70mm f/4L IS USM @37mm

Share Your Best High-Contrast Shots!

Once you've captured a great high-contrast shot, share it with the *Enthusiast's Guide* Community! Follow @EnthusiastsGuides and post your image to Instagram using the hashtag #highcontrast. You can also search that hashtag to see and be inspired by other photographers' shots.

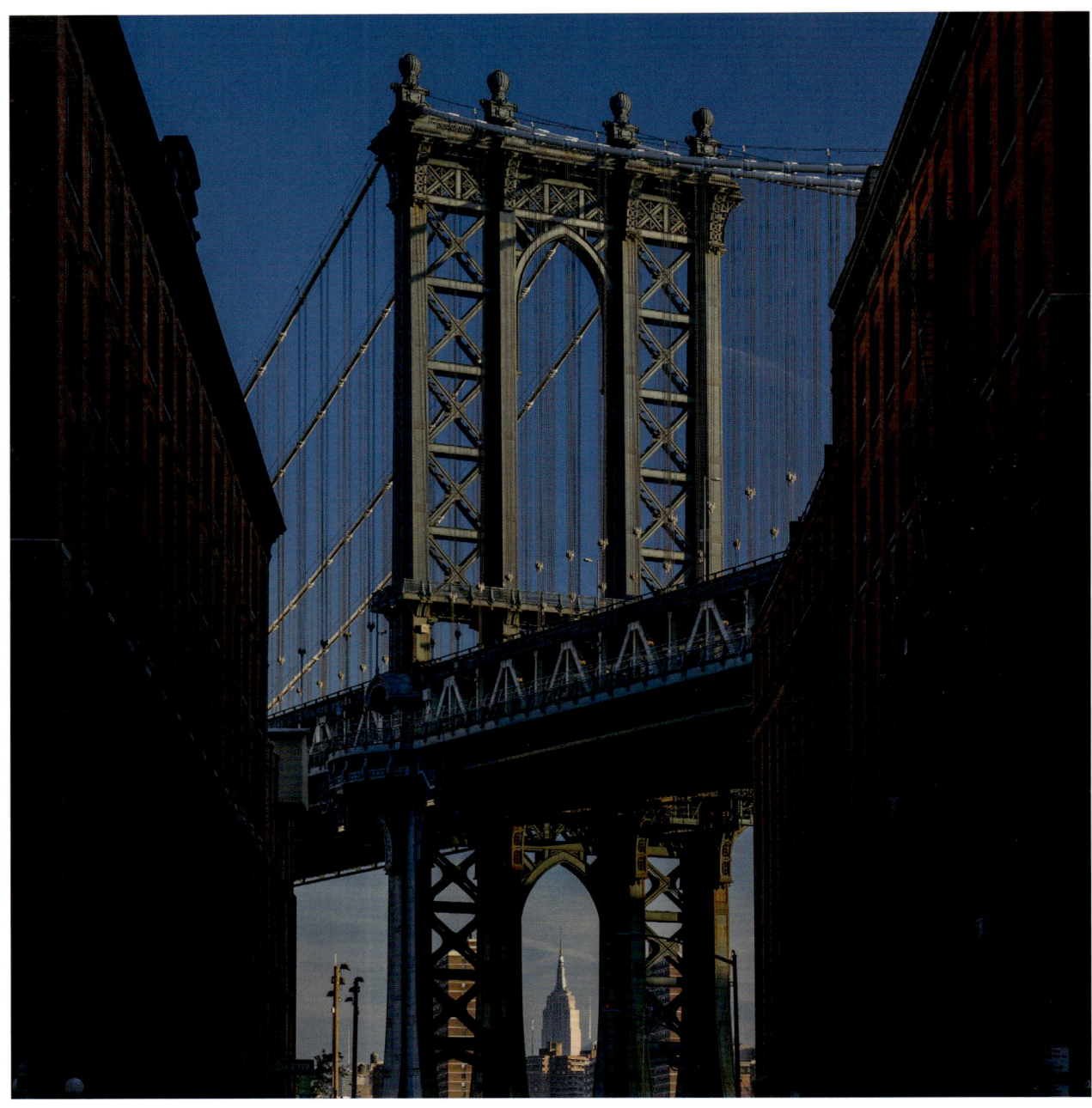

45.2 Shooting RAW images will allow the shadows to be brightened and the highlights to be adjusted in post-processing to maintain detail in both the brightest and darkest areas. **1/15 sec.; f/11; ISO 100; Canon 5D Mark IV; TS-E90mm f/2.8**

Another solution is one that we discussed in chapter 37: HDR. If your subject isn't moving, HDR is a possible solution (though better light is preferable). Shoot a series of bracketed images covering the exposure range necessary to capture details in both the shadows and the highlights. Those images will then need to be blended together, either with an in-camera feature or an image-processing program. The final image should be able to show detail from the darkest shadows to the brightest highlight. Remember, this technique is best accomplished from a tripod with a subject that has no movement.

If your subject is within flash range, fill-flash may be an option. Where this solution will most likely come into use is with portrait photography. If your subject is within 10-15 feet (3-5 meters), a built-in or add-on flash can be very helpful in equalizing the brightness level. If the problem is that part of your subject is in the sun and part is in the shadows, the flash can help fill in the shadows.

To start, you can try turning on the flash and shooting a test shot to see how well your camera's automatic TTL (Through The Lens) system works. If you find that the automatic setting for flash power is too much, you can reduce it with the Flash Exposure Compensation option. The power of the flash is controlled by the TTL system, but this override will allow you to adjust the power of the flash up or down. In most cases the TTL system provides a bit too much light for a portrait. The idea of adding flash is to fill in the shadows and give a highlight to the eyes, but not to go too far. Many photographers find that a Flash Exposure Compensation setting of -1 to -2 is about right. Try shooting without any adjustment first, and then try a -1 setting, followed by a -2 setting. Check your results, and go with what looks best to you.

If you are shooting a series of images and find that the TTL meter and the flash power are inconsistent, you may need to try using the manual flash option. You'll need to have a flash with manual capabilities for this. Try shooting with it at different power settings (full power, 1/2 power, 1/4 power) to see what works. With a manual setting, you'll get consistent exposures with every shot. However, if you change the distance between your flash and your subject, you'll need to adjust your power setting.

A final element that will help in high-contrast scenes is if you are recording in the RAW format. As discussed in chapter 39: Shooting RAW, the RAW file format contains the original uncompressed data from the sensor, which will contain the full range of brightness recorded. With this information and a little work in an image-processing program, you should be able to lighten the shadows and "pull back" the highlights to see the maximum amount of detail.

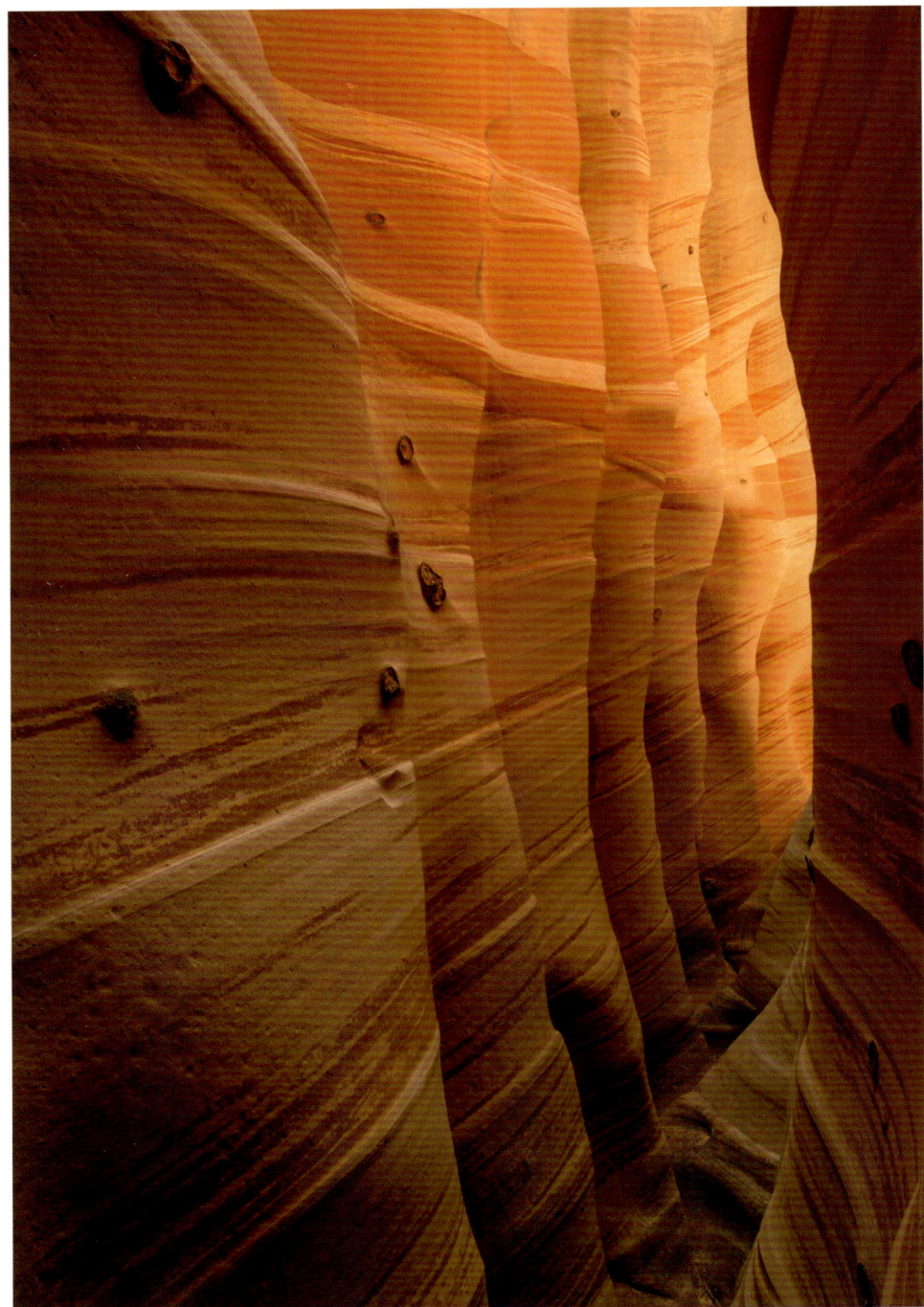

45.3 As the light works its way deeper into this slot canyon, it loses power. Light at the entrance is very bright, but deeper in the canyon, it's quite dark. Post-production software can help to close the gap between these two extremes.
1/4 sec.; f/22; ISO 100; Canon 5D Mark III; EF 24-70mm f/2.8L II USM @31mm

46. BACKLIGHT

WHEN A SUBJECT has bright lights or a bright background behind it, it's backlit. These situations can prove tricky in metering and exposure because excessive light will fool the camera's built-in light meter. The solution to this problem will depend on what your vision is for the final image and whether you are using a manual or automatic exposure mode.

When a subject is backlit, you have a few options for rendering it. First you can expose your subject normally, in which case the background will likely be blown out and there will be few visible details in that portion of the image. On the other hand, you can expose for the background, which will likely render your subject very dark—perhaps a silhouette. Finally, if the conditions allow, you can straddle the highlights and the shadows so that you show detail in both the bright and dark areas. This may be impossible in many backlit situations; it just depends on the range of brightness and the sensor's ability to record it. In every case, shooting with a RAW file type is an advantage because it captures the most amount of information to work from.

Achieving any of these styles of backlit photographs can be achieved with either an automatic or manual exposure mode. If you want to work with any of the auto exposure modes, start by taking a photo without any adjustments to see how it does without modification. Study the result using the histogram information to see if there is enough information represented in both areas of light and shadow. If the photo needs to be brighter or darker, there are three options for modification: the metering modes, the AEL button, and the Exposure Compensation.

Working with the Metering Modes

Check to see what metering mode your camera is in. If it's in the multi-segment style metering mode (Evaluative/matrix), it's likely reading the bright background as a significant light source and is making your image dark as it compensates for the large area of brightness. If you want to base your exposure on a specific subject in front of that light source, you may want to try the spot meter. The size of the spot-metering area will vary with different cameras. With some cameras, there will be a circle at the center of the viewfinder delineating the area; others will have no information. Using the spot-metering area and any of the exposure modes, position the spot meter over your primary subject to establish a meter reading.

The spot meter is a highly centralized reading of the scene that will allow you to read a relatively small subject's brightness while disregarding the surrounding area. It should be noted that the spot meter is calibrated to read light in the same way as the other metering modes: 18% gray, but in a smaller area. This means that you'll need to be aware of the brightness of your subject and you may need to make further adjustments using either the AEL button or by adding flash.

Using the AEL Button

Using any of the auto exposure modes, you reposition the camera so that it's framing the subject and not the backlight, lock that exposure in by pressing the AEL button, and then recompose the image. With this process you can get the exposure you want and the composition that looks best—you simply need to point the camera at an area of average brightness before pressing the AEL button. Keep in mind the object or scene you are basing the exposure on doesn't need to be part of your final image. You can use anything that gives you the reading you want, and then lock that in with the AEL button.

Setting an Exposure Compensation

After shooting an initial test photo, you can lighten or darken subsequent images by dialing in an adjustment with Exposure Compensation. Brightening a backlit subject likely requires an adjustment in the +1 to +2 range. Take a few test shots and check the histogram to achieve correct exposure.

One more bonus solution, for subjects that are reasonably close to the camera, is using the flash. Each of these solutions will have their own pros and cons. Give each of them a try and see what works best for you.

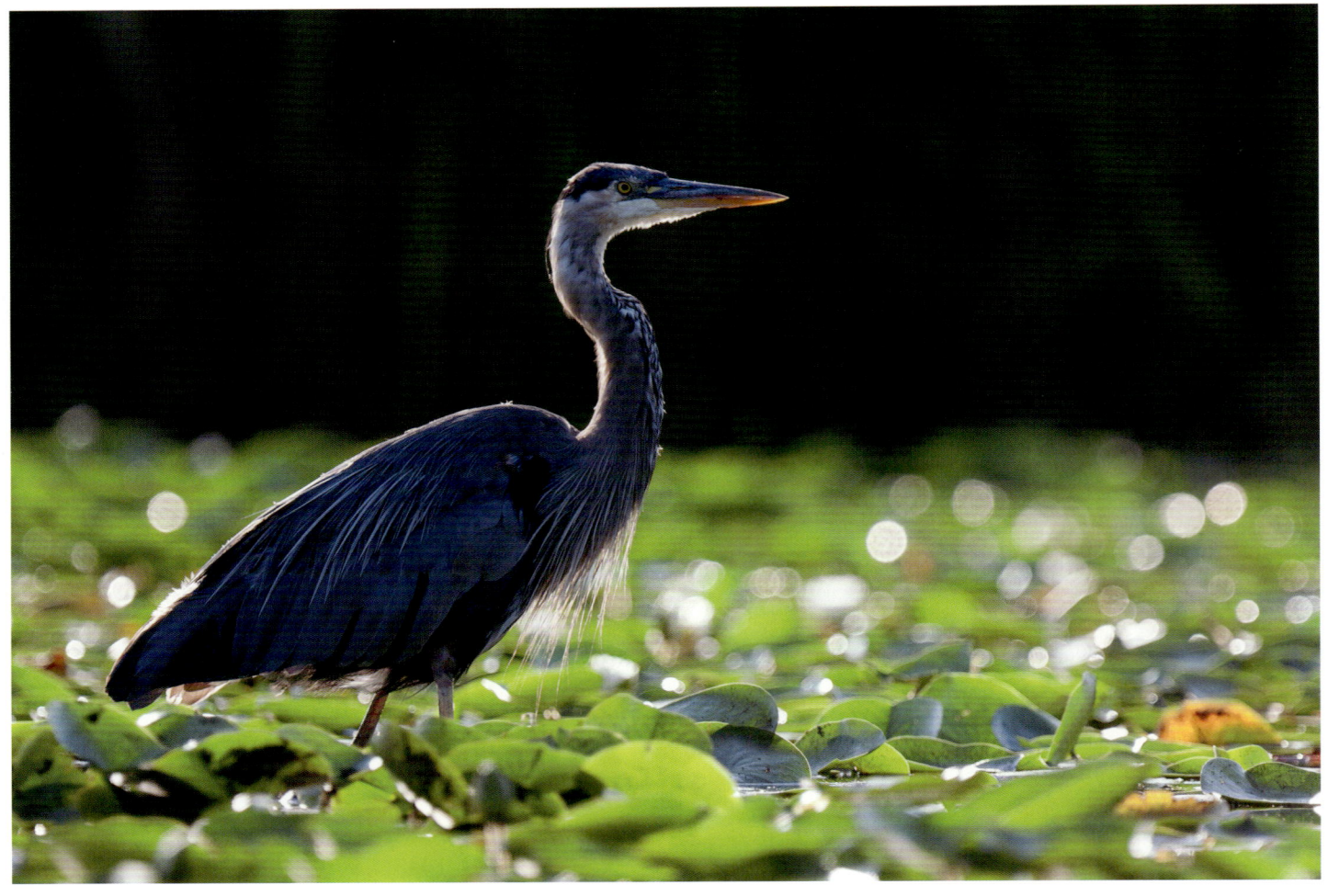

46.1 Backlight situations can be very visually dramatic. If captured correctly, the subject can easily be seen with highlighting that separates it from the background.
1/500 sec.; f/4; ISO 200; Canon 40D; EF 300mm f/2.8L IS USM + 1.4x Extender II @ 420mm

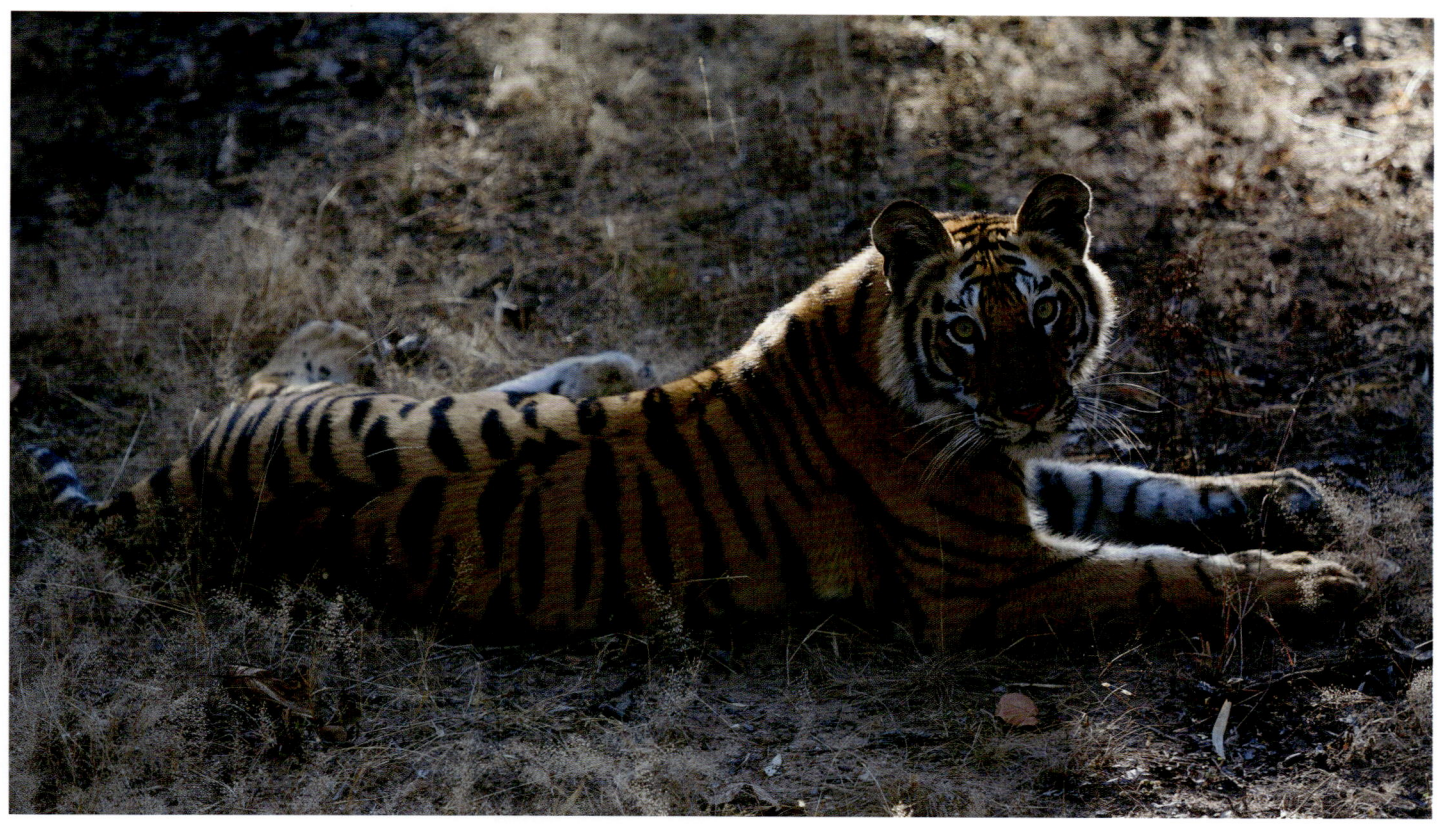

46.2 Whenever possible, shoot your backlit subject against a dark background to make it stand out with highlighted edges.
1/400 sec; f/4; ISO 500; Canon 5D; EF 70-200mm f/2.8L IS USM + 1.4x Extender II @ 230mm

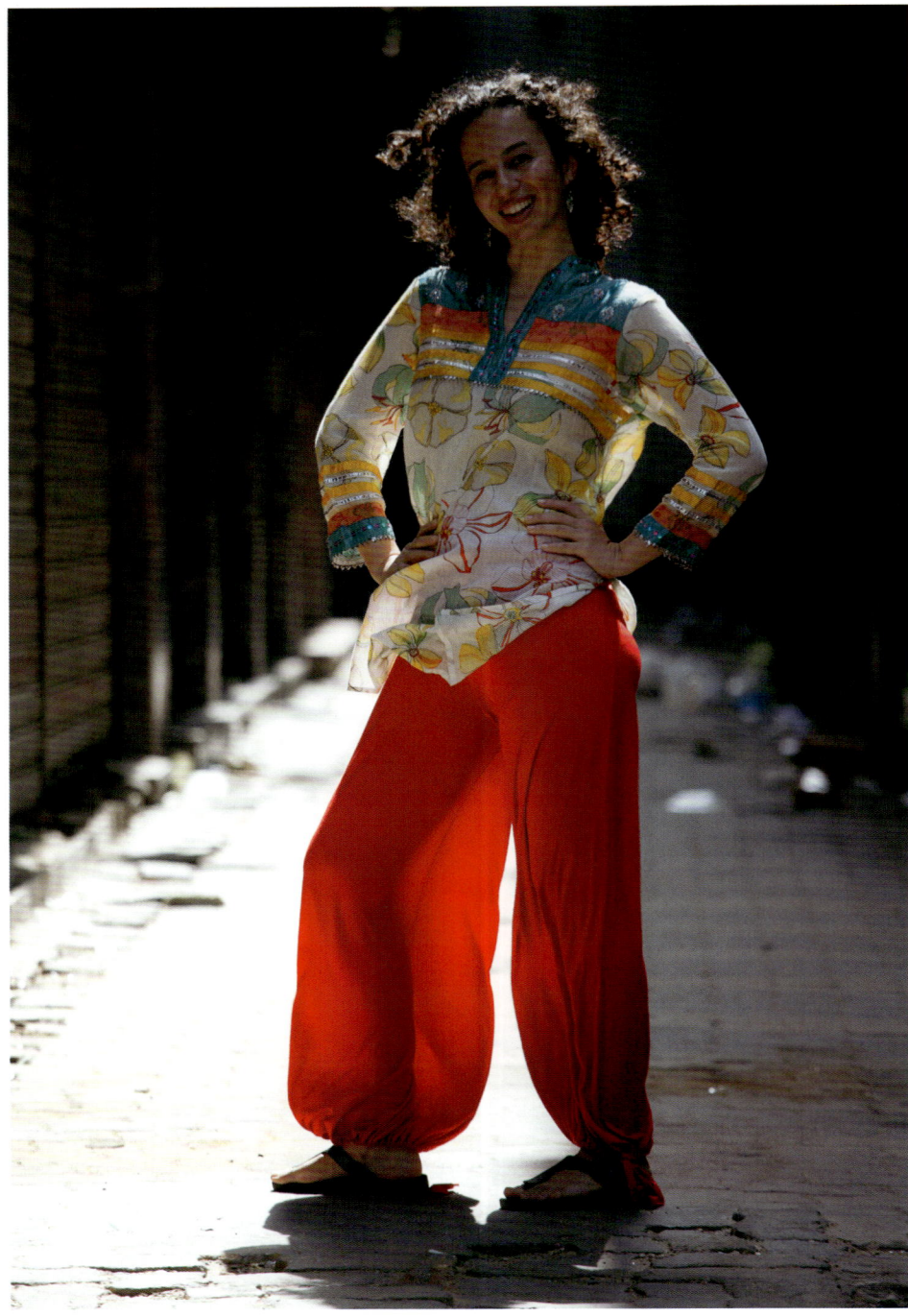

46.3 It's a special situation when your subject is illuminated by backlight, but because of your lens's angle of view, you can't see the light source. Using this alignment to your advantage, find a dark background and your subject will "pop" out from it thanks to rim lighting.
1/250 sec.; f/4; ISO 200; Canon 5D Mark II; EF 70-200mm f/4L IS USM @ 185mm

47. SILHOUETTES

SILHOUETTES ARE ONE of my favorite techniques for illustrating a simple concept or idea. This technique puts a subject in front of a bright or colorful background so that the subject appears in dark shadow. Silhouettes work best with subjects that have a distinctive shape. A common choice is the profile of a face or the human form. The second key is the background. It should be bright and uncluttered. This effect can be created in the studio or in the field if the conditions are right. With a subject that is totally dark and without detail, the image is simple, yet mysterious.

One of the most important elements in achieving a good silhouette is keeping it simple and clean. This means avoiding distracting elements in the silhouettes shape. The beach is a popular place for silhouettes because there's lots of open area in the background. To reduce the size of the background, use a telephoto lens. The narrow angle of view will make it easier to isolate your subject with a clean background.

If you are in one of the auto exposure settings (P-Program, A-Aperture Priority, or S-Shutter Priority), chances are your exposure will be too light. To darken it up, you could use any of the techniques we've already discussed, but exposure compensation will likely be the easiest. Dial in a -1 or -2 exposure compensation and see how that looks. If the background has color, like the sky just after sunset, its colors will deepen and become more saturated when you underexpose the scene.

If you are in manual mode, underexpose the scene by one to two stops. You can do this by looking at your exposure indicator and adjusting your camera settings so that your exposure indicator is at -1 or -2 rather than the typical setting at 0. Silhouettes can vary quite a bit in their style and look, which means the exposure can as well. A manual exposure mode will give you the most control because you can adjust your settings to make the image brighter or darker according to what you want the photo to look like.

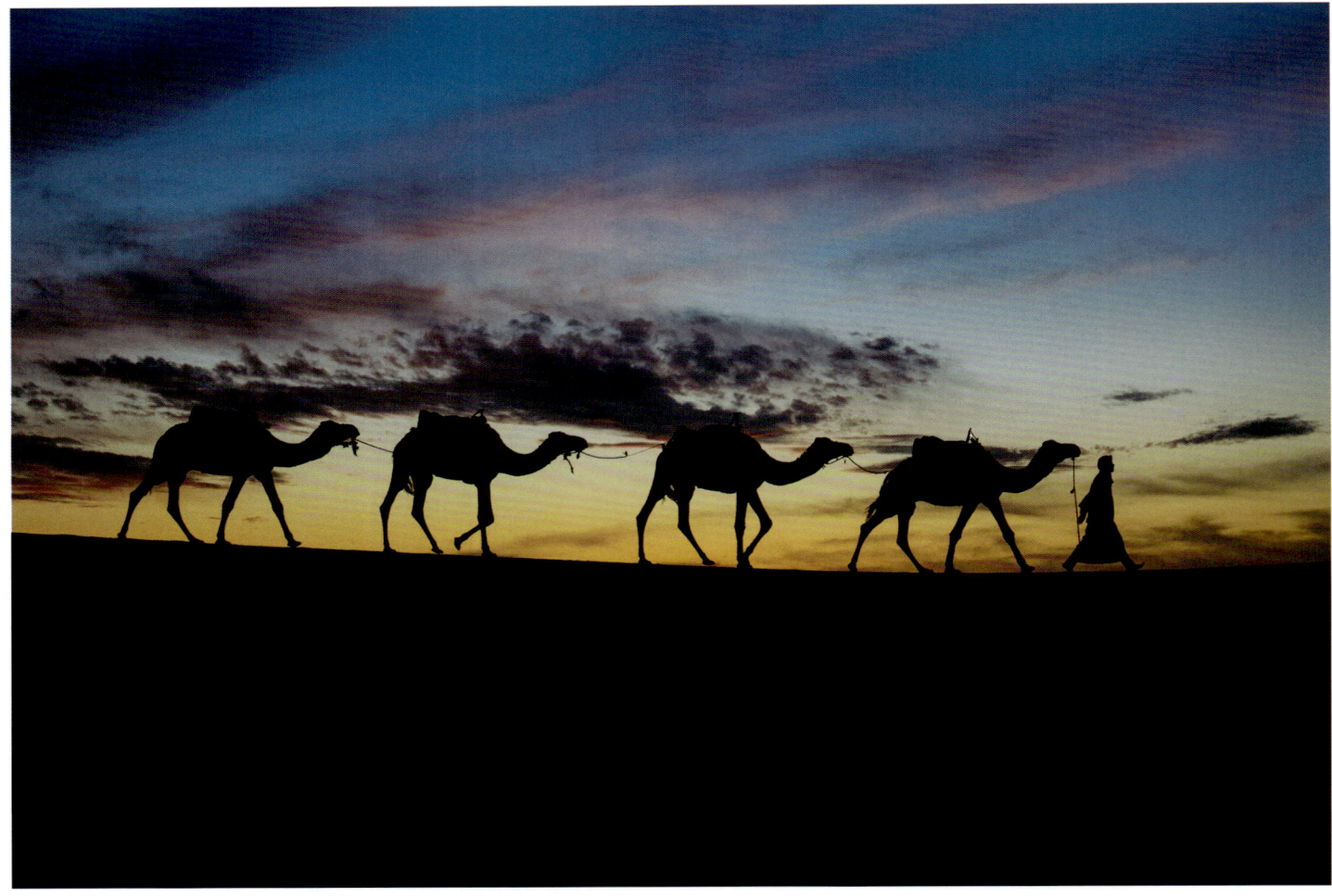

47.1 Silhouettes are special in their simplicity and mystery.
1/400 sec.; f/4; ISO 400; Canon 5D Mark III; EF 70-200mm f/4L IS USM @ 70mm

Share Your Best Silhouette Shots!

Once you've captured a great silhouette shot, share it with the *Enthusiast's Guide* Community! Follow @EnthusiastsGuides and post your image to Instagram using the hashtag #silhouette. You can also search that hashtag to see and be inspired by other photographers' shots.

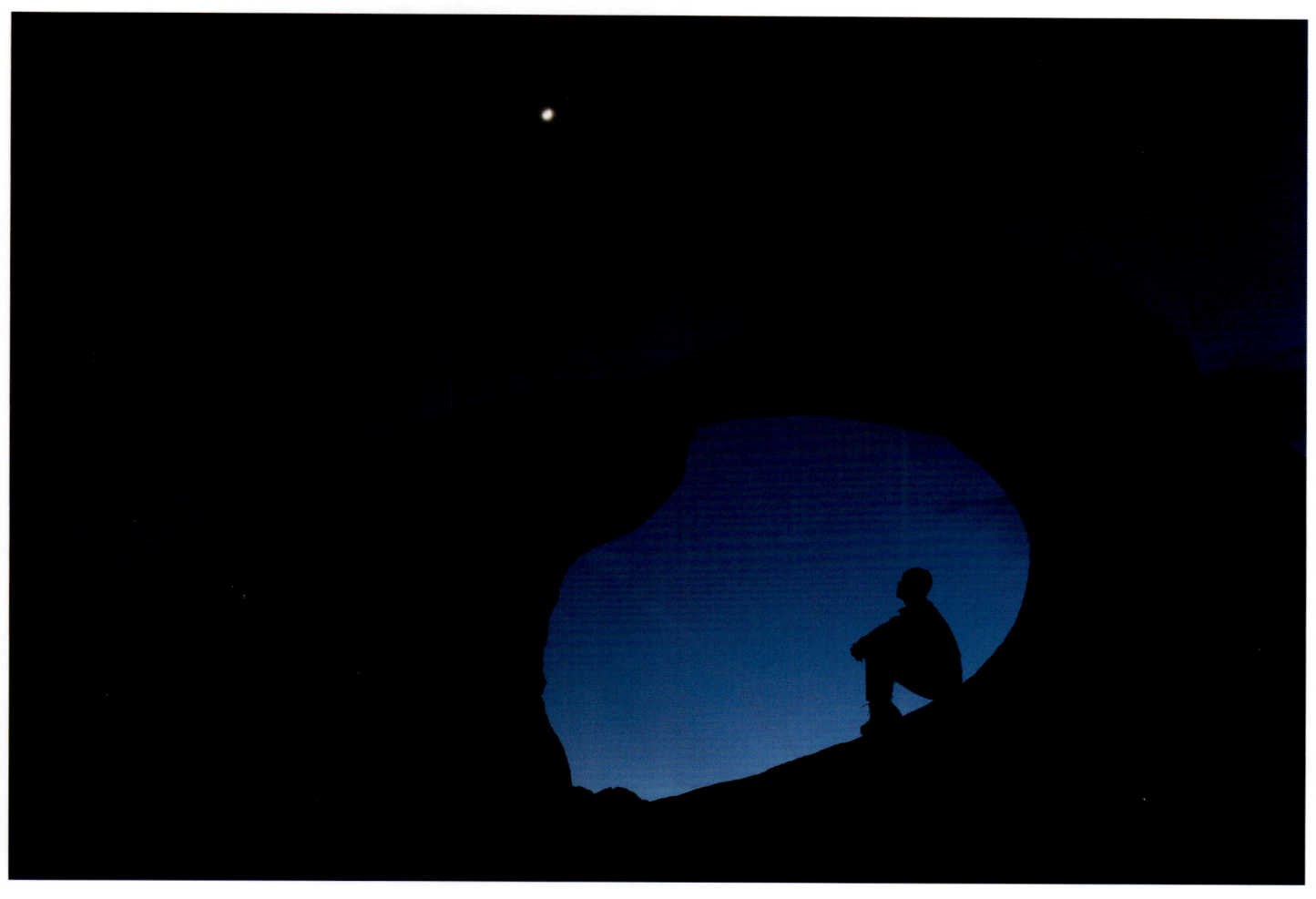

47.2 Silhouettes.
5"; f/16; ISO 50; Canon 5D Mark III; EF 17-40mm f/4L USM @ 17mm

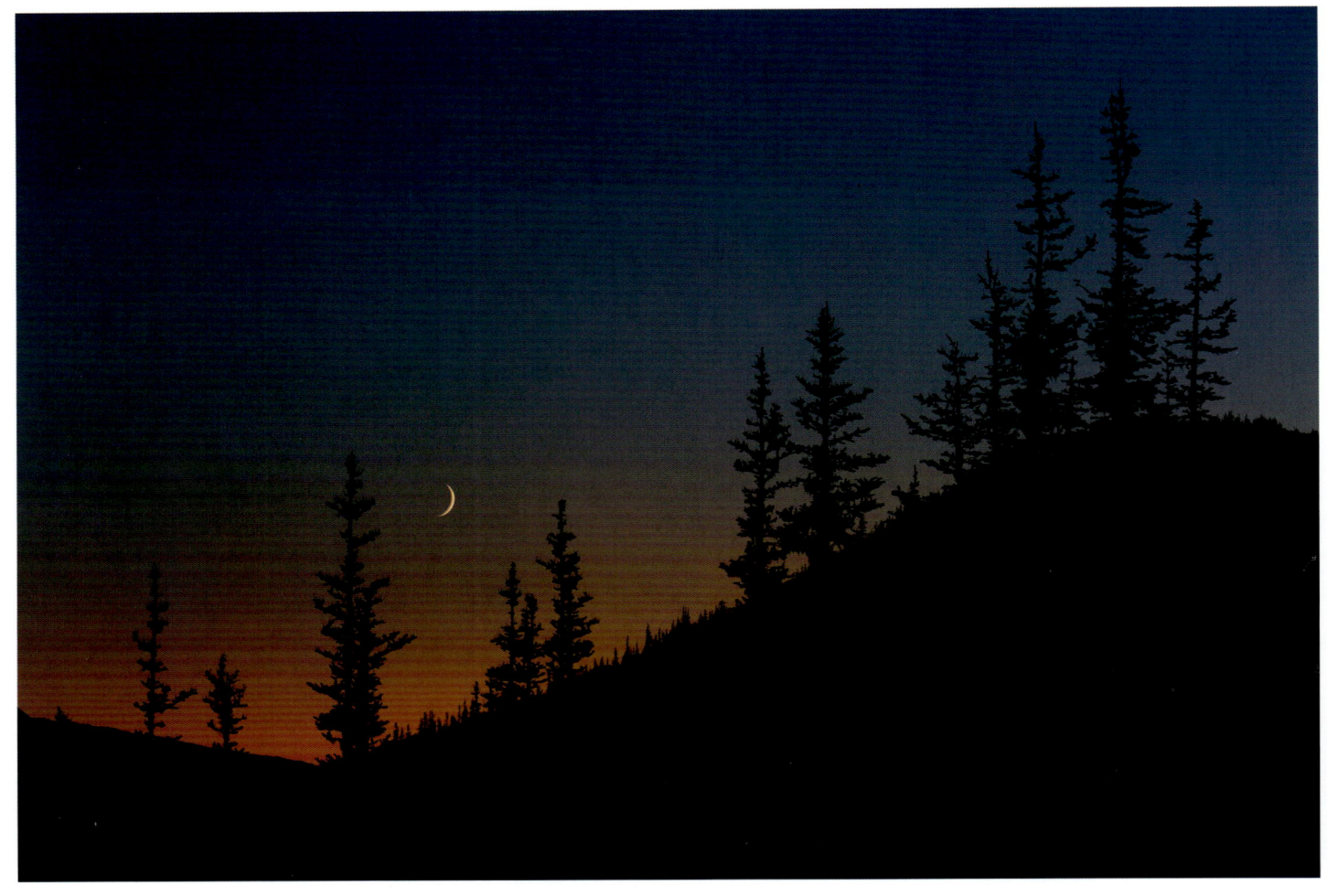

47.3 Silhouettes.
1/2 sec.; f/11; ISO 100; Canon 5D Mark III; EF 70-200mm f/4L IS USM @ 116mm

48. ADDING FLASH

FLASH PHOTOGRAPHY IS easily one of the most complicated topics in the photographic world. Since we only have one chapter to work with it here, we're going to try and keep it simple. Flash photography can be broken down to three basic setup options: in-camera flash (camera with a built-in flash unit); add-on flash (a camera with a flash attached to the hot shoe on top of the camera); and off-camera flash (any situation where the camera will be triggering a flash or flashes which are not mounted to the camera). We'll discuss the first two examples.

When using flash, one of the first considerations should be an awareness of the ambient light level. In dark situations, your flash will be providing the main illumination. In scenes with a fair bit of light, your flash will supplement the natural light and add a bit of fill light to the shadows.

Built-in Flash

The built-in flash can be very convenient, but may lack a number of features that will allow you to exert much control over it. To start with, built-in flashes are not very powerful, and thus have a very limited range in how far they will reach. The built-in flash is quite small and runs off the same batteries as the rest of the camera, and flash units are notoriously battery hungry. In general terms it can be quite effective if your subject is less than ten feet (three meters) away. It can be used for subjects that are farther away

than that by raising the ISO level, but you face rapidly diminishing returns when you do. The light source for built-in flashes is quite small, and subjects illuminated by the flash will exhibit very strong and distinct shadow lines, which are often viewed as harsh and unflattering in portrait photography.

These flashes normally work by automatically adding as much light to the scene as the camera thinks it needs. The system it uses is called Through The Lens (TTL) metering. It fires a test flash just before the photo is taken, and the light bounces off the subject, back through the lens, and onto the sensor. The camera uses that information to determine how much light the photo will require. When the camera shutter opens again, the flash fires and the real photo is taken with the predetermined amount of flash.

A problem can arise when the subject is too far away to be illuminated with the flash, even at maximum power. Your camera may have a warning that lets you know there is a problem, but you'll notice the issue when you review the image. A second problem is subject reflectivity. The camera's TTL system is much like the light meter in that it expects everything to be middle-tone gray. When subjects fall outside this range, the camera/flash will try to fix it. The resulting photo may be too dark or too light. Finally, the TTL system is set for a programmed "correct" amount of flash—which

may conflict with your idea of how much flash a subject needs.

Shots taken with the in-camera flash can be less than ideal, but Flash Exposure Compensation can be used to guide the TTL system to a more appropriate power setting. TTL systems are computers that operate using data with the goal of lighten up enough of the photo so that it's of average brightness. For the police forensic photographer or the insurance claims adjuster documenting a scene, this works just fine. When a photographer is trying to illuminate a subject so that it looks good, the full TTL setting is often too much power for the scene. We end up with photos that look like they have been taken at the department of motor vehicles: great for positively identifying a suspect, but not exactly pleasing to look at.

With Flash Exposure Compensation you can dial down the automatically controlled light level by as much as your camera will allow. Most cameras will allow you to reduce the output up to three stops in 1/3-stop increments. Locate this feature on your camera and run a test with photos at the standard TTL setting, then at -1, -2, and -3. Many cameras will also allow you a +1 setting. It's doubtful that this setting will look good, but give it a test and see what you think. Many photographers have found a happy medium by setting the Flash Exposure Compensation somewhere in the -1 to -2 range.

On-camera Flash

An optional flash, or speed-light, will typically be much more powerful and have more features than the built-in flash. These units slide into the hot-shoe mount on the camera. This standardized mounting system features several pins that are used to communicate with the flash through pins on the mounting foot.

In general, add-on flashes are about three to five times more powerful than built-in flashes, which means they can illuminate subjects that are farther away. Beyond being able to light subjects from afar, that extra power comes in handy when firing your flash in rapid succession. A more powerful flash will only need a fraction of its power for a standard shot, so it can keep up when you're firing multiple shots in a row.

Another advantage of a more powerful flash is the ability to bounce the light off a light-colored ceiling, wall, or other surface. Bouncing the light effectively increases the size the light source. One of the problems mentioned with the in-camera flash is the small size and the harsh shadows it creates. The add-on flash is better, but only by a small amount. Bouncing the light increases it. Just make sure that the surface you are using to bounce off of is white (or close to white) and not too far away from the flash unit. When bouncing light, it's only effective if the light will bounce close enough to the subject to actually illuminate them. The wall or ceiling should be no more than 5-10 feet (2-3 meters) from the flash.

With an on-camera flash, there are many accessory diffusers that will effectively increase the size of the light source and soften shadows. These are portable, and can be very effective at improving the look of an image. Flash Exposure Compensation applies here as well. The controls to adjust this feature may be on the flash unit or controlled from the cameras menu system.

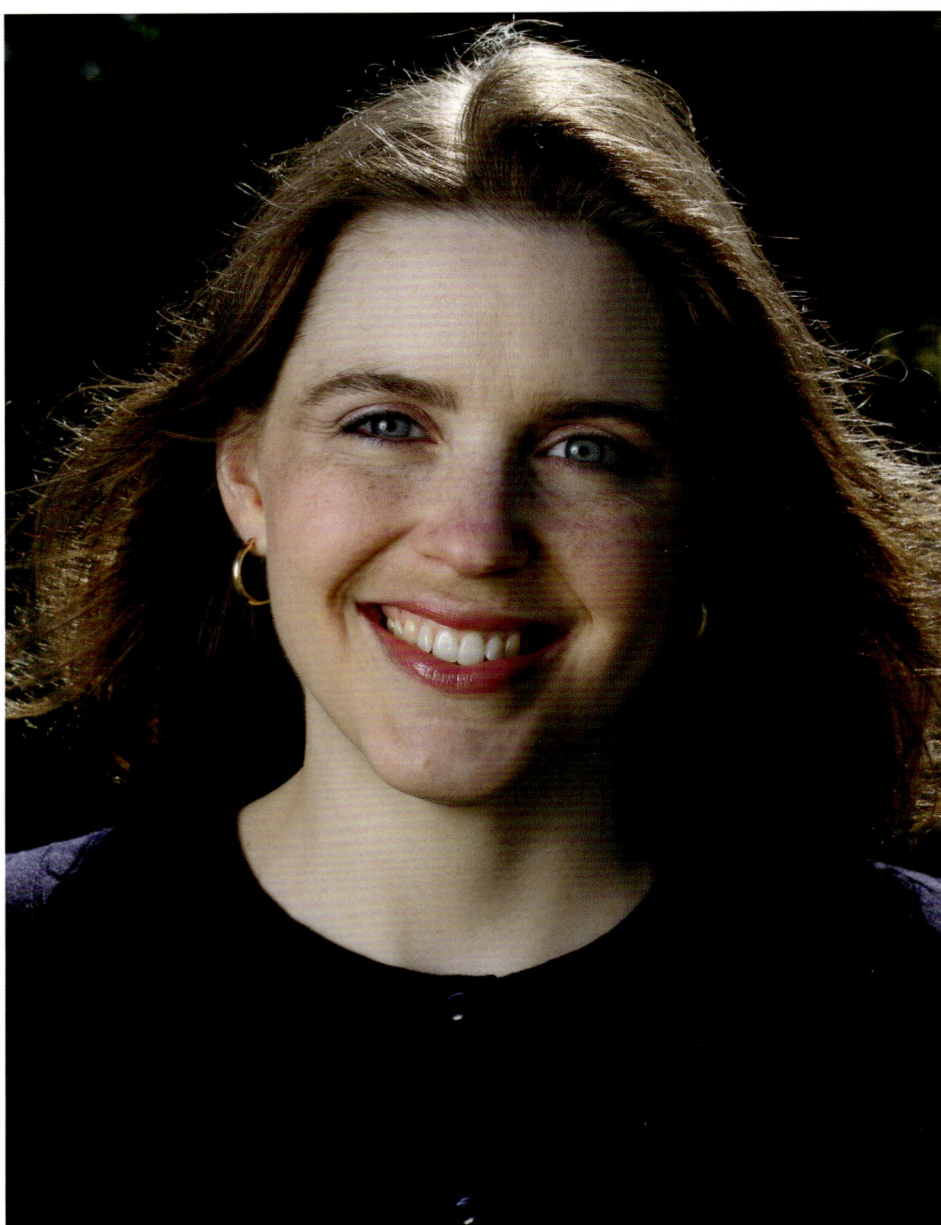

48.1 Adding flash is a subjective choice, but it can only be helpful if your subject is within a reasonable flash range. Portraits are a great opportunity to use flash. Try experimenting with the Flash Exposure Compensation mode, if your camera has it.
1/250 sec.; f/10; ISO 100; Canon 7D; EF 50mm f/1.4 USM

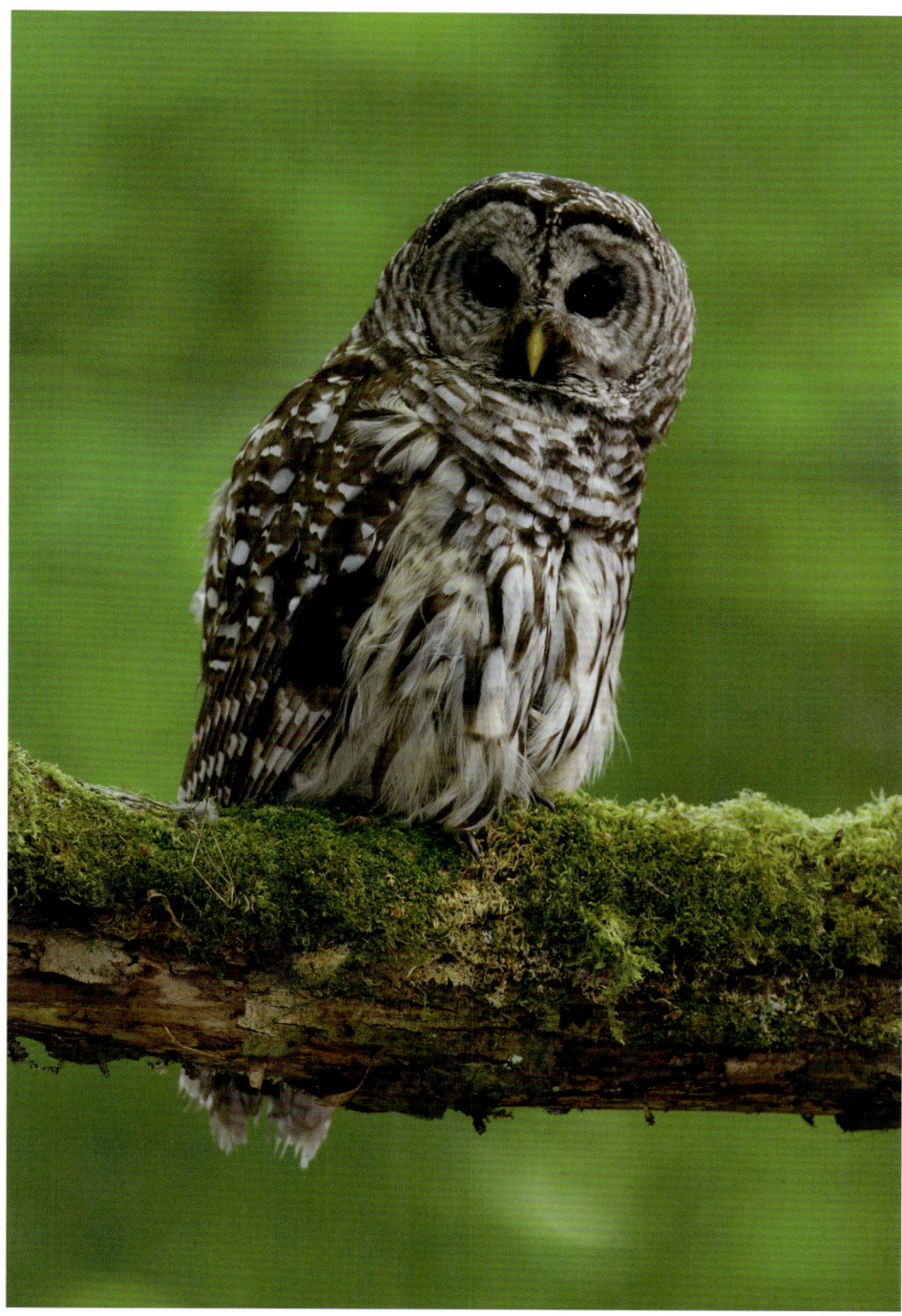

48.2 Any subject with important features "lost in the shadows" can be improved with the proper bit of fill-flash technique.
1/125 sec.; f/2.8; ISO 1600; Canon 7D; EF 300mm f/2.8L IS II USM

49. HANDHOLDING THE CAMERA

BLURRY PHOTOS CAN'T be fixed in post-production and are unacceptable a vast majority of the time, so getting sharp photos by properly holding the camera is very important. If an image would be better shot from a tripod (and a tripod is available), you should use it. But many situations are not suitable for tripod use, and you'll need to do the best you can holding the camera yourself. How well you can do this is very important because the better you are at holding the camera steady, the slower a shutter speed you can use, which will allow you to use a lower ISO for less noise. So the better you are at holding the camera, the better the final photograph will be.

The right hand will obviously go on the main grip of the camera. Hold your left hand out, palm up. Now lay the lens into the palm of your hand. As you hold the camera up to your eye, resting the viewfinder on your eyebrow, your left thumb should be pointing upwards, with the lens cradled in your left hand. Both elbows should be pushing in on your torso. Now look for something to brace yourself against, like a wall, pillar, tree, or post. Ideally you're looking for something to lean your shoulder or back against. The next best thing would be a chair to sit in or a table to rest your elbows on. The idea is to get something rock solid as close the camera as possible. If there is a pillar or wall to lean against, you can put your back to it, lean your shoulder on it, or push your right or left forearm up against it as you hold the camera.

When it's time to fire the shutter you'll want to be as still as possible. Settle into a relaxed, but firm, position. Take a couple of deep breaths and let your heart rate settle down. When it's time to shoot, take a deep breath in, breathe out, hold still, and fire the shutter. Take a few shots at a shutter speed you're confident with for handheld shots, and check the results. Now adjust your settings for a slower shutter speed and try more test photos, checking them for sharpness as you go. At some point, you'll see that you're starting to get inconsistent sharpness. Now you know your limit.

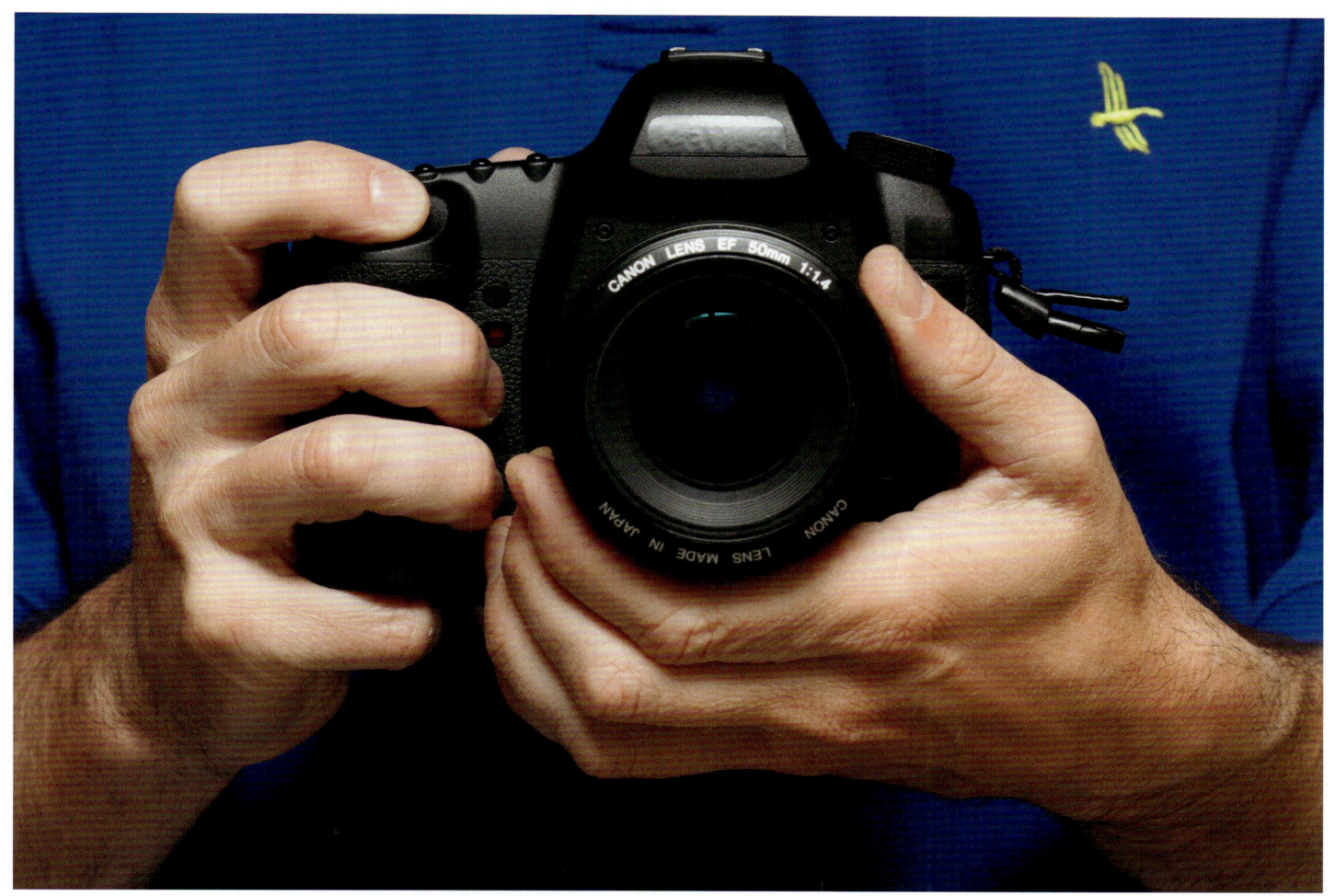

49.1 Proper handholding technique is important for shooting at the slowest of shutter speeds. With the camera firmly gripped, use your elbows to push in on your torso for a solid shooting platform.

INDEX

# #

18% gray 12, 15–16, 135

A

action 80
Adobe 121–122
    Lightroom 121–122
    Photoshop 121–122
advanced ISO settings 62
AEL (Auto Exposure Lock) button 67, 101, 135
aperture 2, 4, 12, 20, 30, 41–47, 52, 65–67, 73, 80, 87, 90, 92, 109
Aperture Priority mode 60, 67, 70–72, 98
aperture unit 43
art 1, 41
astrophotography 28
Auto Exposure Lock (AEL) button 67, 101, 135
auto exposure modes 2, 66–67, 98
auto ISO 60–62, 68

B

background 90
backlight 135–136
base ISO 56, 58, 90
blinkies 19
blur motion 23, 34–39, 83–85
bracketing 102–103
bright scenes 12
brightness 98
brightness histogram 18
Bulb 29

C

camera movement 34
center-weighted metering 15
close-up shooting 66
CMOS (Complementary Metal Oxide Sensor) 27
color channels 18
compression 110

D

dark scenes 12
depth of field 43–46, 50–51, 53, 67, 71, 87–88, 92, 95
diffuse light 4

E

electronic shutter 27–28
equipment 129
EV (exposure value) 8
expansive depth of field 22, 47–48
exposure 2–3, 8, 29
exposure compensation 67, 70, 98, 135
exposure control 28
exposure indicator 73
exposure modes 2, 65, 98
exposure time 26
exposure triangle 2, 20
exposure value (EV) 8

F

f-stop 42–43
film 55
filters 104
first curtain 26
flash 66–67, 129, 133, 135, 143–145
Flash Exposure Compensation 143
Flexible Program 67
focal length 44, 90, 95
focus distance 95
focus lock 50
focus options 50
focus point 50, 87
focusing distance 44
freeze motion 20, 30–33, 68, 80

G

Graduated Neutral Density filter 104

H

handholding the camera 39, 60, 87, 146–147
hard light 4, 7, 11
HDR (high dynamic range) 102, 104, 106–107, 133
Hi ISO settings 58
high contrast 4, 130–131
high dynamic range 102, 104, 106–107, 133
high ISO 58
highlights 8, 18
histogram 18–19
hyperfocal distance 95

I

imaging software 121–122
in-camera 110
International Organization for Standardization (ISO)
    4, 12, 20, 30, 56–59, 66–67, 80, 87, 146
ISO 4, 12, 20, 30, 56–59, 65–67, 80, 87, 146

J

JPEG 110, 112–113, 121–123

L

landscape 22, 66, 88, 95
lens 41, 52, 55, 87, 129
light 1–2, 4, 55, 97, 125
    characteristics of 8
    colors of 8, 10
    direction of 8
    hard 4, 7, 11
    natural 4
    quality of 2, 8
    quantity of 2, 8
    range of 8, 29
    size of 8
    soft 4, 6–7
light meter 4, 12–14, 18, 73, 77, 80, 97–98
Lightroom, Adobe 121–122
Lo ISO settings 58
low light 125–129

M

macro 51
Manual exposure mode 12, 60, 73, 75–76
maximum aperture 42
maximum depth of field 87–88
maximum sharpness 92
mechanical shutter 27
metering modes 12, 15, 135
mirrorless camera 26
moving subjects 36–38
multi-segment metering mode 16–17, 135

N

native ISO 56, 58, 90
native sensitivity 56
natural light 4
ND filter 104–105
night 66
noise 57–59, 146

O

optimum exposure 20
overexposure 19

P

panning 34, 36–38, 69, 83, 86
Program Shift 67
Photoshop, Adobe 121–122
pixel 18, 26, 28, 123
portrait 20, 50–51, 66, 90
post-processing 121–123, 132, 146

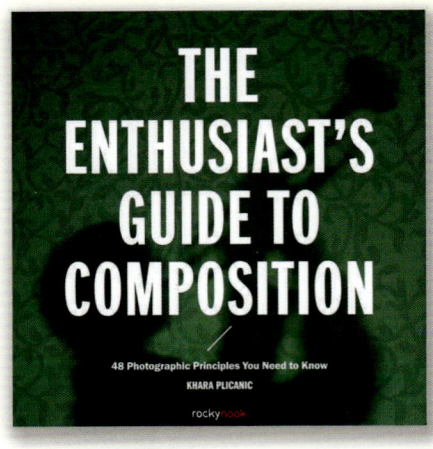
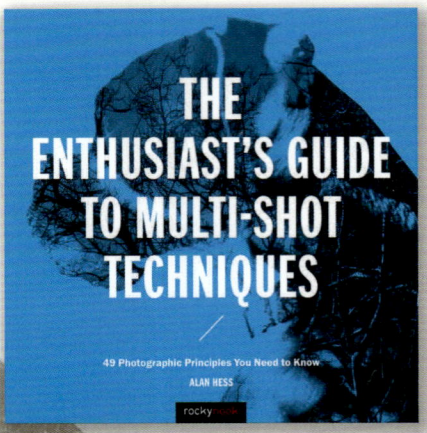
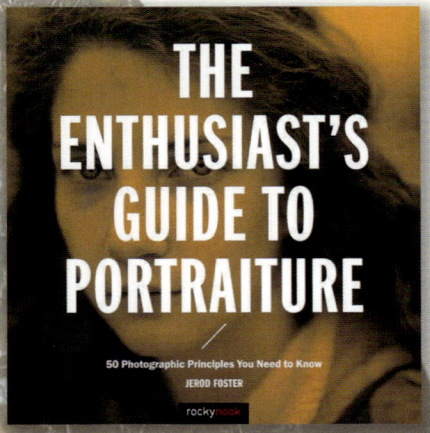